KT-574-702

Preface

The summer of 1994 saw the fulfilment of one ambition after another as 15 of the finest players ever to pull on navy blue jerseys gave patiently of their time while I asked questions they have all answered 100 times before. The fulfilment of those ambitions for me also meant a long, laborious summer of transcribing notes for one young lady, my wife Nicky, who put in hours of unpaid work as we sorted out page upon page of notes and hours of tape recordings. She's not a rugby fan so it must be love and since we met when she was a copy typist on the newspaper I worked for as a reporter, it's nice to know I'm still not the only person who likes the sound of my voice.

It was also a summer in which, working at home, I finally perfected my side-step and body-swerve as our very own crash-tackling midfield partnership Sean (5) and Craig (2), tried to obstruct every attempt to reach the keyboard. These skills last received serious attention in the late seventies which is why it was appropriate that the interviews began on March 9 in Jedburgh visiting John Rutherford in his office and ended on September 15 in Andy Irvine's office in central Edinburgh. Those two great inspirations wore their hair long throughout their playing days, a side effect of which was at least one fairly tragic photograph (to the horror of all concerned still apparently in circulation) of the Lawside Academy XV of that era - a team which contained three Ferries. Cousins Steve and Andy looked no better than I with their flowing locks.

It was John Rutherford in whose likeness I played with my collar turned up, all the while rehearsing the art of half bending forward while clutching the bottom of my shorts - usually when opposing locks or props were passing at anything approaching pace. Andy Irvine was, however, the man who diverted this young football fan, one among thousands, to rugby. I remember at some stage reading that Irvine was 5'10" tall and 12 1/2 stones in weight. On reaching the former aged 16 I would willingly have taken up smoking to ensure no further development had not nature intervened. Having attained the appropriate height some bulking up was required and the target weight was reached around a year later. Sadly the right build does nothing for an innate lack of ability and these days Irvine's relative condition remains an inspiration as I attack the target weight from a different direction.

The book also provided an introduction to a man with whom I had felt a stranger connection - the first player from "the past" with whom I had felt an affinity. Having been christened Kevin John Ferrie and as a proud nationalist, the name KJF Scotland struck a chord long before I discovered that he was a player worthy of consideration

iii

alongside and indeed to some minds at least, as it turned out, ahead of full-backs of the calibre of Gavin Hastings and, indeed, Andy Irvine. A man of supreme dignity he managed to avoid looking at me as if I had three heads when I explained that self-styled connection on our first meeting.

Among the other interviews, every one of which was memorable, the biggest mistake was pointing out to Ian McGeechan that England's opening tour match in South Africa was on television live that afternoon which had the effect of minimising conversation for the next hour or so and the best arrangement was seeing Gordon Brown at a sevens tournament, which meant missing out on having to watch all those early meaningless ties before catching up on things in the closing stages of the competition.

The concept behind this work was that of Scottish Rugby managing director Sean Lineen, himself a source of endless inspiration thanks to his endless enthusiasm and energy allied to his status as a 1990 Grand Slam hero. His brainchild itself bore a hugely successful competition which ran in the first half of 1994 after our highly respected panel of The Scotsman's Norman Mair MBE, The Herald's Bill McMurtrie and 1984 Grand Slam chairman of selectors Iain MacGregor had selected the side.

The book is an unashamed tribute to all those selected so enough self-indulgence. Where possible I have left the stories to be told in the words of the subjects themselves.

Kevin Ferrie

September, 1994

Acknowledgments

The photograph on page xii is published by kind permission of The Scottish Rugby Union; 14, 19, 48, 49, 78, 110, 114, 119, 126, 190, 202 by Colorsport; 20, 30, 36, 72, 81, 100, 148 by The Scotsman and Evening News; 180 by Adam Elder of Scotland on Sunday; 195,199, 201 by Bob Thomas. All other photographs by Gordon Fraser.

Contents

Preface iii

Acknowledgements iv

Foreword by Matthew Gloag vii

Introduction ix

15 Ken Scotland 1

14 Andy Irvine 13

13 Scott Hastings 27

12 Ian McGeechan 41

11 Keith Robertson 55

10 John Rutherford 69

 9 Gary Armstrong 83

 1 David Sole 97

 2 Colin Deans 111

 3 Iain Milne 125

 4 Andy Reed 139

 5 Gordon Brown 149

 6 John Jeffrey 163

 7 Finlay Calder (Captain) 177

 8 Iain Paxton 191

Foreword

*by Matthew Gloag, corporate director of Matthew Gloag & Son Ltd.,
The Famous Grouse finest Scotch whisky, sponsors of the Scottish rugby team*

We are delighted to be associated with this celebration of Scottish Rugby. 'The Famous XV – Scotland's All Time Rugby Greats', charts the rugby careers of fifteen of Scotland's finest and most celebrated players.

The result of a painstaking selection process by an experienced panel of judges, in conjunction with a competition run in Scottish Rugby magazine, this book is a first. It details the pride, passion, determination, success and disappointments of the fifteen selected players and will make excellent reading for all Scottish rugby fans.

Through its sponsorship of the Scottish Rugby Team, together with its planned support of the Rugby World Cup next year, The Famous Grouse is firmly committed to International Rugby Union. Perceived as dynamic, hard, yet fair, with high entertainment value, the quality and popularity of the sport complement The Famous Grouse Finest Scotch Whisky.

At a time when World Rugby is enjoying increasing popularity in all corners of the globe, this book is a truly nostalgic trip through some thirty years of Scottish rugby. The Famous Grouse and Scottish Rugby magazine are proud to be associated with 'The Famous XV – Scotland's All Time Rugby Greats' – which we believe is a fine reflection of Scottish rugby.

Introduction

Well over 200 players donned the dark blue between 1964 and 1994 and in the series which ran earlier this year Scottish Rugby magazine whittled down the contenders to six for each position — some were chosen in more than one position. The final selection was made by a panel comprising three men with unrivalled knowledge of the Scottish game — The Scotsman's rugby correspondent Norman Mair MBE, The Herald's rugby reporter Bill McMurtrie, and Ian MacGregor, who was Scotland's chairman of selectors in the 1984 Grand Slam season which ended the long years barren of rugby honours. Their reasoning is set out below.

Ken Scotland, the only player whose international career began in the Fifties was the man who popularised attacking full-back play and worthy of his place on footballing ability alone. Gavin Hastings was an automatic choice as reserve full-back.

The 30 years over which our competition extended was hardly a vintage period for Scottish wing play. Two out-and-out wingers, Dave Shedden and Billy Steele, ended up in the shadow side. A place had to be found for the incomparable attacker Andy Irvine, and Keith Robertson's all-round brilliance, getting the very best out of a fairly slight frame, got him in on the left.

The younger Hastings, over the years the less noticeable of the brothers whose international careers have been almost perfectly synchronised, was readily accepted at outside centre. What proved slightly more difficult was finding the perfect foil — Sean Lineen? David Johnston? Alan Tait? Jim Renwick? Ian McGeechan's all-round talent and great vision, recognised by the British Lions selectors through two Test series in the Seventies, ultimately made the latter-day coaching guru the obvious choice.

Discussion was minimal at halfback, although it was noted Roy Laidlaw would probably be the unanimous choice among the 1984 Grand Slam squad. Laidlaw walked into the shadow side and there was little debate over the inclusion of the late Jock Turner as the back-up stand-off.

David Sole or Ian McLauchan? A majority decision favoured Sole's athleticism over set-piece and scrummaging ability. Colin Deans was a unanimous choice at hooker, with Kenny Milne in the 'second XV'. On the tighthead side it was inevitably a lengthy assessment of the relative strengths of Sandy Carmichael and "The Bear". In the event Iain Milne was at first only provisionally selected until it was clear that the rest of the pack contained the sort of line-out and loose players to allow for "the luxury" of his inclusion as an out-and-out scrummager, providing a set-piece cornerstone. That may seem almost contradictory to the reasoning behind Sole's selection on the other side, but the front-row which performed so superbly in the first World Cup, represented the most balanced unit we have fielded there.

It was accepted that Scotland have rarely had classic second-row giants of the sort other countries seem able to produce at will. "Broon Frae Troon" was always likely to feature. In the past two seasons Andy Reed has not once, but twice transformed Scottish line-out play and the big man's athleticism saw him in as the principal middle-of-the-line jumper. Chris Gray, his towering performances on the 1990 tour of New Zealand not to mention that season's Grand Slam very much in mind, was chosen as the second choice front-jumper with the ubiquitous and marvellously unpredictable Alistair McHarg alongside.

Only at full-back has Scotland enjoyed such a rich vein of talent as in the back-row in recent times. Though he did not appear in a single Test for the Lions, there was easy unanimity that John Jeffrey should wear the no.6 shirt. On the other flank came perhaps the longest discussion. Finlay Calder's workrate got him in by the narrowest of margins, operating off the back of the line-out and packing down on the right-hand side. David Leslie was the second-choice no.7 with his regular partner Jim Calder alongside him. Paxton or Beattie? Probably the factor which swayed it was that in 1983, when both went on the Lions tour of New Zealand and the selectors had the chance to put them under the microscope, Paxton consistently won through.

We left the selection of captain until after we had chosen the side — there was never going to be any shortage of quality. Finlay Calder captained Scotland only four times, yet he was the unanimous choice of our panel to lead the Famous XV. Calder and 1966 captain Mike Campbell-Lamerton, whose side won 2-0 in Australia before losing 4-0 to the All Blacks, are the only Scots this century to lead the Lions to Test series wins. Between 1966 and 1989 it is fair to observe that the Wallabies had become a rather different proposition.

The '89 Lions won in the most difficult of circumstances and Calder and coach Ian McGeechan, another member of the Famous XV, share the credit for turning things round after defeat in the first Test - traditionally regarded as a touring side's best chance of victory. Calder came under intense personal scrutiny at a time when rugby players were just beginning to discover the downside of the dramatic increase in interest in the sport amongst the modern media, midway between the first two World Cups. The Wallabies had been semi-finalists in the first of those World Cups and were, two years later, to become world champions. Coach Bob Dwyer was in the process of polishing his gold and green machine. That Calder led his men through that toughest of tests, or more precisely two of them, bears everlasting testimony to his qualities as a captain. His wonderful sense of humour, which he demonstrated both in adversity and in triumph as a skipper would surely allow him to appreciate the tongue in cheek reasoning of one of our selectors who observed that Finlay had to be captain because he is the "only one who can deal with all those prima donnas."

Typically he has outspoken views on everything from his own selection in The Famous XV and as its captain, to Scotland's future prospects, and these comments are peppered throughout the book

The winning entry in the magazine's competition, by the captain of Orkney Rugby Club, Iain Rushbrook, had 13 of the 16 selections correct. In-depth analysis of all the entries bore out Finlay Calder's assertion that the only player who would have been regarded as a certainty by all of his fellow contenders was stand-off John Rutherford. Of those who entered almost 83% selected the Selkirk star at no.10, with Colin Deans proving the second most popular candidate being included in almost exactly 80% of the line-ups.

Gary Armstrong (73.75%) was next, with Gordon Brown nudging ahead of Andy Irvine a little over the 70% mark. However, as expected, the non-selection of Jim Renwick, who with ex-Hawick team-mate Deans is jointly Scotland's most capped player, having made 52 appearances for his country, was the one which threw most people. He was the sixth most popular selection, polling inclusion in close to 67% of sides.

1990 Grand Slam stars John Jeffrey (64%), David Sole (57.5%), Finlay Calder and Scott Hastings (both 54%) slot in thereafter. Ahead of Iain "The Bear" Milne (35%), are no fewer than six more controversial omissions from our Famous XV, Sandy Carmichael (45%), David Leslie (44%), Gavin Hastings and Alistair McHarg (both 41%), Iwan Tukalo and Ian McLauchlan (both 36%). The only Famous XV selection among that group was Keith Robertson (36%) who, interestingly, was chosen by almost an identical number of people as Scotland's most prolific try-scoring left winger of the 30 years to which the competition was confined, Iwan Tukalo.

The low percentage of selections picked up by Iain Paxton (30%), was a reflection not of any unpopularity on his part, but of the tremendous range of choice available to our competing selectors at no.8.he did pick up most nominations, but stacked together were Derek White (21%), Jim Telfer (20%) and John Beattie (25%) with Peter Brown and Rob Wainwright also appearing in some sides.

It was perhaps unsurprising that the two members of the Famous XV to gain least "support", so to speak, were those at the most extreme ends of the 30 year spectrum. Ken Scotland (18%), happily acknowledged his inclusion as crossing something of a "time warp", having played just a single match in 1965 to make himself available for selection, while Andy Reed (10%), Scotland's tour captain in Argentina, had played only four Test matches when the competition was launched.

The Famous XV	The 2nd XV
15 Ken Scotland	15 Gavin Hastings
14 Andy Irvine	14 David Shedden
13 Scott Hastings	13 Alan Tait
12 Ian McGeechan	12 Jim Renwick
11 Keith Robertson	11 Billy Steele
10 John Rutherford	10 Jock Turner
9 Gary Armstrong	9 Roy Laidlaw
1 David Sole	1 Ian McLauchlan
2 Colin Deans	2 Kenny Milne
3 Iain Milne	3 Sandy Carmichael
4 Andy Reed	4 Chris Gray
5 Gordon Brown	5 Alistair McHarg
6 John Jeffrey	6 Jim Calder
7 Finlay Calder (Captain)	7 David Leslie
8 Iain Paxton	8 John Beattie

Mr. Scotland

15 - K. J. F. Scotland

Back in the late fifties and early sixties amateur sportsmen still merited that title and, in relation to the sport of rugby, none has ever been more appropriate than that conferred upon Mister Scotland. A decade or so before JPR Williams had been heard of another of the great full-backs of the post-war era was instantly recognisable by his initials - KJF.

As for that surname: "I think I had heard every possible joke about it by the time I left primary school. I don't think it ever did me any harm, though."

Raised in the nation's capital Kenneth James Forbes Scotland was a man born not only to play rugby, but to play a major role in transforming the way it was played. "Environment has a lot to do with success in any walk of life. I was brought up very close to Goldenacre, within 100 yards. I was always around the ground. There's always this thing in a youngster that you want to ape your heroes. I had a lot of the advantages of being at boarding school without the disadvantages of being away from home," he reckons.

In every sense that proximity created the sort of all-round balanced individual perfectly suited to international rugby. "Because I lived so close to the ground I was always being exposed to a lot of different sports. I never played formal football but did play a lot of what you would call tanner ba' stuff. You can play that where you can't play rugby on a concrete playground. I got a sense of balance from football you don't get in rugby."

Though rugby was always his passion it was a circuitous route which brought the man recognised as the world's first great attacking full-back to the position in which he was to gain fame. "The attacking full-back thing was not something I was conscious of. It really evolved over a number of years," he says.

Fundamentally though he puts it down to the fact that he never really thought of himself as a full-back, as such, being, in effect, a frustrated stand-off. "Rationalising with the benefit of hindsight I probably always thought of myself as a stand-off. I played all my school rugby there, so when I did play full-back I was always anticipating what the opposing and indeed our own stand-off was going to do. It was a bit like a game of chess. It gave me the split second ahead of somebody who wasn't thinking that way."

1

In essence, having as a youngster been used to making things happen, Scotland was unprepared to be restricted by the limitations of conventional full-back play as it was then.

"The basic attributes of a full-back in the fifties were to catch and kick, preferably with both feet. You had to put the ball out on the full. Forwards were quite simply looking for someone who didn't make mistakes."

Scotland, himself, does not credit himself with the "first attacking full-back" tag, although he does recognise that he may have increased the profile of such a style.

"There had definitely been people who were adventurous full-backs and I would have learned by watching them but I have only really rationalised it since I stopped playing. Full-backs in the fifties, if they fielded a loose kick in the middle of the field, they might run and link up. For me the next step was to come into a three-quarter line in an attacking position."

It was actually only the Scottish international selectors, in the somewhat befuddled manner which some believe has generally tended to be their trademark over the years, who first saw Scotland as a full-back.

"The move certainly wasn't planned and probably would not happen that way nowadays. In my second year in the army I was called up as a reserve for the international trial and on the letter, in brackets, it said 'full-back'.

"I arrived to be a reserve for the trial and the whites full-back called off. When I was called into the Scotland side after the second trial I had only had two games at full-back. The only time I had played there before was two and a half games in my first season in the school first XV before they moved me first to centre, then to stand-off."

Such a selection for his country was, to some extent though, a sign of the times. "Nowadays you might well look for your number one footballer to be at full-back, but in those days he was at stand-off. Then you were looking for someone dependable, but not particularly fast at full-back. The best ball players were at stand-off. the fastest men were on the wing. But there were good footballers at full-back.

Last line of defence — saving the Lions versus the All Blacks, a sequence from before the days of instant replay

"In those days stand-off and full-back were much more interchangeable than now. Stand-off, centre and full-back were always linked, whereas nowadays it tends to be full-back and winger — although I never saw myself as a centre.

"At centre there has always been a premium on head-on tackling and I find they tend only to get the ball when others have finished with it. They are never in control of the game, in my opinion. Centre is the most difficult position to play well. It's easy enough to get through games, but the really top ones who stand out have been few and far between."

He felt he had been selected because, quite simply, he could catch and kick reliably, but there was one added irony before he took over, literally as well as metaphorically, as Scotland's no. 1.

"It said something about the selection in those days, even although the selectors were beginning to recover from the terrible reputation they had in the early fifties, that on my debut I played at full-back, whereas Mickey Grant was at stand-off.

"He was the full-back who had missed that first trial and he was playing in that position for Harlequins, while I was a stand-off in the army. In the second trial we were getting ready to go out on the field when we realised that we had both just automatically put on the wrong shirts. I had the no. 6, he had the no.1."

A historical point emerges with the recollection in that the numbering was different, Scotland explaining that the full-back was no.1 until around 1960 when the numbering

First line of attack — releasing Arthur Smith for a memorable try v Wales at Murrayfield, 1961

was reversed after the no. 8 became known as the no.8 instead of middle of the back-row.

Grant won the last of his four caps that day, the selectors opting for four different players in that position that season, despite the fact that the first two matches were won. Scotland moved on to become a man who played a major role in transforming rugby. Perhaps the selectors did know something after all, or maybe they just got lucky.

"I actually thought Mickey had a great game in Paris that day, despite having taken a lot of punishment," Scotland recalls.

He was not so impressed with his own early showing at a time when matches were still played at Stade Colombes, long before the Parc Des Princes jinx emerged.

"I remember that it snowed very heavily for quite a bit of the game and the Scottish forwards played extraordinarily well. I missed a penalty in front of the posts which only rose high enough to hit the bar. I wasn't very popular and wasn't playing well."

Then that little bit of luck which can transform sporting careers, came Scotland's way, again in every sense. "Earlyish in the second half Jacques Bouquet miscued clearing from his own line. The ball came bobbling towards me. I picked it up and dropped a goal.

"It was just a reaction having been in that position so many times before, no conscious thought came into it. I then got a penalty which kind of settled the game which was never going to be a high scoring one...mind you, there hardly ever were high scoring games in those days."

It was January 12, 1957 and a new star was born. Scotland was the first player to score all of Scotland's points in a win on his debut for 19 years - something of a template for fellow Edinburgh native Gavin Hastings' six penalty effort in the 18-17 win over the same opposition the best part of three decades later.

The new boy may have been a novice at full-back, but that is not to say that he had not already given some thought to the possibilities of making things happen from that position.

He had arrived on national service in the Royal Signals, after leaving school and, naturally, slotted into their XV at stand-off, arriving just ahead of the then inevitable brilliant Welsh fly-half "strangely enough, named Evans". Said Evans had to make do with playing at full-back, at least to begin with - "although we interchanged a bit."

"I wouldn't say I was ever conscious of changing anything," Scotland says of the innovations they introduced. "But it definitely started in that good regimental side. We worked on some moves where he would take the ball directly from the scrum-half down the blind-side and so when I was at full-back I would do that too."

Those embryonic ideas were further developed at Cambridge University, although despite having been capped it took a little while for Scotland to get the chance to work on them, in the first XV at least. "I had been capped before I got to university and so had become known as a full-back, but I couldn't get into the team. Times were hard," he laughs. "I got there as third choice."

Ahead in the queue, already established, were South African David Millard, a Blue from the previous year and Welshman Alan Prosser-Harris. "Standards were pretty high in the post-war period. Students were much more mature coming in because of national service," says Scotland, who was himself 21 on arrival. There was, though, a large-scale clear-out at the end of that season and as he earned his Blue the light blue line-up carried tartan flair. "Gordon Waddell became the stand-off. I was the full-back. We developed a lot of moves at that time. It was the first time we developed a set move of me coming into the line outside the outside centre at pace.

"Because it was a novelty it created a lot of opportunities. People didn't catch on for a long time. We had a good combination and the captain was a centre. You needed to have two centres who are selfless to make it work, because at that time centres tried to do a lot more than they do now."

An inherent advantage for the students was that as well as the top class fixture list they boasted in those days, they could train twice a week: "We trained and practised a lot."

The initial reticence of the Cambridge selectors in relation to their international recruit was, to a large extent, in keeping with his own assessment of his selection. "My first cap was probably a bit fortuitous, it didn't come as a result of years of concentrated work, but it had been the climax of my ambition since about the age of seven or eight."

He had been 20 years old on his debut and the following season found himself out of the side on the return of previous incumbent Robin Chisholm, who had missed the 1957 championship through injury. At club level Scotland was on his travels again after winning his Blue, since the University season ends after the Varsity match in December and had short spells with both London Scottish, who won the Middlesex Sevens with him in the side and Ballymena, during an early posting with his Midlands-based employers. In the meantime Chisholm picked up another injury in the Ireland game which allowed Scotland to play in the Calcutta Cup match, then traditionally the season's finale.

That match was drawn 3-3 and was the first time in five international appearances Scotland hadn't scored. The focal point of the 1959 season was selection for the British Lions tour of the Antipodes and although the Scots lost to France and Ireland, their full-back secured his place on tour returning to scoring form in the last three matches, including his side's penalty in that year's 3-3 draw with England.

"You know I played against them seven times and never won, but we had three draws with them in that time," he says, his words still tinged with regret.

A Lions tour Down Under was, however, the pinnacle of any career. Ken Scotland's was no exception. "It was an absolute treat to go to Australia and New Zealand with the

Lions and play in that back division alongside players like Tony O'Reilly, Dave Hewitt, Phil Horrocks-Taylor, Peter Jackson and Dickie Jeeps," says a man who suddenly found himself projected to stardom.

"In New Zealand the level of interest was phenomenal. To us coming from the UK where rugby was very much a minority sport, you didn't tend to be recognised in the street, but there it was like being Willie Bauld walking along Gorgie Road all the time.

"The whole country was like that - particularly the small towns when we played provincial games." It was something of a culture shock for a man used to the more staid world of the Scottish game, albeit he was already something of a rugby nomad.

"I must admit I enjoyed the rugby more than the attention. I can understand what people say about living in a goldfish bowl. It can get a bit wearing, having said which this was an opportunity for us to be doing what we wanted.

"We were away for five months which was probably best done as a student with no attachments as I was at the time. The exams could wait!"

He was made to work at his rugby, though, as one of the most versatile backs, turning out in 21 matches of the 33 on the five month trip, in the days of no replacements. "I even played at scrum-half in emergencies against the Junior All Blacks and the Maoris. I got away with it."

Here too was the opportunity to develop attacking full-back play on a global stage, at the highest possible level. "There was a lot of development on the running full-back ploy there. It was a bit of a novelty to them altogether."

Scotland's first job was to win the Test place from Terry Davies - a man who had been well established in the Welsh international side since 1953. "He was very much in the traditional style of full-backs. In the JPR mould under the high ball, he kicked well with both feet."

Scotland, however, ended up playing in five of the six Tests, both matches against Australia as well as the first and third against the All Blacks at full-back, but switching to centre for the final test in New Zealand.

"At the very top level, particularly the Lions, opportunities to attack from full-back coming outside the outside centre, were very limited. Like all tactics it was always one which was slightly more successful at a lower level. International rugby is such a stalemate there is so little room for the backs."

As he points out, that was even more the case then. "At line-outs the backs could stand right up to the line and at scrums right up to the tunnel.

"Certainly we scored a try in Australia, just a straightforward coming into the line and creating a try for Tony O'Reilly in Brisbane. In another of the top provisional games I created a try for Peter Jackson, but against Canterbury I got myself carried off. Their winger read the move a bit better than my inside centre..."

After a brace of comfortable wins against the Wallabies the Lions were to lose the first three Tests of the four Test series against the All Blacks, yet this was in no way a humiliating sequence. Indeed it was the home side who were humiliated in the series opener. Scotland's own recollections sum up the dignity of the man, giving little indication of the storm of controversy caused by the result and the way it came about, via the relentless place-kicking of Don "The Boot" Clarke.

"It's pretty fruitless to get too worked up about that now. There have always been questions about different interpretations, but I wouldn't say refereeing was a major issue on that tour, although the referee wasn't very popular that night.To be fair, though, he wasn't very popular with the New Zealanders either."

For a more vivid account of a match that many New Zealanders were reported as having been embarrassed to have won, it is worth drawing from the history of New Zealand international rugby "The All Blacks" by the great Kiwi rugby writer T.P.McLean.

"Sadly a controversy raged over the standards or refereeing. It was then the habit of new Zealand referees to go overboard in awarding penalties. In the first Test more than 20 went against the Lions. With fewer than 12 minutes of play left the Lions led 17-9. When Don Clarke placed a 50-yard goal and, five minutes later, another from 45 yards, the mood of the crowd changed dramatically. The chants of 'Black! Black!' turned to 'Red! Red!'

"At Clarke's sixth and final penalty, two minutes from no side, the jeering of the All Blacks was almost venomous. The experience jarred Wilson Whineray, just settling into his long reign as captain. And it angered some of the Lions, too, some of whom grossly misbehaved at the formal dinner that evening, throwing oyster shells and salted peanuts about the dining room and mocking the accent of Gordon Brown, president of the New Zealand Rugby Union, as he declared that, 'within the framework of the rules', the referee had done his duty."

Though it is impossible to imagine Ken Scotland being among those who, in the modern vernacular, lost the place, he does provide some flavour of the emotion that was felt.

"Can you imagine that," he says, laughing ruefully and shaking his head at the thought some 35 years on. "It's the only time I've ever seen tears shed in a changing room," he adds - typically refusing to name names. "We'd got to 17-9 up with quarter of an hour to go and Don Clarke then slotted three penalties, at least two of which were controversial."

Scotland missed the second Test in Wellington through injury, when another dubious decision helped wreck the Lions chances, a knock-on which never was allowing the home side to set up a close range scrummage from which they scored the winning try. The All Blacks produced their best performance of the series to seal it with a 22-8 win in the third Test in Christchurch, four tries to nil.

However Scotland regards the fourth Test win as the high point of his career, despite finding himself switched to centre. "I suspect playing me at centre was a decision to try to get the best balance they could in the side." Suffice to say the Lions roared back.

"To win that Test was very emotional. We were pretty drained by that time. It was a big effort and we hadn't had the best of luck in the first two Tests. This time it was the absolute reverse of the first Test where we lost 18-17, having scored four tries to none."

By that statement what Scotland means is that the result, not the respective performances of the combatants, was reversed. The Lions won 9-6, through three unconverted tries by Jackson, O'Reilly and Bev Risman, while Clarke, this time, could muster only two successful penalty strikes.

"They were not vintage All Blacks. The standard of back play wasn't that high," he says. One exception, though, provided a glimpse of the future in terms of a key to Scottish success in 1990.

"I played against Sean Lineen's father Terry in the Tests. He was probably the most dangerous of their backs. But I never had to tackle my opposite number in the entire Final Test, which I found pretty amazing. It was just the way they played, but if I had been up against me I would certainly have had a go. I always feel it's worth having a go at anyone out of position in the centre because it's all about angles," he says, also conceding that at 5'10" and 11 stones he did not present the most imposing of barriers.

The Lions performance in that last match, with Scotland in a play-making role albeit out of position, was testimony to his approach as the men most closely around him, both wingers and the stand-off, got the vital tries.

His record of 27 Scotland caps and five Lions Tests without an international try hardly ties in with the image of the world's first attacking full-back, but he did not see his job as being to touch down.

"I always looked at myself as a provider of scoring opportunities. I think particularly later on this was the case. When I first came into the line from full-back the opposition didn't know what to do so I did score tries. But then they learned and I had the winger coming in at me. They would aim to take man and ball and it often worked painfully well.

"I was lucky to play with some great finishers - Tony O'Reilly and Arthur Smith. Peter Jackson was another one with a real nose for the line, even though he wasn't that quick."

The fact that there were only four Scots in the party meant that the Lions tour was hardly the platform for domestic success that the 1983 and 1989 tours would prove to be, but Scotland did go close to major success in the early sixties.

Scotland, the individual, believes that Scotland, the rugby nation, has a slightly unfair perception of that time. "That period in Scottish history has probably been written down more than it should be. From the mid-fifties we started winning just about as many as we lost which, to be fair, was just about the height of ambition at that time. At the start of each season there was little thought about winning anything like Grand Slams and Triple Crowns. Each game was just a unique international occasion, more so than now."

Unlike any Scot in the last quarter of a century he had the experience of winning in Paris not once, but twice — on his debut and again in 1963 (11-6) when he contributed a penalty, a drop goal and a conversion. The 8-3, 1962 win against Wales was the last at the Arms Park for 20 years. "People used to come and ask me all the time what it was like to win in Cardiff, but that stopped after 1982."

But those matches against England provide bitter memories, even although he lost only four of the seven matches he played against them during a time when they were consistently the best side in the championship. Probably people don't remember it, but in both 1961 and 1962 we played England with the chance of winning the Triple Crown."

The 1961 defeat was hard enough to bear as Scotland went down 6-0 with their full-back's old Lions colleague Horrocks-Taylor - he of the marvellously put compliment once paid by Irishman Mick English 'Horrocks went one way, Taylor went the other and I was left tackling the hyphen' - scoring a penalty and setting up the game's only try. But in 1962 it was real agony, with Scotland feeling real personal responsibility for the failure.

"I don't think we played for the Triple Crown again at Murrayfield until 1990. It was one of the most disappointing moments in my career. We had done the difficult thing, beating Wales and Ireland away, but we never beat England...anywhere!

"In that match I had two opportunities to kick penalties that would have made it 6-3. It was a severe disappointment because we knew, going into the match, that Hugh McLeod, who hadn't beaten them in nine meetings and Arthur Smith, who'd faced them seven or eight times without a win, were playing their last matches. It was so galling not to do it for them.

"Looking back on it now a win that day would have transformed in a way the image of that era of Scottish rugby as we look at it 30 years on. I could have done it with one kick..." he says with a shake of the head as he thinks about the final effort from some 35 yards out, five yards in from the touch-line. "It wasn't a cutting the throat job, but it was one you'd think you had a good chance of getting over.

"The chances I had weren't easy, but I struck them well. However like putting at golf sometimes they all go in and other times they seem to keep fading away from the hole." To rub salt into the wounds he sent over eight of nine attempts for his club Leicester against Birkenhead Park a week later "and I kicked no better."

For the most part, though, Scotland thinks of his rugby career as a period of almost endless pleasure. "All games have their good and bad moments, but I almost always enjoyed every game at every level. I can remember some cracking games at school and

in particular one game for Leicester against Swansea when we won 29-3. The sheer elation of beating a Welsh side by that margin in their own backyard was probably second
only to winning a Test in New Zealand."

Though by no means on the scale of the modern day player transfers, he candidly
admits that rugby opened doors. His first job after leaving Cambridge was arranged by
one of his first Scotland team-mates, hooker Bob MacEwen, with a company in the
English Midlands which also employed his former Lions colleagues O'Reilly (who was
of course to go on to big things as head man at the Heinz conglomerate) and Horrocks-
Taylor.

However some remained permanently shut, as he discovered when work took him
and his family to Aberdeen, effectively terminating his international career. "It said a
lot about Scottish club rugby at the time. I was currently captain of Scotland when I
arrived there, but couldn't join either the club with the best fixture list, Aberdeen
Grammar School FP or the one with the strongest side, Gordonians."

His choice was Aberdeen Wanderers or Aberdeenshire. "The captain of
Aberdeenshire at the time was a very go-ahead fellow so I went there. I really enjoyed
playing there, though and there were some good young lads, but the standard was basically too low to keep me in condition for international rugby. Aberdeenshire have
always been around division V or VI since the national leagues came in and the standard was around the same then.

Ken Scotland today — a contented man at Paxton House, Berwickshire.

"I had always felt that what you really needed was a very hard game every Saturday. At University and at Leicester I was very lucky to have that."

Aberdeen's isolation was also a factor. "I think anyone will tell you travelling becomes the first sickener when playing top class rugby and at Aberdeen you are out on a limb and incessantly travelling."

He grimaces at the thought that Aberdeen is still without one major club, even allowing for the fact that Aberdeen Grammar and Gordonians are, at least, now open. "My ability was eroded by being there. To stay at the top level you've got to be testing yourself all the time at that level. I was only 26 when I went there so was still ambitious to play at the highest level there was."

He even considered making regular trips to Edinburgh from Aberdeen to return to his alma mater, but with a young family and on the roads of that time the travelling really would have been too much. Indeed it is one of the great ironies that his name is so closely associated with Heriot's FP.

"At Leicester they had a special tie for playing 20 first team games. I played for Heriot's FP between 1956 and 1967 and if they'd had something similar I would have struggled to get one of those ties," he reveals. "My appearances were just about the 20 mark, but you'd have had to include sevens tournaments."

That said, back in Edinburgh, he was chairman of selectors when Andy Irvine's side lifted the first division title in 1979, rating his successor as Scotland captain not only as a great player but as "a superb club captain."

Scotland's rugby career ended in low-key fashion. After captaining Scotland through the 1963 Five Nations (beating France and Ireland and losing to Wales and England), playing twice at full-back and twice at stand-off, he was dropped for the 1964 season. After the 1965 trial he got back in for one game, which for the purposes of the Famous XV, was fortuitous. "That one appearance in 1965 got me into your last 30 years. I'm a bit of a time warp, but it's very flattering."

Since his retirement he has continued that nomadic existence, and the wanderlust has passed on to the next generation. Middle son Iain is in England, playing his rugby for the Midland Bank, youngest son Alastair "was quite good" but now works in Stavanger, while oldest son Robin is still in Edinburgh playing with Heriot's FP, where he has appeared in the first XV, having captained the school.

After some 20 years in the building trade KJF made a career switch in the eighties which took him to Arran, working for the National Trust and "having great fun helping with the running of the rugby club there."

By a strange coincidence, although he stresses he has no involvement, rugby is now on the up and up in Berwickshire where he and wife Doreen are now based, Ken having taken up the position of executive director of the private independent trust which looks after the historic stately home, Paxton House.

Career Statistics: K. J. F. Scotland

1957 France 0 Scotland 6 (1DG 1 Pen); Scotland 9 Wales 6 (1 Pen); Scotland 3 Ireland 5 (1 Pen); England 16 Scotland 3 (1 Pen).

1958 Scotland 3 England 3.

1959 France 9 Scotland 0; Scotland 6 Wales 5 (1 Pen); Scotland 3 Ireland 8 (1 Pen); England 3 Scotland 3 (1 Pen).
Australia 6 British Lions 17 (1 Pen); Australia 3 British Lions 24 (1 Pen, 1 Con); New Zealand 18 British Lions 17; New Zealand 22 British Lions 8; New Zealand 6 British Lions 9 +.

1960 Scotland 11 France 13; Wales 8 Scotland 0; Ireland 5 Scotland 6 (1DG); Scotland 12 England 21 (3 Pens).

1961 France 11 Scotland 0; Scotland 5 South Africa 12; Scotland 3 Wales 0; Scotland 16 Ireland 8 (2 Con 3 Pens); Scotland 0 England 6.

1962 Scotland 3 France 11; Wales 3 Scotland 8 (1 Con); Ireland 6 Scotland 20 (2 Pens 1 Con); Scotland 3 England 3 (1 Pen).

1963 France 6 Scotland 11 (1 DG 1 Pen 1 Con)* ; Scotland 0 Wales 6*; Scotland 3 Ireland 0* + +; England 10 Scotland 8 (1 DG)* + +.

1965 France 16 Scotland 8 (1 Con).

All appearances at full-back except: + Centre + +stand-off. * Captain

CAPTAIN'S COMMENT

On The Famous XV: "Roy Laidlaw was saying to me, after the team was announced, that he'd love to have had a game because they've got a few handy players in the Reds. We've been privileged in the past 10 years in particular to see enormous talent and to pick one side. Well, it's one man's opinion against another, of course it is."

Superstar

14 - A. R. Irvine

Andy Irvine always wanted to play on the right wing. At least he did before he started playing rugby. Right up until his teenage years the man who inspired a generation of young Scots to play rugby, who was in every sense Scotland's first rugby superstar, was a football fanatic idolising Denis Law, Jim Baxter and Pele. "Yes...there's a big difference between the right wing at football and at rugby," he muses now.

As a youngster in Edinburgh in the days not long after a very different Famous Five from the one he became associated with, his affiliation lay across the capital at Tynecastle with just the occasional trip to the East End to watch Hibs. Rugby was not an option until he went to George Heriot's School. "I was more or less forced to play it, although I think it worked out quite well."

With more than a trace of humour Irvine explains his own assessment of the appeal of football and indeed why he believes he took more naturally to football and rugby than to sports like tennis, cricket or golf. "I was always better with my feet than my hands," he smiles, aware that the ensuing comments about his proficiency under the high ball are inevitable.

He shares the view of fellow Heriot's FP Ken Scotland that playing football was a vital component in his development. "I would agree about the balance football gives you and it also gives you vision."

It is a great curiosity, however, that the man who took on the mantle of attacking full-back for both club and country, growing up in the city where his predecessor was among the leading sporting stars, never saw Scotland play. "I just missed seeing him play," Irvine reveals. Yet the pair share another similarity in the way they came to play major roles in the evolution of full-back play. Irvine, like Scotland, arrived at the position almost by accident - if a little earlier in his career. "I played at centre all through school," says a man who was capped at schoolboy level in the midfield.

"I only went to full-back a couple of times when people were injured. But after that I wanted to play there because I just couldn't believe the way things opened up. There were so many options."

13

Another option was a move to The Greenyards which arrived at the end of his school-days. "I went there in the summer of 1970. I got pally with a couple of the Melrose boys who'd been in the Scotland Schools team, George Elliot and Jim Henderson and they invited me down to play in the Border Junior Sevens for Melrose Colts. I was free to go and we won a few titles. We kept in touch over the summer and in the August they asked me to go back down because the Grand Slam of Border Junior tournaments was on. I was then selected for the Melrose senior seven for the Kelso Sevens and that's when Heriot's stepped in and said they didn't really want me to play there. I then had to think about where I was going to play, but there was never really any doubt. You always feel a degree of loyalty to your school and a couple of my pals were at the FPs as well."

Representative honours came unexpectedly quickly thereafter. "I was in the Edinburgh side within three months of leaving school. I picked up the Evening News one night and my picture was on the back page. I thought 'That's strange' and then read about being selected for Edinburgh. I didn't know anything about it till then."

However with Colin Blaikie - Scotland's full-back throughout the previous year's Five Nations Championship - still at Heriot's he was stuck with playing on the wing, both for club and district. "I never enjoyed playing on the wing, simply because you don't get much of a game out there. It's pretty constrained. Given a choice I'd rather play at my school position of centre than on the wing. I remember playing there two or three times for Heriot's later in my career when we had some injuries and the best cover

Irvine on his way to the line for the Lions in New Zealand, 1977, supported by Bill Beaumont and Tony Newry.

from the seconds was at full-back and enjoyed it. But I couldn't have played there regularly. I was always too greedy. I made Keith Robertson look like a philanthropist when I played at centre," he laughs.

That said he is critical of those who are not confident enough to take men on, and take the often easier option of the pass. "Not enough players now want the ball and are prepared to have a real go at people. There were a lot of instances when I put the winger in when I had a 50/50 chance of scoring myself but there are a lot who won't take the responsibility at all now. I like to see guys who are willing to take people on."

As he embarked on his senior career Irvine's wait to play his preferred position wasn't a long one - at any level. At the beginning of the 1971-72, on Blaikie's retirement, he established himself as the Heriot's and Edinburgh full-back. By the end of that season he found himself sitting on the bench for the Calcutta Cup match. In that game a young man from Gala by the name of Arthur Brown was making his fifth appearance for his country and he ended the season established in the side after a fine performance, the penalty goal he scored in a comprehensive 23-9 Murrayfield win taking his overall tally for his country to 13 points. The superstitious may take note of that figure. He never played for Scotland again.

Irvine, whose talent was further recognised in selection for the bench for the Scotland/Ireland v England/Wales match to celebrate the beginning of Scotland's Centenary season, was always going to gain selection for his country. At that stage, though, there was little chance of him gaining a regular place at full-back ahead of the talented and highly dependable Brown. That was until New Zealand arrived for their tour and in their clash with a Scottish Districts XV Brown suffered a broken leg.

Irvine was worried that an indifferent performance against France at B level might have damaged his chances, in a match played in Inverness by way of petty SRU retaliation at having been invited to play the two previous away matches in remote parts of the Pyrenees and the Alps.

Chosen for the junior side in the trial before the All Blacks match he put in an exceptional first half performance before further endangering his prospects by picking up a knee injury which was to trouble him throughout the build-up. Nonetheless come the day of the game he was sufficiently fit to put in an outstanding display of his art, attacking frequently from deep defensive positions, as the gallant Scots were beaten 14-9.

Irvine was aware of the immediate comparisons with his Heriot's predecessor Ken Scotland and he is aware of the debt he owes to the man who, in effect, made it acceptable for the full-back to be viewed as much as an the first line of attack as the first line of defence. "It must have been so boring in the days when a full-back was just a stopper," Irvine groans. "I don't think there's any way I would have played there in the Fifties and Sixties." He also acknowledges the importance of having the right players making the decisions, his views again parallelling those of Ken Scotland.

"You have to have a good stand-off to be able to play full-back. It only works if you're in a side that wants to involve you. I was very lucky in that I played with three genuinely great stand-offs.

"For much of my time at Heriot's I played with Fraser Dall who I thought was a wonderful player. With Scotland the most enjoyable time was after John Rutherford came into the side. The only man I ever encountered who was better than John was Phil Bennett. He was unbeatable.

"People like Mike Gibson and Gareth Edwards tell you that Barry John was better. I didn't play with him so you have to respect the views of players of that calibre. But I only did it for a couple of seasons. I often wonder if he would have kept Phil Bennett out. Barry John had a very good couple of seasons and a great tour of New Zealand with the 1971 Lions. But he struggled on his first Lions tour in South Africa in 1968. Phil sustained his form for a long period through the Seventies when Wales won everything.

"The stand-off is the key to everything," Irvine adds. "He's vital because he's the one who basically calls all the moves although I must admit I had a bit of a failing in that I used to make the odd suggestion...every minute or two!"

He notes with regret: "I think that great player as Gavin Hastings is, he could have reached greater heights had he been used more." Perhaps slightly less so, but important all the same in Irvine's view, was having the right sort of combination at centre to release an attacking full-back. "At club level people like Harry Burnett and Jimmy Craig were top quality players and great passers of a ball and at international level, of course, I was fortunate to be playing with Jim Renwick," said Irvine who also made his debut alongside Ian McGeechan.

Describing the two as "very similar players" Irvine is puzzled as to why McGeechan received due regard at international level, but Renwick, relatively speaking, did not, in spite of his record haul of caps. "Geech was never dropped by Scotland, but Jim was," he notes. "Jim was vastly under-rated by the selectors in my view. Just one Test for the Lions..." That said, when Irvine picked the best Scottish and British Lions sides during his career he selected both for Scotland, only McGeechan for the Lions.

Irvine firmly subscribes to the view that given that calibre of player behind the scrum the Scottish philosophy revolved far too much around the front five, yet he offers other explanations for the lack of consistent success which led to a collective reputation as the worst of travellers.

"I don't want to be cruel here, but we never had the sort of quality of back-rows they had in the Eighties. We had one or two good players at various stages, but we never had three good back-row forwards at the same time. I think you'll find if you check that David Leslie's record in terms of winning matches was probably phenomenal, but he missed an awful lot of games In my opinion one of the all time great wing forwards and desperately unfortunate not to have made a Lions tour. I'd love to have played behind some of those good back-rows of the Eighties - they were really exceptional."

Irvine does point out, however, that Scotland's Seventies style was as attractive as that of any side. "We probably ran the ball more than most sides and gave away too many tries. We quite often gave two or three away and we were particularly poor defending around scrummages. Gareth Edwards used to score one down the blindside every time."

He is very much aware of the reservations which are always raised over his own defence, but such comments never really got to him. "Everybody gets knocked all the time. I just went out to enjoy my sport. Don't get me wrong I absolutely hated to lose, I've got a very competitive instinct. But I always believed there was no point in playing if you're not enjoying it."

He is, though, an advocate of squad systems and believes that in a sport like rugby selection should be left until much later, thereby allowing the choice of horses for courses. In the mid-seventies there emerged something of a debate as to whether Irvine's flair or the reliability of Bruce Hay with Irvine moved to the wing, would suit Scotland better. With few top class wingers around the selectors experimented and Irvine agrees with the principle, if not necessarily the timing which was, by necessity, somewhat random.

"If it was a wet, miserable day with the wind blowing then I would have picked Bruce Hay ahead of me at full-back," he says candidly. However he believes there is a great deal of mythology about who are the great defenders and who are not."There are assumptions made about that. For example I always enjoyed playing against the big, fearsome crash tackling centres. When they hit you they really hit you all right and that's what people noticed. But four times out of five they would miss as clean as a whistle. All the great tacklers are the ones who will sometimes miss you. Similarly, when it came to back row forwards I referred laying against the big men rather than the likes of Jean pierre Rives or at club level Hawick's Billy Murray who had the ace and reactions to close you down.

"The other side of that is someone like Phil Bennett. He wasn't noted for his tackles, but what he would do was to show you the outside and he always had the pace to close you down. He would then just grab hold of you and haul you in. I remember one time against Wales getting clean through and Phil was the only man I had to beat...I was never going to score!"

Irvine believes that in attempting to change things, as Scotland sought to add away victories to their perennial successes, meanwhile attempting to take some sort of moral stance on the Gordon Brown case, the selectors shot themselves in the foot.

"I think the Famous Five was dissolved prematurely. The treatment of Gordon Brown was just short of horrific. The SRU made a fool of themselves. There were also Ian McLauchlan and Sandy Carmichael who were both left out and then came back later. They were probably left out a year too soon."

As for the opportunities to achieve real successes in a Scotland shirt, they were few and far between with two cracks at Triple Crowns, both at Twickenham, the only realistic chances. "We tended to beat England at Murrayfield and lose at Twickenham, where we had those two Triple Crown matches. In 1973 we lost quite comfortably but I'll always maintain that we won the other one in 1975. Dougie Morgan missed a kick from 20 to 25 yards out that would have won it. But they were also awarded a try when the ball was put over me and I had to turn and race back against Alan Morley. I've spoken to him since and he agrees he never got to it - but it was given.

"We came as close as that. Sometimes winning and losing is on a knife edge. Look at the 1990 Grand Slam game, for example. It was pretty fortuitous the way the ball bounced for Tony Stanger."

As Irvine struggled in pursuit of what would prove to be his Holy Grail, Five Nations success with Scotland, so the personal tributes flooded in. His talents were introduced to a much wider global audience in 1974 when he was part of Willie John McBride's Invincibles squad as the British Lions toured South Africa.

"That whole 1974 tour was a pure bonus for me. I think I was the second youngest - about a week older than the youngest there. For me it was like a holiday trip to Disneyland. Only two or three years earlier I'd been keeping a scrapbook with these legends in it. I played more games on tour than anyone else."

He ended the tour a Test hero - albeit as a right winger - having scored seven points on his Lions Test debut with three successful kicks at goal in the third Test which proved the series decider, then scored a try as well as a penalty in the final Test to help preserve the Lions undefeated record in a 13-13 draw. However Irvine was mature enough to fully appreciate how well things went for him - a message driven home by one of his room-mates, English lock Chris Ralston midway through the tour.

"I'd played about eight games and he'd played about three," Irvine explains. "I was buzzing with how wonderful things were, but he said it was a dreadful tour and all he wanted to do was go home. I couldn't believe it but he told me to think about it. 'You've played in almost every match while I'm just a spectator out here.' Willie John was captain so tended to play a lot. Roger Uttley was being used in the back-row on Saturdays but was getting extra games on the Wednesdays at lock. Chris was the unlucky one."

Even on the happiest of tours Irvine had learned about the need to keep every member of the party involved. Indeed the trip to South Africa played a huge part in his rugby education. "A lot of people don't know this, but many of the moves that Heriot's and Scotland used were the ones I learned on Lions tours, almost all from Phil Bennett"

Irvine was also deeply impressed by the straightforward approach of the coach on that tour - Irishman Sid Millar.

"Sid was a forward and I'm not one for forwards coaching backs...I think it's like a geography teacher trying to teach maths. But give him credit for this. We were working on back moves and some of the senior Welsh backs were pretty well running things. Sid couldn't really teach these boys anything about back play, but he came over and involved himself.

"What he did was to take a stop-watch and just got us to cut out the moves to work on getting the ball out to the wings as quickly as possible. We had real pacemen out wide, people like JJ Williams and Clive Rees. Sid just checked on the time it took from Gareth getting the ball to it being touched down. He improved our speed by a second and a half. That doesn't sound like much, but Sid reckoned that a good player could cover 12 yards in a second and a half. That means you could give a flanker a 10 yard start from the base of a scrum and he still couldn't get across by the time you've put a man over in the corner."

Irvine was to establish himself as one of the game's most stylish performers in two subsequent, less successful, Lions tours. He played in seven of eight Tests between the trips to New Zealand in 1977 and South Africa in 1980. On the second of these trips Irvine was originally left at home due to a torn hamstring but amidst an injury ravaged tour he was sent for after the opening Test. Three days after arrival he was in the Saturday side against Transvaal. A further week later he was in the Test side. Even a fully fit Irvine probably couldn't have turned things around for the sadly depleted Lions, however and he never had the opportunity to do so anyway. However after the series had been lost he scored a try in the final Test as the Lions salvaged some pride.

In retrospect, considering the problems which beset the tour, the series defeat was probably inevitable. Certainly the management was spared much of the criticism which

Finding a gap versus Wales in 1977

was directed at their counterparts of three years previously - in particular skipper Phil Bennett. Irvine, however, is fierce in his defence of his friend and captain. "I would question the judgment of a lot of the pressmen," he says of the reporting of the 1977 series. "I know they've got a job to do but there are only two or three whose views I really respect. I've got one or two articles by New Zealand scribes that present a very different version of that tour to the one which was transmitted to Britain."

Long before he embarked on his final Lions tour Irvine had already established himself as Scotland's first true rugby superstar - a player whose exhilarating style was popularising the game across the Scottish social spectrum in a way that had never happened before. Among the small percentage of Scots in whom he did not inspire a burning desire to be at Murrayfield on international day was his mother, however. As her son became one of the country's most famous ever sportsmen, making what was briefly a record 51 appearances, she saw him play just once. Her bemusement was such that after the thrilling 1974 Calcutta Cup match won by Irvine with the final kick of the ball, she asked her son which side had won, complained good-naturedly about the vast crowds in attendance, then suggested that she would, in future, simply watch the televised highlights.

In the late Seventies, however, another television programme arrived which could hardly have been more appropriate and despite Irvine's protestations that he was not a natural all-rounder, he made quite an impact. His first crack at the competition, featuring the top performers in a string of different sports, allowed to compete in a range of different events, other than their own sports, came in 1978.

"I really enjoyed 'Superstars'," he says. "The only thing that really disappointed me was that I didn't have time to work on it. For example I'd never used a bow and arrow before or been in a canoe. But I couldn't take the prize money that was on offer and had a job to do, whereas some of the professional sportsmen trained hard for it."

Irvine had no great difficult in turning down the cash. He was used to substantial offers by that stage, having had a number of approaches from rugby league."But I am fairly sure I could have won if I could have worked at it like some of the others who were getting the money. Brian Jacks from judo was not a household name but because he trained specifically for 'Superstars' he picked up something like £50,000 so it was worth the work he put in. It might well have been different if we'd all had the same preparation

"What I really enjoyed was meeting the other guys from different sports - people like Mick Channon the footballer, racing driver Stirling Moss and boxer Herrol Graham. On one occasion I shared a room with Tony Knowles. That was entertaining to say the least," Irvine laughs. Around that time the snooker star's antics featured prominently and regularly in the tabloids. "As soon as the gun went off I was as competitive as anyone, but I never trained for it and there's a real technique to things like cycling, archery and paddling a canoe."

Irvine did his sport proud, nonetheless, eventually finishing third in the British final and gaining an invitation to the World final. He then established firmly where his priorities lay by turning down that glamour trip to the USA because Heriot's had a vital league match at around the same time, in Spring 1979. He was invited again in 1982, finishing second in the British event. However Irvine ultimately had reason to regret his participation in the contests.

"It was the 'Superstars' that finally crocked me for rugby. I had to win an 800 metres to win the overall thing and as I say I was very competitive once the events got under way. I went flat out and that's what finally wrecked my achilles tendon. Had I not taken part I might have played international rugby for another two or three years. Then again I might have gone down to Goldenacre that night and done the same damage. However it was on the tartan track I really hurt myself. We played Fiji the next month and I had been captain at the time and was still only 30, but that let Peter Dods in."

For all those of us who were drawn to rugby in the Seventies by Irvine's dazzling brilliance, one of the great twists of sporting fate is that, having sat on the bench just once previously some 12 years earlier — Andy Irvine would come so close and yet so far to being involved in the triumphs of 1984 — a first Triple Crown in 46 years, a first Grand Slam in 59 years. Yet Irvine is not a man haunted by the knowledge that he might have been involved in the latter in particular had either of two players injured in the first half, required to go off at the interval. Indeed in his autobiography he spoke of a strange sense of relief at not receiving the call after two years absence from the international arena. Certainly it would have been a tragedy had any lack of match fitness on the part of such a great player contributed to the Grand Slam slipping from Scotland's grasp that day. In any case, as previously noted, he had by that stage learned to appreciate the good things.

"I never looked on missing out in 1984 as in any way ironic. In some ways I was very unlucky towards the end of my career, but then you look at someone like David Leslie. I had 10 years on the trot and went on three Lions tours. He missed so many games over the years through injury and was never selected for the Lions. David played in the Triple Crown and Grand Slam matches, but I'd rather have had things my way than his.

"Anyway I wasn't alone. Jim Renwick missed out through injury in the Grand Slam season. I would love to have been involved though," he adds. "But it was always inevitable that I would miss out somewhere down the line. I wouldn't swap my career with anyone. I suppose Gareth Edwards or Phil Bennett had more wins to savour, but I loved every moment of my career."

From a dazzling array of performances there is further irony in that one of the matches which saw him at his worst is best remembered for the way in which he turned things around.

"I suppose that 1980 win over France is the most obvious one to mention among the games I enjoyed," he admits. The crowd had actually begun to get after their hero after over an hour which had seen him miss umpteen kicks at goal including one almost under the posts in a generally nightmarish display. Just as there are golfers whose putter can suddenly, inexplicably get hot, so Irvine was a player given to bursts of inspiration and this was the definitive display. In the closing 12 minutes he scored two tries in two moves with which any French three-quarter line would have been ecstatic, the first of them started as well as finished by Irvine. For good measure two penalties and a touch-line conversion were put over as a beaten looking Scottish side found themselves winning, going away. Little wonder that the shell-shocked French did not win at Murrayfield for a further 14 years.

He also went out on a high at home and abroad, his final Five Nations game being the spectacular win over Wales at Cardiff, before he led Scotland to Australia where they claimed their first Test win on tour. In terms of achievement, though, the greatest success of his career, in his own view, came a year earlier, when he led Heriot's FP to the national league title - the first side in six years of the Championship to deny Hawick.

"The games that gave me most enjoyment were club games against the likes of Hawick, Gala or Watsonians. We were quite often real underdogs and I always felt I was under more pressure there. I also enjoyed it even more because I was at the centre of everything, taking the penalties and the drop goals, calling the moves. In internationals it was different because everyone was an accomplished player doing his own job. I never used to get much sleep before Hawick games and that was down to excitement rather than fear. I never thought of them as a dirty side, but they were hard."

Audrey snaps one for the family album in 1979 when Andy went to the Palace to receive his MBE

In particular the autumn friendlies with The Greens stand out in his memory as great occasions.

"We usually played them on the last Saturday before the leagues, in good weather late in September. I used to get more worked up for that game than for internationals. Even in those days, when Hawick won seven out of the first eight titles, we used to beat them regularly at that time of year. It was a different story for the regular New Year game, though.

"One of the greatest moments was lifting that title in 1979, although one of the biggest disappointments was a year later when we should have won it again, but lost to Stewart's Melville FP at Goldenacre on the last day as Dougie Morgan scored four penalties.

"A lot of the enjoyment of success with Heriot's came from the fact that these were the guys you were training with week-in, week-out. Some of them weren't great rugby players by any means. A couple of them were very ordinary, never got a sniff of the Edinburgh team, but these were the players who always turned out at training. Never missed a session because they knew they couldn't afford to. But when it came to heart and commitment they were second to none and they were very much a part of our inaugural Championship winning side.

"It meant a lot to help these boys be involved in something like our title success. It's the great thing about rugby. Some pretty average players can play a vital part in a winning side."

Irvine's Heriot's also played a champagne style of rugby, drawing crowds the like of which may never be seen again at Scottish club matches. "I always believed the best place to attack from was a scrum in your own 22," he says, providing an insight into his entire way of thinking. "Especially if the other side attacked your scrum because that meant their back-row was still bound on. Always scrums, mind you, not line-outs because then there are forwards around cluttering things up.

"We used to score an incredible number of tries from deep positions. Even if it is expected players still get so much room to play there and we had Bill Gammell who would always score from any range if you gave him a sniff of the line. I remember one in particular when we scored following a scrum about four or five yards out under our own posts. It's so much more satisfying to see a winger go the length of the field and score rather than the no.8 scoring from a pushover."

He believes pace throughout a back division is a vital ingredient alongside handling ability and vision. "It helps when people have to watch everyone the way they did when we had the likes of John Rutherford, Keith Robertson, Jim Renwick and myself in the line. They couldn't take the risk of laying off anyone because we all carried a threat and that lets you create overlaps."

However good the backs may be he would still always prefer to be involved than isolated, as he saw it, on the wing. However as he ponders his selection for the Famous XV, in the knowledge that he would never actually have to play as a winger again should he choose not to, he is philosophical. "Better to be selected out of position on the wing than not to make the team at all," he reckons.

These days he still has a keen involvement in the game, doing occasional work with the Heriot's back division and, according to his colleagues in the Scottish Classics line-up which toured South Africa in 1994, still able to turn on the style when the occasion demands. "I paid for that though. When I was young and fit I preferred those hard South African grounds, but the achilles tendons played up for ages. It doesn't bother you during a game, but afterwards..."

It's not that long, though, since he still felt capable of doing a turn at club level. "I enjoy watching certain games these days. For the first few years after I stopped I had a lot of trouble watching. With Scotland there wasn't much you could do about that, but with Heriot's it was just a case of bringing the boots along the next week.

"I remember one time in the late Eighties, one of the seasons Kelso won the title, we were facing relegation. We had an end of season match against Jed-Forest and Alan Lawson and I both came back. They had Gary Armstrong at scrum-half and Roy Laidlaw at stand-off. They were strong favourites but we won with plenty to spare. It was fantas-

Irvine today, a successful professional man still fit enough to tell current Division One players on a Golden Oldies tour just to give him the ball and leave the rest to him.

tic to be able to do that," he says with relish. "You could do it at club level, but as I say, internationals were a slightly different story."

Achilles tendons undeterred by several flights of stairs to his office high above Edinburgh's Charlotte Square, Irvine, who with wife Audrey has three daughters - Jennie, Sara and Nicola and a son, Jamie - has since turned his competitive instinct to building a highly successful career with Chartered Surveyors - Jones, Lang, Wootton.

Of the rugby he does watch he isn't overly impressed, but there is always hope.

"Of the present international sides the only one I really respect for their style of play is obvious - Australia! The second best would be France, although one of the best displays I've seen was New Zealand against us last season (1993/94).

"A lot of people were livid coming out of there considering our display, but I said we should forget how bad we were and accept that they played some absolutely fantastic rugby. I still love the game," he says, with just a slight reservation. "I do get a wee bit frustrated with some of the boring ones."

Career Statistics: Andy Irvine

1972 Scotland 9 New Zealand 14 (2 Pens).

1973 France 16 Scotland 13; Scotland 10 Wales 9; Scotland 19 Ireland 14; England 20 Scotland 13 (1 Con); Scotland 27 Overseas XV 16 (1 Pen 2 Cons).

1974 Wales 6 Scotland 0; Scotland 16 England 14 (1 Con 1 Try 2 Pens); Ireland 9 Scotland 6 (2 Pens); Scotland 19 France 6 (2 Pens 1 Con).

South Africa 26 British Lions 9 (1Con 2Pens) +; South Africa 13 British Lions 13 (1Try 1Pen) +.

1975 Scotland 20 Ireland 13 (2 Pens); France 10 Scotland 9 (3 Pens); Scotland 12 Wales 10; England 7 Scotland 6; New Zealand 24 Scotland 0+; Scotland 10 Australia 3 +.

1976 Scotland 6 France 13 +; Wales 28 Scotland 6 (1 Try); Scotland 22 England 12 (2 Pens, 2 Cons); Ireland 6 Scotland 15 (4 Pens).

1977 England 26 Scotland 6 (2 Pens); Scotland 21 Ireland 18 (2 Pens); France 3 Scotland 23; Scotland 9 Wales 18 (1 Try 1 Con).

New Zealand 16 British Lions 12 (1 Pen); New Zealand 9 British Lions 13; New Zealand 19 British Lions 7 (1 Pen); New Zealand 10 British Lions 9.

1978 Ireland 12 Scotland 9 +; Scotland 16 France 19 (1 Try)(1); Scotland 0 England 15; Scotland 9 New Zealand 18 (1 Con).

1979 Scotland 13 Wales 19 (3 Pens 1 Try); England 7 Scotland 7 (1 Pen); Scotland 11 Ireland 11 (1 Try 1 Pen); France 21 Scotland 17 (1 Try 1 Con 1 Pen); Scotland 6 New Zealand 20 (2 Pens).

1980 Ireland 22 Scotland 15 (1 Pen 2 Cons); Scotland 22 France 14 (2 Tries 1 Con 2 Pens); Wales 17 Scotland 6 (1 Con); Scotland 18 England 30 (2 Cons 2 Pens)*.

South Africa 26 British Lions 19 (1 Pen); South Africa 12 British Lions 10; South Africa 13 British Lions 17 (1 Try).

1981 France 16 Scotland 9 (1 Pen)*; Scotland 15 Wales 6 *; England 23 Scotland 17 * (1 Con 1 Pen)*; Scotland 10 Ireland 9 (1 Pen)*; New Zealand 11 Scotland 4 *; New Zealand 40 Scotland 15 (2 Pens 1 Con) *; Scotland 12 Romania 6 (4 Pens) *; Scotland 24 Australia 15 (5 Pens 1 Con).

1982 Scotland 9 England 9 (2 Pens)*; Ireland 21 Scotland 12 (1 Con) *; Scotland 16 France 7 (3 Pens) *; Wales 18 Scotland 34 (4 Cons) *; Australia 7 Scotland 12 (1 Pen 1 Con) *; Australia 33 Scotland 9 (3 Pens) *.

All appearances at full-back except + on wing. * Captain [1]Replaced by Alistair Cranston.

CAPTAIN'S COMMENT:
On his successors as Scotland captain: "Off the pitch David Sole is just one of the nicest men, but on it.... There are precious few of them but he's the kind of bloke that you'd be quite happy if he married your daughter. He's a good, hard man. I don't know how much it had to do with the public school stuff, the early morning runs and all that nonsense. Two of the hardest men I ever played with or against - David Leslie and David Sole - were products of Glenalmond College. Gavin is the biggest thing, if not in UK certainly in Scottish rugby and has been for some time. I phoned him about a trip to Mull recently and said 'OK Gav, three-line whip on this one.' 'Oh aye, very good Fin,' he said. 'Well I'm speaking at a dinner at Kyle of Lochalsh at 7.30pm so if you can get me from Mull to Kyle of Lochalsh then I'll come. I said 'Ach, no problem', put the phone down and immediately arranged a flight from Tobermory to Kyle of Lochalsh. So I phoned him back and said I'd got it organised. 'Oh no,' he says. 'You're joking.' But we took him across to Mull where we played in the most horrendous conditions - on a mud patch in the middle of the island. We were there to officially open the clubhouse, but the work hadn't been completed so he got a cold shower in the dressing room then changed and away to speak at Kyle of Lochalsh. I don't honestly think that Will Carling would have done that. Gavin is just the perfect ambassador for Scottish rugby"

Little Brother

13 - S. Hastings

Several of their colleagues have recounted the freshness the Hastings brothers brought to the Scotland dressing room on their arrival in the mid-eighties. They speak of a confidence, bordering on cockiness, but they do so with great affection because, as another of the debutants that day, Finlay Calder, sums up: "They were winners!"

Gavin and Scott took to international rugby as if born to it, but it is little wonder that the pair felt so at home on January 18, 1986. Not only did they have one another for company at Murrayfield that day, but all around them were very familiar faces.

"The great thing for me was that I was playing alongside David Johnston, who I was playing club rugby with at the time," says Scott. "A few years previously I had been a schoolboy on the terraces cheering on the likes of David and John Rutherford and here I was playing alongside. "John had actually been a PE teacher at Watson's while I was there. He didn't teach me directly, but he had taught Gavin." Clearly they had the perfect pedigree for the success that was to come their way.

In reviewing Scott's career "hard-hitting centre" and "Gavin's brother" are the two descriptions which are most commonly linked with his name and while they don't exactly rankle with the brilliant Watsonians back, nor do they present much of a picture of a man who has won a half century of caps and whose presence was deemed by the opposition to have turned a British Lions Test series.

It is natural to regard the Hastings brothers, who have formed the solid core of the Scottish back division since 1986, as two halves of the same whole. Having made their debuts together that year, against France at Murrayfield, they then, remarkably, went on to win their 50th caps together against the same opposition, again in their home town, a little over eight years later. Yet, as Scott points out, despite latterly playing almost every competitive match together, for Watsonians, Edinburgh, Scotland and the Lions, they have not exactly lived in one another's shadow, as rugby players or as individuals.

"Our rugby careers never really came together until our first international," he reveals. As youngsters the Hastings brothers, all four of them - Graeme is the oldest and Ewan the youngest - did, of course, learn their sport together.

27

"It didn't really matter what time of year it was. If Wimbledon was on we'd be out with the tennis racquets, if the Open was on it would be golf." Dad, Clifford, played for Watsonians, though and was, of course, instrumental in getting the boys involved there. The sight of the four of them kicking a football about on the Myreside back pitches became a familiar sight on the Saturday afternoons of the early seventies.

"Instead of going to watch football it was on with the tracksuits and down to Myreside. We were brought up going there every Saturday afternoon if there was a home game."

They may not have been following the masses to Tynecastle, but it is fair to say that the Hastings quartet were not overly concerned with the performance of their own Maroons, either.

"Even when the game was going on we'd be playing football on the back pitches and occasionally we'd go across to see what the score was. After the game we'd go across the road, get our crisps and coke, watch the football results and then it was out onto the hockey pitches until we got chased off them. They weren't too big and had good size goals."

The good news for Watsonians and, perhaps, for Scotland is that the next generation is on its way. "It's quite funny now, my young son Corey comes down to Myreside and all the kids play with him. He's emulating some of my childhood in many respects. He's become part of the luggage. Comes everywhere with Jenny and me...in the kit-bag."

Rugby, though, began in the back garden of the family home. "Because there were four of us there always used to be three against one," Scott says, evenly. "No, no, never two against two. We always had to pick on somebody."

A tight-knit bunch in early days, they began to go their separated ways on arrival at George Watson's College. "The family is very strong," says Scott. "But we're not particularly close, just good friends more than anything else. We're quite happy just to phone each other up for a chat and have never been ones for family feuds and arguments, we just got on with it. But we see each other as friends more, we value that."

In terms of blazing a rugby trail Scott gives the credit to Graeme. "He laid the groundwork, playing for Scottish Schools, I think against Philippe Sella around 1978. He was a centre, while Gavin and I played most of our school rugby at stand-off. But Graeme kicked it all off playing age group rugby for Edinburgh Schools under-16s. So when Gavin came along it was very much a case of 'Here's Graeme's brother. He's bound to be a good player.' That was the same in many respects for myself."

Scott quickly found out that the family name might help open the odd door, but once in the room he had to make his own presence felt, failing to gain selection for the Scottish Schools after his first trial, although he would go on to captain them.

Family man — Jenny, Corey and Scott on a rugby day out

Graeme would play for the Watsonians first XV and have an involvement with the national under-21 squad, before emigrating to Australia where he met and married Jacqui who, to keep the Scottish rugby connection going, comes from Melrose.

"After school we all went our different ways. Gavin made strides with Watsonians and Edinburgh and the like, studying at Paisley Tec before going on to Cambridge. I went to Polytechnic in Newcastle-upon-Tyne and Graeme went to college in Crewe, for some unknown reason. I think he thought he could catch a train from there to Australia or something."

Graeme continued his career and was, ironically, the first Hastings brother to make contact with another player with whom Scott's name was to be inextricably linked.

"In 1980 or thereabouts, Graeme played for Victoria, who were very much the Cinderella rugby state in Australia, where they play a lot of Aussie Rules, cricket and rugby league. In one of their matches they came up against the New Zealand province Counties.

Proud mother Isobel pictured with her sons before their fourth caps in their first international season, 1986

"I think if you'd told the Counties centre that day, Sean Lineen, that he'd end up creating an international record for centre partnerships with his opposite number Graeme
Hastings' brother on the other side of the world and would end up being his best man
he would have thought you were crazy.Sean became a very, very close friend."

Graeme's presence in Australia has added extra flavour to tours "Down Under" for
his younger brothers - all three of them. Ewan continues to play rugby but never really
aspired to following in the family business, so to speak.

"I think in many ways he must regard himself as the black sheep of the family, but
he's had as much enjoyment following us around. He came out and supported us on
Scotland's tour of New Zealand in 1990 and just had an absolute ball," Scott says, indi-
cating that his little brother has clearly decided to make the best of his "Hastings
brother" notoriety."He's not maybe as keen on the game as Gavin and myself are, but
he still likes being part and parcel of it."

As for the middle two brothers: "Certainly up until our middle twenties rugby did
mean everything to us."As single guys playing international rugby you put a tremendous amount of dedication into your sport. Now I would like to think I'm putting in the
same amount of dedication, but I've got to strike a balance with work and family values
now."

As a teenager there was no such distraction, but while the success of his brothers
gave him something to aim for it is remarkable that he and Gavin played so little rugby
together."It wasn't the Watson's way to push you into the First XV until fifth or sixth
year and there are three years between us.

"After school we went our separate ways and got away from home, which, I think, was
good for us. It was never a case of getting out of the shadow of an older brother, though.
It's never been that. I just took the decision that I thought it would do me good to get
away from Edinburgh where I was born and bred and I think Gavin felt the same."

So it was that Scott found himself with the Newcastle Northern club, as a stand-off,
learning to make decisions under pressure against some of England's top clubs."At that
time, as a youngster, it was tremendous to play against the former England stand-off
Alan Old of Sheffield and Steve Smith the 1980 Grand Slam scrum-half, who was with
Sale. We also faced sides like of Orrell, Otley and Waterloo, who were among the top
clubs in England back in 1982, as well as London Scottish, Irish and Welsh and made
trips across the Border to the likes of Gala and Hawick, which kept the Scottish connection going."

That connection was also maintained through the national under-21 set-up with players like Dougie Wyllie, who was already involved in the senior squad, Adam Buchanan-
Smith and Alan Tait, both of whom followed Scott into the Scotland side with the latter
going on to superstar status in rugby league.By the time he got back to Scotland he was
highly experienced in almost every back position, bar centre.

"I had played on the wing in my first year at school and again their for Northumberland," he says, slightly sheepishly with the 1993 New Zealand nightmare still fresh in the memory. "And I was at fly-half for the Anglo-Scots. I remember playing at centre for Scotland under-21, but my second game there was the Scotland trial and the third was my debut against France."

On his return to Watsonians in 1985, he found himself at full-back, with Gavin still south of the border, but the current Scotland centre pairing of David Johnston and Euan Kennedy were in place in the Myreside midfield, though during Gavin's holidays he would switch to stand-off.

"There was a fair bit of chopping and changing but when you're young you can handle that and at club level you can get away with it. It's a different kettle of fish at international level as I've found," he says with a pained expression as he ponders that appearance on the left wing against New Zealand in November 1993 during the 51-15 record mauling.

In 1985 he was also picked for the Scotland training squad and, having at last now played a few games alongside Gavin, would probably have accompanied him on that summer's development tour of the USA and Canada, but was unavailable.

However Gavin did, indirectly, give him a leg up towards the international side. "He had played a couple of games for Scotland B and was likely to be selected for Scotland B to play Italy the week before the Varsity match when he was due to get his first Blue. He had a hard decision to make but opted to make himself unavailable for the B side and that was when I got my chance to step in at full-back."

The part he played in that 9-0 win at Old Anniesland did enough to earn a place in the international trial the following January which was to provide the probables Blue XV with a horrendous shock.

"It was a great time. Suddenly I was selected for Scotland B, then Gavin played his first Varsity match. I celebrated my 21st birthday in December, Christmas came and went, we walked into the trial and, bang - the Reds stuffed the Blues. I've always taken the view that it doesn't matter who you are playing against, you've always got a chance of beating them...of coming off the pitch having played better than them. That's all you have to do. The David and Goliath story has been repeated over and over again in sport. I genuinely thought we could beat the Blues."

As with so many of the great moments in international rugby in recent years, Scott remembers his debut international as, above all else, a very special family day.

"I was nervous and excited about the occasion and I was determined to enjoy it. It was great getting all that recognition on the television in the build-up." But the big moment was just that final surge into the limelight.

"As a youngster international rugby made such an impression on me and running down the tunnel was something I'd always wanted to do. Euan Kennedy wrote me a fantastic letter and all he talked about was running down the tunnel...what it had meant to him and what it would mean to me. It was a kind gesture from Euan and I certainly will not forget the experience."

As mentioned he was alongside David Johnston that day: "He'd been one of my boyhood heroes. I'm now very friendly with him. I think he's got a very exciting rugby brain and coaching talent."

As to the match itself it began in the most bizarre circumstances, with France taking a quick line-out on halfway after Gavin's kick-off went direct into touch and scoring in the left corner. "I was standing with John Beattie going 'What the hell happened?' and he didn't know either. We weren't aware of the rule that you could take a line-out rather than a scrum or kick again.

"We hadn't a clue what was going on but fortunately we kicked off, Gav kicked a penalty and suddenly 4-3 didn't mean an awful lot. That maybe brings us to the great debate, namely what's greater a try or a penalty, but it was 4-3. At the end of the day Gav kicked six penalties, a new world record — not a bad debut and we won 18-17."

It looks like a sidestep coming on for Edinburgh against the touring Australians in 1988.

From a personal point of view there wasn't a great deal of involvement, but Scott was grateful to John Rutherford's consideration. "He was great. We were playing a bit of a kick and chase game and on one occasion he just turned to me and said 'Right, you're doing this one', gave me the ball and I banged the high ball up. I think we even got a penalty out of it. Without a doubt he was settling me in. It was great encouragement.

"I was playing against Sella who must have had around 30 caps at that time. I must admit in all the years I've played against Sella, although he's a great player, he hasn't created too much against Scotland. When you consider the damage he's done against other international teams I like to pride myself on that."

It was a strange championship in 1986. Scotland's previous two campaigns had ended with a Grand Slam in 1984 and a whitewash in 1985. This season was something of a transition, yet it came very close to being another Grand Slam year.

The only hiccup was in the second match at Cardiff Arms Park when Gavin had an off day, while Paul Thorburn launched a penalty, subsequently measured at some 70 yards, to inspire Wales to a 22-15 win, despite the fact Scotland scored three tries to one. "But Gavin kicked well again against England. He's never been one to dwell on a bad day," Scott records.

This time though, despite the fact that Gavin had just broken his own record by scoring 21, with five penalties and three conversions, the younger brother had his own reason to celebrate as he went over to score his first international try during the 33-6 humbling of the English.

"That England game was one of the most satisfying I can remember because we'd worked at a game plan. We'd discussed things which went almost to the letter on the pitch. The planning and preparation all came good."

The following year Scotland were building towards the first ever World Cup. In the second championship match, against France, Scott claimed another international try, but from that point things started to go wrong. Despite scoring 22 points in the Parc Des Princes Scotland lost by six points and although they beat Wales a fortnight later Scott was injured and forced out of the Calcutta Cup match, though there was some consolation with big brother's first penalty making him the fastest century-maker in International Board history. "I broke my cheekbone against Wales. The same one as forced me out of the Lions tour in '93."

Come the summer and he was desperate to reclaim his place in the side - perhaps too eager! "It was the worst possible situation. We were two days off the plane when I pulled a hamstring two and a quarter hours into a training session. Scottish rugby's come an awful long way from that day.

"You wouldn't now find a Scottish squad training for two and a half hours the second day after a trip round the world. It wouldn't happen, but the coaches were part of the learning process too. I was tired after a long journey. Nowadays I know when to stop, but as a young lad who had only six days prior to the opening game against France I wanted to impress the coaches."

He finally did get on in the second qualifying match against Rumania, but set the target which Michael Dods just about pipped by earning a cap for eight seconds on the pitch as a blood replacement for Gavin against Ireland in 1993. "The big question is how many seconds did I actually last. John Rutherford had a long tournament compared with me. He lasted minutes, I lasted seconds."

Insult was added to injury when manager Bob Munro insisted on throwing Scott out of the team hotel a day ahead of the rest of the side. "The players pleaded with him because they felt I should still be part of it, but he stuck to the decision because he felt the New Zealanders would home in on the fact that we would have 27 players when we sent for a replacement and not 26 as the tournament rules stated. The management of that tour left a lot to be desired. It was a real kick in the teeth for me."

It was a doubly determined Scott Hastings who returned to the side in 1988, but he again missed the Calcutta Cup match and Scotland were spared a whitewash only by France's Murrayfield hoodoo. That year was completed by a thrashing at the hands of the Wallabies, who had been well beaten by England a week earlier, but Ian McGeechan had, by then, just been appointed as Scotland's coach.

Just as significantly for Hastings was that Lineen had arrived in Scotland for a rugby-playing holiday, only to be plunged into the international scene, courtesy of a long-lost Stornowegian grandfather. " '88 sort of passed by. It was a season of change. '89 was different, as much as anything else there was the chance of a Lions tour."

Results started to come again with only one championship defeat that season, inevitably in Paris, and while the epithet "scavengers" was heard for the first time, from England manager Geoff Cooke after the 12-12 draw at Twickenham, it was clear that the whingeing was based on concern that Scotland were becoming a force to be reckoned with.

Eight Scots went on that summer's British Lions tour, Scott among them and it was to prove something of a watershed for Scottish rugby. "We were the first brothers to go on a Lions tour this century. I think that although we'd only been playing for three or four years an awful lot had happened and this was just another step up the ladder. But I was only 24 and very aware of pulling on a jersey that had been worn by some of the greatest rugby players in history. Being there was fantastic. It is the only time a rugby player gets the chance to find out what it is to be a professional athlete. I just wish I'd been born a few years earlier and could have gone on one of those six month tours."

He revelled in the experience: "If I had the opportunity to play rugby union for a living I would, but unfortunately I don't."

The social aspect also appealed. "The opportunities touring provided were great. Things like diving off the Great Barrier Reef were an unforgettable experience. You don't have a great opportunity during the Five Nations to get to know your opposite number. Maybe just a quick couple of beers across the table after the game. But that changes on a Lions tour. I got to know the likes of Rob Andrew and Brendan Mullin extremely well.

"The management were going to stand for no cliques. Finlay Calder as captain made that very clear. "Ian McGeechan got the very best out of the players. Maybe not the backs just so much because it was a relatively short Lions tour, but if we'd gone on to New Zealand as they used to, I reckon he could have got the very best out of them."

He was unavailable for the first Test, which the Lions lost, because of a hamstring problem, but would return for the remaining Tests to make his presence well and truly felt. The Scots had taken a tremendous level of fitness to Australia. "We got Douglas Morgan and Derrick Grant to take twice weekly training sessions before we left. One in Edinburgh, one in the Borders, for all the Scottish Lions."

His appearance in the second Test marked another family landmark as the Hastings became the first brothers to appear in a Lions Test side together and they combined for the vital score.

Then the youngest member of the Scotland side, Scott and his captain Colin Deans examine the Calcutta Cup with Miss Lorna Antonini, whose father was one of the donors, before the centenary match in 1986.

By the time the decider came around the Australian press was hurling accusations left, right and centre. "Halfway through the tour there had been a punch-up and they were literally calling Dean Richards, the policeman, a 'Paki-basher'. That expression was actually in one of the papers. As to the rough stuff the Australians were just as much at fault as we were.

"The decider was unbelievable. Gavin had his kicking boots on again. Ian McGeechan had got his psychological hat on and had us in just the right frame of mind." The older Hastings scored 15 points, but his brother was credited with the moment which won the series by opposing coach Bob Dwyer, who would guide the Wallabies to the World Cup two years later.

"He was very kind in saying that if it hadn't been for myself Australia might have won the series." The moment in question was a last-ditch, try-saving tackle on the great David Campese.

"I caught Campese coming through the centre. It was literally out of the corner of my eye as I lined up someone else. It was just an instinctive reaction to pull him down. If he'd got through he'd almost inevitably have scored."

Within a year Hastings had made another tackle which most Scots would regard as far more important, but at the time the Lions victory was the greatest moment in his international career.

"When that whistle went...oh!" he says with a sharp intake of breath. "Suddenly the Lions had won the Test series."

It is perhaps no coincidence that in 1993 in New Zealand Scott, having again fractured that left cheekbone earlier in the tour, was unable to add his considerable presence to the midfield for the Test series. That was so disappointing because the 1993 Lions was just about the most enjoyable time I've had in rugby, that first four or five weeks."

The Scottish Lions returned from that 1989 tour very much aware that they were as good as any of the other Home Union players. It wasn't quite the same as in 1983 when John Rutherford spoke of having been a little overawed by the rest until the Scots trained with them. It is hard to imagine either Hastings brother, Finlay Calder or David Sole being overawed.

"I think we all just thought, having trained alongside the English, the Welsh and the Irish, here was an opportunity. We had a lot of experience and here was the opportunity to benefit from the knowledge we had picked up."

It was only in turning down the chance to become a full-time professional athlete, in another sport, that Scott put into words what a lot of them were thinking. "The rugby league offers started coming in but I told them I wanted to win the Grand Slam first." If he thought he was buying himself some thinking time it wasn't much.

He believes the fact that Scotland followed England worked to their advantage, although not in the way some pundits south of the Border might have presented it. The net effect was that Scotland were probably a bit more battle-hardened coming into the 1990 Grand Slam decider.

"It's much more the case with the other countries, as with us, that when you get thumped you want to come back, with all guns blazing. England had been playing some of their best rugby and every team we met had been hammered by them."

Come the glorious day England were as unprepared for the pressure of the situation as the Scots were primed. "England have only got to look at it. Will Carling made some very poor captaincy decisions. If they'd kicked those two early penalties it might have been a totally different game. They'd been carried away with the media hype as well.

"We'd had to work bloody hard for our wins. It hadn't been spectacular rugby by any means, but when you're playing for the championship, the Triple Crown and the Grand Slam and on your home patch nothing was going to stop us winning that one at the end of the day. On the Wednesday night Ian McGeechan had to stop the session short because the backs were working so well that we were getting too excited. He was trying to hold back the adrenalin."

Scott is acutely aware that he was dragged out of position for the try which led England to believe they were on course. "I made the mistake. When we spoke about it under the posts we agreed it was not going to happen again and although Jeremy Guscott scored, what it achieved was to put a steely resolve in our team."

With Scotland 13-7 up the chance for redemption arrived as the supposedly uncatchable Rory Underwood burst through Scotland's midfield. It was time for The Tackle. "I got just the right angle on him to make it." Though that moment in many ways symbolised his contribution to Scotland defensively, Hastings hopes the creative side of his play is not forgotten.

"People have maybe looked at my game and perhaps I'll go down in history as one of the hardest tacklers there's been, but they tend to forget you've made a few breaks as well, or a few diagonal kicks," he says ruefully. "I'd like to think of myself as a player's player, though, maybe not as greedy as I could have been, but running off the ball, supporting the ball carrier."

He knows, though, that he was perhaps destined to be remembered for his defensive style rather than his attacking qualities from an early age. "When I was young I was watching an international on television and Gerald Davies, or somebody like that, did a diving tackle. So when I was playing one of my first games of rugby I was chasing a guy down the touchline and I dived to make the tackle. One of my best pals Calum Thomson still tells the story of my diving tackle for the Watson's JA1s against Morrison's Academy of Crieff."

Having moved on to "Senior Pro" status in the Nineties Scott has continued to be a solid team man - further highs would follow with the New Zealand tour of 1990, where many critics feel Scotland performed even better than in the Grand Slam campaign, despite losing both Tests and the 1991 World Cup.

"We had two more matches that bear comparison with the 1986 game against England in terms of everything going according to plan. The first was the second Test in New Zealand. The day before the game Finlay Calder stopped a training session and said 'Right, if we get a scrum five yards out here's the move we'll do'. It involved Tony Stanger coming in at pace from the blindside wing and taking the ball from the back row. New Zealand had used a similar ploy with John Kirwan in the past and the whole team agreed on that tactic. When the moment arrived the move went like clockwork." New Zealand narrowly won the match, but Scotland had successfully taken them on at their own game.

"The other occasion it went like that was in the build-up to the World Cup quarter-final against Western Samoa when Jim Telfer stopped training two days before the game. He presented a situation and said if we were there we had two choices, either to kick for touch or put Gavin in on a short ball and try to burst 10 yards over the gain-line. We went for the second option." The opportunity presented itself early on and Hastings senior's breenge set the tone for the game against the Samoans who had developed a fearsome reputation for the physical nature of their play. "That's great rugby when it works. It gives you great satisfaction. The execution couldn't have been better," says Scott.

Since 1990 touring has lost some of its allure as his career develops and family life becomes increasingly important, leading to his decision along with various other senior members of the Scotland side to miss the 1994 tour of Argentina, but deep down, even although "we don't get paid enough" the relish for the real top level stuff is what makes players of Scott's calibre have long careers in the international game.

"The 1995 World Cup is going to be huge," he was enthusing a year ahead of the event. "We were fit for the 1987 tournament and were again among the fitter sides in 1991, but the others have caught up. I don't know how we're going to stay ahead, but it's down to attitude and pride in performance."

Career Statistics: Scott Hastings

1986 Scotland 18 France 17; Wales 22 Scotland 15; Scotland 33 England 6 (1 Try); Ireland 9 Scotland 10; Scotland 33 Romania 18 (1 Try).

1987 Scotland 16 Ireland 12; France 28 Scotland 22 (1 Try); Scotland 21 Wales 15; World Cup - Scotland 55 Romania 28 [1].

1988 Ireland 22 Scotland 18 (1Try) ; Scotland 23 France 12;Wales 25 Scotland 20; Scotland 13 Australia 32.

1989 Scotland 23 Wales 7; England 12 Scotland 12; Scotland 37 Ireland 21; France 19 Scotland 3; Scotland 38 Fiji 17; Scotland 32 Romania 0.

Australia 12 British Lions 19; Australia 18 British Lions 19.

1990 Ireland 10 Scotland 13; Scotland 21 France 0; Wales 9 Scotland 13; Scotland 13 England 7; New Zealand 31 Scotland 16; New Zealand 21 Scotland 18; Scotland 49 Argentina 3.

1991 France 15 Scotland 9; Scotland 32 Wales 12; England 21 Scotland 12; Scotland 28 Ireland 25 (1Try).

World Cup - Scotland 47 Japan 9 (1Try); Scotland 51 Zimbabwe 12 (1Try); Scotland 24 Ireland 15; Scotland 28 Western Samoa 6; Scotland 6 England 9; Scotland 6 New Zealand 13.

1992 Scotland 7 England 25; Ireland 10 Scotland 18; Scotland 10 France 6; Wales 15 Scotland 9; Australia 27 Scotland 12 ; Australia 37 Scotland 13.

1993 Scotland 15 Ireland 3; France 14 Scotland 3; Scotland 20 Wales 0; England 26 Scotland 12 [2]; Scotland 15 New Zealand 51+.

1994 Scotland 14 England 15; Ireland 6 Scotland 6; Scotland 12 France 20.

All appearances at centre, except + on wing. [1]Replaced by Richard Cramb; [2]Replaced by Kenny Logan.

CAPTAIN'S COMMENT:
On the importance of winning for Scotland:
"Unless you perform on the paddock the rest is irrelevant. I don't care how much your club is prepared to pay you to stay, whatever, you perform on the paddock and then you've got some kudos. If you don't you're wasting your time. I believe most players in the first division are good enough to play for their country — the litmus test must be whether they are good enough to win for Scotland."

Coach

12 - I. R. McGeechan

As a child of the Sixties it is hardly surprising that, in his youth, Ian McGeechan found for himself the perfect narcotic. Not that 'Geech' was a carefree member of the free love brigade, far from it. He and wife Judy met at school, in 1964, and having married five years later, have celebrated their silver wedding anniversary.

But, in his mid-twenties, at around the time its profile was on the up and up McGeechan did discover that stimulant. One which he badly wanted to try; which at first he felt he could give up relatively easily, but which became increasingly addictive; a habit which he began to feel he was in control of, just as it began to take over his life; which provided extra energy; which made him, in his leisure time at least, care about little else; which even let him feel years younger.

Thankfully this is not the sordid tale of how another top Scottish sportsman of the Seventies followed athlete David Jenkins into steroid abuse and disgrace. It is how the adrenalin charge provided by Test rugby somewhat belatedly became Ian Robert McGeechan's raison d'etre and brought him, as well as Scottish and British rugby, magnificent glory. "It was like a drug," he says of life after his first season in the Scottish international side. "I just wanted it again - couldn't get enough of it."

The young McGeechan took a convoluted route to a career in top level rugby union, via soccer, the family game naturally enough, rugby league at primary school and indeed cricket, four or five years at the Yorkshire County nets, no less. "Especially being a stand-off I think the cricket and soccer helped quite a lot," he reckons now. "The cricket helped with my hands and the soccer helped my kicking."

His opportunity to play top level rugby, after a sound apprenticeship at Headingley, Yorkshire's biggest club at the time, was a long time in coming, which perhaps ensured he appreciated it all the more when he did get his chance. "My first trial was in 1968. I was 21 at that stage. There were occasional games with the Anglos, but really it was only one game a year against Edinburgh or Glasgow. I played in four trials before I was picked."

Nor was it even as a direct result of one of those trials that he was finally selected since his first appearance came in the meeting with the All Blacks late in 1972. "It took two retirals and four injuries and they eventually got to me," is McGeechan's recollection.

It was a dream come true for a lad born and bred in the heart of Yorkshire, whose first taste of rugby was of rugby league, at primary school, but who was never allowed to forget his roots and indeed whose accent retains a Scottish twang - "I have been in and out of Scotland non-stop for the past 26 years!" - despite the fact he has lived almost all of his life south of the border.

Father Bob was a regular soldier, born in Glasgow and educated at Queen Victoria School in Dunblane, who was in turn the son of a Scottish soldier. The young McGeechan was brought back on regular visits to ensure he knew exactly where he came from.

Consequently there was never the slightest doubt over his natural allegiance and he made sure the SRU were aware of his qualifications while his on-field performances guaranteed that he held official interest. "There were some enquiries after one good performance against London Scottish.

So to Murrayfield and the toughest baptism imaginable. His impressions of that first match were of a game which was over in a flash, despite the fact that he had a reasonably gradual build-up during the Kiwis tour. "I actually played against them three times in four weeks - for the Rest of Scotland and the North of England, prior to the Test match. It was very tough, but a good grounding."

Like a number of the players who represented Scotland at A level and competed effectively against the All Blacks side in the 1993/94 season, a week before virtually the same group of New Zealanders provided a 51-15 Murrayfield drubbing to a Scottish side containing the best performers from among that A side as well as the nucleus of battle-hardened internationalists, McGeechan was to discover the All Blacks have an extra gear which is only located for full Test matches. "They had immense physical presence and the pace was up again for the Test. The game just went like that," he says, with a click of the fingers.

Scotland, who have never beaten the All Blacks, went pretty close, their new stand-off registering the first of three drop goals in his first four internationals, with another new boy, a 21-year-old Andy Irvine, adding two penalties in a 14-9 defeat which wasn't completed until the dying stages. "We were unlucky that day. A late interception try by Sid Going sealed it for them."

A second cap, a second drop goal (v France) and a second defeat, early in another of those win-less sequences for Scotland, this time the venue providing the jinx in the shape of the Parc Des Princes and McGeechan thought that could well be that. His chance had come because of an injury to Colin Telfer, but when Telfer regained full fitness for the meeting with Wales McGeechan expected the worst. "As a player you never really think you are going to get capped until it happens. You always need a bit of luck to get selected which I suppose I had in the end, but when Colin got fit again I thought 'Well at least I've got a couple of caps.'"

Very much a stand-off with his club Headingley at the time that was an understand-able feeling, however the selectors showed vision in finding room for him at centre. Although McGeechan did alternate between the two positions he went on to win 20 of his 32 Scotland caps and make all eight of his British Lions Test appearances, in the centre. "When they put me in at centre that was a hell of a boost to my confidence...I realised they wanted to keep me in."

His recollections of that first meeting with the Welsh are very similar to those of the man who was, eventually, to follow him into the navy blue no.10 jersey. "They were all legends like JPR, Gerald Davies, Gareth, Mervyn Davies," he says.

As for John Rutherford, Wales were to provide McGeechan with some happy memo-ries, including that day, as Scotland won 10-9 to deny them the Triple Crown. "It was very special beating Wales so early on, especially when they were winning everything. You know I think the only time in the seventies the Welsh didn't win the Triple Crown was when we beat them."

That win may have been McGeechan's first non-scoring cap, but it provided the start of a very special run as Scotland began a winning sequence at Murrayfield, which lasted throughout the remainder of Bill Dickinson's reign as "adviser to the captain"/coach and ended only with defeat by Wales as they did collect the Triple Crown in 1977.

Scotland went to Twickenham seeking a Triple Crown themselves that season but a team boasting a fine, but at that point still very youthful, back division, supplemented by the introduction of the pugnacious Dougie Morgan - whose conversion had separated Scotland and Wales on his debut - lost out, despite Billy Steele's brace of tries. However McGeechan had settled in for a run of appearances which would only be broken by an injury-enforced absence at the 1978 Calcutta Cup match.

"Looking back the Irish game of that season was another of the highlights of my career. I got another drop goal, but I enjoyed it particularly because it was the first time I really felt I'd come to terms with the pace of international rugby. I felt as if I was in control and could influence things, even although Mike Gibson, who was at the height of his powers, was in the Irish side that day."

Having established himself during a historic season, a sixth cap was collected as an SRU President's Overseas XV were beaten at Murrayfield in a match to mark the union's Centenary, McGeechan had developed a very different attitude to Test rugby in the space of a couple of months. At the end of the 1973/74 season a British Lions tour would beckon, but by now a craving for Test rugby was all the motivation Geech required. "The only thing I was conscious of was of having the experience going into the second season and just wanting more. I was training four or five times a week even then...I just didn't want to be dropped!"

Test rugby had taken years off him too, at least in the eyes of the rest of the world. "It was quite a good thing that Andy got his first cap the same day as me because everyone tended to think I was 21 as well. I think they thought I was five years younger all my days, so I was still playing international rugby when I was 32 or 33 years old and no-one really though much of it. I always kept myself in pretty good shape mind you and was never overweight, either."

Quite the reverse in fact and although in those days 5'10" and 11 stone 7lbs wasn't quite as small for a centre as it is considered now: "I was always very aware that the first tackle was very important. At my size I didn't want people running at me all day so I had to stop them first time."

It is hardly surprising, though, that the 27-year-old performed in the 1974 Five Nations Championship, during which Scotland again won both home games against France and England and lost twice away, with a maturity far in advance of a player with just a single season of international rugby behind him. No surprise either that he was selected for the British Lions squad which was to set a standard which may never again be matched by a British touring side.

Alongside the 'Mighty Mouse', Ian McLauchlan, McGeechan was one of only two Scots to play in all four Tests as Willie John McBride's "Invincibles" imposed themselves on the rugby-besotted Afrikaaners of South Africa. Gordon Brown missed out on the last Test through injury. After Billy Steele played in the first two Tests he fund himself replaced on the right wing by Andy Irvine, whose kicking prowess was felt particularly necessary following Phil Bennett's failure to convert four of their five second Test tries.

"It was a huge bonus at the end of that season to be going on tour with players of that level," said McGeechan just a couple of weeks after returning from a reunion hosted by the Northern Ireland Tourist Board just outside Belfast, to mark the 20th anniversary of that history-making tour: "That was wonderful - just like being on tour again, only shorter and without having to play the rugby.

"It was an amazing tour - undefeated for three and a half months. There was no television either, so people were coming 1000 miles to watch the games. There was intense interest and we just played tremendous rugby. There was incredible passion. As the tour went on every side we played was just desperate to be the one to end our run. One of the great things was that the Test side remained the same right through apart from Andy Irvine coming in for Billy Steele and Gordon Brown dropping out for the last game. There was also a great spirit in the midweek side. They were determined not to lose the unbeaten record."

That last fact alone set a standard which McGeechan was anxious to maintain and prior to the 1993 Lions tour of New Zealand, his second as coach, made the attitude of some of his charges difficult to accept. "That was not particularly easy to take. For some players in 1993 it just wasn't important enough. I couldn't understand that."

For McGeechan it was impossible to underestimate the sense of pride at pulling on the red shirt of the Lions and at the end of those 15 glorious weeks the Lions had become the first and almost certainly the only British Isles side in the 20th century, to go undefeated through a Test series against either the All Blacks or the Springboks undefeated, South Africa saving a little face by drawing the final Test 13-13.

"It's only when you come away from a tour like that you realise the achievement." South African administrators had been so desperate to beat them their players even had to face being jailed. "Before the second Test the Springboks were put in prison so they couldn't read the papers," is McGeechan's recollection of the level of intensity.

For men like McBride, McLauchlan, JPR, Edwards, Gordon Brown and Merv the Swerve, who had been involved in the 1971 tour of New Zealand which had seen the All Blacks beaten 2-1, with the fourth Test similarly drawn, legendary status was assured.

Newcomers like McGeechan and Irvine found themselves, for the first time, with global reputations. They had achieved their success against all the odds, at a time when administrators were largely unaware of the significance of playing at altitude, despite the fact that the Mexico Olympics had been some six years earlier.

"Altitude was just something we had to put up with. There really wasn't a lot of thought went into it. We did sleep a heck of a lot more when we were at sea level, though. I'm talking about as much as 16 to 18 hours a day. But when we were at altitude we just seemed to cope. And we took a lot of salt tablets."

From the high veldt to the coast the Lions faced all-comers and McGeechan's pride in his own condition was given the most rigorous of examinations as his versatility was put to full use by the management. He certainly couldn't complain about being bored, despite the length of the tour.

"There was only one game I wasn't changed for in 22 matches. I think I played in up to 16 matches." The 1974 Lions won many new friends as well. "We played a game in one of the townships in East London. There the coloureds and the blacks just said they were so pleased we'd come and they were behind us in the Tests."

Like so many Scots before him and since, he returned home from a Lions tour knowing he was worthy of playing with and against the world's best and there was absolutely no sense of anti-climax.

"Coming home from a tour like that you're just determined to stay in. In 1974, 1975 and 1976 I was playing my best rugby. You find out exactly what the others can do on a Lions tour. The Scots tend to come out of it well and I think there were more of us on that trip than for a long time. In the press we tended to be written down a bit, but that changed. Mind you after that 1972 game against the All Blacks we didn't lose again at Murrayfield for such a long time that had to have an effect."

The nadir of McGeechan's international career was also reached during that period, however, as Scotland's tendency to go into their shells continued. "Losing to England in 1975 when we had the chance to win the Triple Crown was probably the lowest I ever felt in a rugby match. To be 10 to 15 points better and not show it...we were the best side in the championship. We only lost by a point in Paris when Andy missed a late penalty and Dougie missed one at the very end against England when we lost by a single point again." To this day he can feel the pain of that Twickenham defeat as he looks back and he is certain that a single crucial away win could have transformed Scottish fortunes.

Another sad memory away from home in 1975 was a second Test defeat at the hands of New Zealand, this time in Auckland on a saturated pitch, during his only tour with Scotland as a player. "The waterlogged Test was a terribly frustrating game. The conditions were just appalling. The ball was floating on the pitch. It was such a let down. All that way for that. The game should never have been played, but of course we were on a plane the next day..."

Fortress Murrayfield may have been impregnable, at least to other Europeans, between 1972 and 1976, but Scotland could not find a way to reproduce that unbeatable form away from home. "Bill Dickinson was the first person in there to organise and take responsibility away from the players. Jim Telfer had done it when he was captain. Bill had the organisation and good rapport, particularly with the front five."

Indeed the front five dominated things, perhaps a little too much, with personalities such as the 'Mighty Mouse', Broon frae Troon, Sandy Carmichael and, of course, the utterly unpredictable Alistair McHarg all in the middle of long international careers. "At first we were well organised up front but lacked experience behind the scrum. We were intimidated a bit by the front five," says McGeechan...and he was on their side!

"By the mid-Seventies it was balancing up a bit, though. We played a lot of running rugby. The game we lost to Wales in '77 for example (oddly enough the match which ended the unbeaten Murrayfield run) we played some great rugby. I said 'To hell with this lads let's have a go at them.' We ran them ragged. In the end they beat us 18-9 but we made them look quite ordinary."

He is speaking, of course of the great Welsh side which won the second of three successive Triple Crowns that year and was only prevented from matching those Triple Crowns with Grand Slams by a powerful French side in Paris.

As he talks about his playing career McGeechan constantly points towards the lessons which created arguably the greatest coaching brain Scottish, perhaps even British rugby, has known. For example his renowned use of video technology had its roots in the work done by Bill Dickinson way back in the early seventies.

"He was very well prepared and he used a lot of reel to reel video tapes. I found that very useful as a player, sitting there in a back changing room at Murrayfield, just watching our own performances even. What you do and what you think you do are often very different. The positive side of that is very important."

Irishman Sid Millar, who coached the 1974 Lions was another major influence, as much as anything else in is attitude and the way he controlled situations. Most important of all, though, was to learn from what was happening on the pitch and particularly from mistakes.

"The Eighties Scottish side was more miserly, but the Seventies team played as much good rugby. The problem was just not winning that one crucial match away from home. The experience of that may have helped in the Eighties."

In 1977 another Lions tour beckoned and McGeechan would play in all four Tests, matching the eight appearances of McLauchlan, Brown, Jim Telfer and Mike Campbell-Lamerton, a total surpassed by only one Scot - his fellow 1972 debutant Andy Irvine. "In 1977 the weather didn't help," he says of a tour which was disappointing only by the mighty standards set earlier in the decade. It gets depressing when you're there for so long and it rains every day. But we still didn't lose to a provincial side and we won the second Test, the first Lions side to do that against New Zealand.

"We should have won the fourth, but tactically we lost it a bit. Our forwards were controlling the game but forgot about the quality of ball they were giving us. They were winning the ball at will but were kind of holding it up to show the New Zealanders how dominant they were. Meanwhile they had men waiting in the backs. Graham Mourie and these people just waiting for us in midfield." Another valuable lesson learned: "It made a big impact on me!"

That same year had seen McGeechan assume the Scotland captaincy for the first time, but a heavy defeat by England (26-6 at Twickenham) followed by the loss of the Murrayfield record to Wales, meant that Dougie Morgan took over for 1978.

When Alan Lawson was preferred to Morgan for the 1979 campaign following the whitewash in 1978, McGeechan was restored to the captaincy and although he failed to secure a win in his final season he finished with a flourish, even in defeat. "My last game was in Paris, three tries each, we really took the game to them," is his memory of a game which finished 21-17 to France.

There was also a last defiant dart at the Auld Enemy as he finally came away from Twickenham with something and knowing he had really imposed himself upon England on their own turf.

"My biggest regrets are not winning a Triple Crown when it was available in 1973 and 1975. By 1979 we had hardened up again, but that was a good English side that went on to win the Grand Slam the following year. They scored from the very first touch of the ball, but in the later stages of the game I took great pleasure in going right up the line of our forwards asking them to speed up the game and in letting them know we knew they were exhausted and we had them. We didn't quite end up winning, it was a 6-6 draw but they knew they were knackered."

Though it is clear that McGeechan possesses the desperate need of the Celt to beat the English, he sees his upbringing south of the Border as having been something of an advantage in terms of his general outlook. "It's meant that I've never been too parochial. Being brought up in England means I have a very healthy respect for English club rugby. To develop on international terms you have to see teams in that context which is why under Jim Telfer as director of rugby we will continue to look outwards, towards Australia, New Zealand, France.

OVERLEAF
He played a bit, too — for the British Lions and Scotland.

"Of course the desire is there to beat England. Every side playing England wants to beat them and when you know you've got your own team working well as a captain as I did in 1979 I believe you should stand up front and really put the challenge down on the field. You've then got to back that up by winning ball and running it."

As he bowed out of international rugby McGeechan was a man enthused, rather than jaded by his experiences, despite the fact that Scotland failed to win a single match in his last 10 appearances and the fact that that last 1978/79 season saw yet another brave, but losing performance against those All Blacks.

On his final appearance at stand-off prior to Rutherford's emergence McGeechan came within an ace of snatching a draw for Scotland with a late drop goal, having already put one over to set a new record of eight in international rugby (a mark since overtaken by John Rutherford). However opposite number Doug Bruce lunged desperately at him to charge the ball down and Bruce Robertson deepened Scotland's gloom on a dark day in Auld Reekie, by racing to the other end to score a try which provided New Zealand with a flattering 18-9 margin - echoes of Sid Going's interception score some six years earlier.

"It was always pretty intense against the All Blacks. You know you have to think all the time," says McGeechan. "There's only Carwyn James has really come out on top against them, but I played against them nine or ten times, beat them as a player and twice as a coach, with the World XV in 1992 and the Lions in the second Test in 1993."

He believes he could not have become involved in international rugby at a better time. "The Seventies was a good decade for the game. It was when rugby really took off with the Lions in '71 and '74.

"By the end of my international playing career when I finished after getting my cartilage out, I wasn't really interested in playing club rugby. Latterly club rugby was just a means to an end. The incentive was international rugby."

He never scored an international try but as he looks back on his career he can do so with great satisfaction, a drop goal in the second Test in Pretoria taking his total international haul to eight. "I'd also like to think I made between eight and 10 scoring passes over the years, which is what I felt my game was about. Billy Steele scored a few and Andy got a few tries on the outside."

He set high standards for himself, standards which doubtless have helped make him the coach he is: "I used to be furious with myself dropping one pass in a game."

Even after seven great seasons at the top then McGeechan was not sated and while he always thought coaching would be second best he wanted to stay involved. "I've been surprised at how satisfying coaching is, more satisfying than playing in some ways. Helping players do things that sometimes even they didn't think was possible."

Just as was the case on his playing debut when McGeechan got involved once more on the international scene his youthful appearance meant that he could give the impression of a maturity far in advance of his years. The chance to be involved again was something he relished and while people speak fondly of the memory of the way David

Sole and the Hastings boys brought an injection of youthful vigour to the scene in 1986, McGeechan brought that same freshness to the coaching scene.

Two years later he was in charge of the team and began the partnership with Jim Telfer, with whom he shares tremendous mutual respect, which took Scotland to the 1990 Grand Slam and the World Cup semi-finals the following year.

That side perhaps reached its peak on neither of those memorable Murrayfield occasions though, in the coach's view, but in between them - in New Zealand in the summer of 1990. "It was frustrating not beating New Zealand in the second Test. People thought we'd had our chance in the first — yet we played even better."

In that opening Test, always the match the pundits expect to be the better chance for a touring side against the All Blacks, Scotland battled well in the first half before New Zealand stretched away. However in the second Scotland led until Gary Armstrong was forced off eight minutes from time. Two penalties by the unflappable Grant Fox gave the Kiwis an undeserved 21-18 win, in a match where they had conceded two tries to one. "The performance was very satisfying, yet unbelievably disappointing. We couldn't have asked any more of them.

"The World Cup in this country was another coaching high. It was just a bit different. The international team generated a magical atmosphere across the whole country for a month. I remember the people queuing for tickets when they suddenly became available. People just wanted to be a part of it. To think that feeling was there because of the Scottish rugby team in a soccer country..."

Unfortunately it was just before that World Cup campaign that McGeechan learned that it is something of a myth that an involvement in international rugby is bound to help your career, at least if you're in the wrong place at the wrong time.

His desire to be involved in the World Cup meant a conflict of interest with the Leeds education authority and it may not be too fanciful to suggest that the perennial reluctance of some of those involved to let him have time off, became stronger following that win over England in the Grand Slam decider.

A change of direction was required, but there were no complaints on either side as what was planned to be a short term appointment at Scottish Life turned into a longer term arrangement when he was appointed as training manager.

With an office base in Edinburgh, coaching London Scottish in his first season out of international harness and having moved the family back to Leeds it's as well that Judy has had a quarter of a century to become used to her husband's frequent absence from the family table, while Rob (15) and Heather (10) have never known anything else.

"I'm not really getting much more family time now, although there's not the same pressure on weekends after the last eight years of never being at home, following on from seven as a player."

For Rob though, there are perks. When one of the biggest sporting heroes in Leeds, Alan Tait, turned up at the door seeking a word with his dad. "As ever, I wasn't in, but he brought a couple of tickets round for one of their matches. Rob was delighted."

Left: Ian McGeechan in today's
familiar guise — coach

Below: A less familiar one than he
would sometimes have liked —
Family man with Judy, Robert and
Heather

Career Statistics: Ian McGeechan

1972 Scotland 9 New Zealand 14 (1DG) +.

1973 France 16 Scotland 13 (1DG); Scotland 10 Wales 9; Scotland 19 Ireland 14 (1DG); England 20 Scotland 13; Scotland 27 Overseas XV 16.

1974 Wales 6 Scotland 0; Scotland 16 England 14; Ireland 9 Scotland 6; Scotland 19 France 6 +; South Africa 3 British Lions 12; South Africa 9 British Lions 28 (1DG); South Africa 9 British Lions 26; South Africa 13 British Lions 13.

1975 Scotland 20 Ireland 13 (1DG)+; France 10 Scotland 9+; Scotland 12 Wales 10 (1DG)+; England 7 Scotland 6+; New Zealand 24 Scotland 0+; Scotland 10 Australia 3.

1976 Scotland 6 France 13; Wales 28 Scotland 6 +; Scotland 22 England 12; Ireland 6 Scotland 15.

1977 England 26 Scotland 6 *; Scotland 21 Ireland 18 *; France 23 Scotland 3 *; Scotland 9 Wales 18 (1DG) +*;

New Zealand 16 British Lions 12; New Zealand 9 British Lions 13; New Zealand 19 British Lions 7[1]; New Zealand 10 British Lions 9.

1978 Ireland 12 Scotland 9; Scotland 16 France 19; Wales 22 Scotland 14+; Scotland 9 New Zealand 18 (1DG)+*.

1979 Scotland 13 Wales 19*; England 7 Scotland 7*; Scotland 11 Ireland 11*; France 21 Scotland 17*

All appearances at centre except + at stand-off. [1] Replacement for JJ Williams. * captain

FOOTNOTE: McGeechan continued to break new ground when at the beginning of the 1994/95 season he accepted a seven-year contract to become full-time director of rugby at Northampton RFC.

CAPTAIN'S COMMENT:
On selection as captain of The Famous XV: "I think it's safe to say that not everyone is a Calder lover, but this is very flattering. When I sat down to pick my XV I selected David Leslie. My son picked Ian Smith ahead of me as well. I've got a lot of time for Ian Smith. He's not dynamic, but if you've played the position you can see he's a very clever player."

Utility Man

11 - K. W. Robertson

The late seventies was very much the era of the Bee Gees, but for all their macho, medallion man posturing there aren't too many rugby players who would have been terribly intimidated by them. In New Zealand though, ever behind the times in everything but rugby, Bee Gee didn't mean a trio of disco dancers, but was a name synonymous with a solo performer. The gentleman in question was perhaps not the sort of individual against whom to blood a 10 stone eight pound debutant, out of position to boot, but in their infinite wisdom that's exactly what the Scotland selectors chose to do.

"Back then they used to weigh you for the match programme. I had to put on two tracksuits and put weights in my pockets to get myself above 11 stone," remembers the new boy that day. Though he was to go on to win the majority of his 44 caps on the wing, Keith William Robertson would always feel slightly vulnerable when out on the flanks.

"I never believed I had the out and out pace to be a winger," he says, admitting to surprise at his selection among these modern greats. "People never regarded me as an out and out winger either."

So to be fair to those selectors who seemed to spend much of the period pursuing Scottish rugby's Holy Grail (pre-Iwan Tukalo and Tony Stanger at least), namely a "genuine" winger who would score regular tries, their confusion over Robertson's best position only reflected his own doubts.

"I always felt a little bit susceptible, especially to blinding pace. You're often left in a one to one situation. Not that he's given to false modesty, mind you! "Don't get me wrong...I regarded myself as a reasonably good winger."

However his own assessment ties in with that of most who closely followed his career. Robertson was one of the few players whose career at representative level was not stunted by the description "utility player".

"I didn't really think of myself as a wing or a centre," says a man, who at one stage or another, played in every position behind the scrum for his club. "More as a player that would hopefully be able to play any position outside stand-off. I liked to think of myself as a good footballer.

"My kicking was never good enough to play stand-off. I came up all through school until I was 16 or 17 years old playing at scrum half and thought I'd play there when I moved up to senior level, but you can't do anything about growing. I went from a smout to being 5'11" almost overnight," he notes with a rueful smile when reminded of the size and weight of the average no.9 in the nineties.

Bulk did not come with height - "I was always light" - and although his own tendency seems to be to consider the midfield role as more suited to his style, he has his reservations on that score.

"After my first cap, through to '81, I worked on putting on weight. Pound for pound I regarded myself as very physical when I did get up to a bit over 11 stone, but it did take its toll. I got a lot of shoulder injuries in tackles. My physique was a drawback at centre.

"Having said that if you gave me the choice of my career over again and playing the game the way I did or whether I'd rather be a big physical straight-running centre and there's no contest!" So say all of us!

However on hearing him describe these doubts about his flat out pace and his own build, it is little wonder that he felt a bit exposed when up against the 15-stone flying machines who began to line up against him with increasing frequency throughout his Test career.

"There were people I wouldn't have liked to have had to face more than once a season. Chris Oti was one of them - a real disaster to mark," is the example he offers. "He was all thighs. His one thigh was twae of mines," - a true Borderer's description.

Bryan George (Bee Gee) Williams was the original prototype for the steam-roller style wing man. As it turned out he was making his final appearance in All Black the day Keith pulled on a navy blue jersey for the first time, but even at this distance the man from Melrose makes no claims about having helped bring that about. What he does remember is coming closer than ever to discovering the true colour of fear. His

The slim young man who
made his Scotland debut in 1978

main concern, though, was not the identity of the opponent, but over his unfamiliarity with the position.

"I played centre for Melrose and the South. I'd only played a couple of game on the wing, but one of them had been against the Anglos, against Lewis Dick who was the incumbent in the Scotland side. I was one surprised boy when I got selected I'll tell you. In fact I was a little bit embarrassed about it. A lot of things go through your mind at a time like that.

"That was the only time I was ever really frightened, not because I was dreading facing Bryan Williams, though. It was just the fear of the possibility of really embarrassing myself. He would have had to run right over the top of me to get away from me that day," says a man, who knows that physical sacrifice he was prepared to make would have meant he would have been unlikely to survive the first challenge if Williams was to get away. "It was a huge worry."

Mixed with the disappointment of losing a match in which Scotland had every chance right up to the closing stages, before Ian McGeechan's potential equalising drop goal was charged down and a try scored at the other end, Robertson's principal emotion was relief at the finish.

"I knew I got away with it," is his candid confession. "I've never been so glad for it to be wet. He dropped three balls when it would have been one on one. I got away with it thanks to the wet and him dropping those three balls, but it was more good luck than anything else.

"I remember the game vividly. I caught one up and under early on and later I took a poor clearance kick, beat Bee Gee and set up Andy Irvine who almost scored. Most importantly, though, I didn't do anything wrong.

"I think I was pretty philosophical afterwards. I knew I hadn't been tested the way I might have been, because he hadn't taken the ball when he'd had the chance to run at me. That's the wee bit luck in the game.

"I remember sitting beside Mike Bigger after the game and saying 'I'm bloody glad I came through that '. He said 'You did a lot more than come through it '. He was just encouraging me but it was nice to hear it. You've either got to be a genius or have a bit of luck - in November 1978 with the weather and a poor set of hands I certainly had my bit of luck."

The genius was to emerge over the next 11 years as Robertson emerged as the man the selectors could always look to when problems arose in the three-quarter line.

Like several other Famous XV members Robertson's early sporting interest was in soccer rather than rugby, for all that he was brought up in St Boswells, so close to Melrose, the club with which he was to become synonymous.

"Unlike today when Melrose work hard to encourage youngsters into the club at a very early age, rugby was not foremost in my mind in primary school. My father John was born and brought up on farms around Kelso and loved his football in his early years while my uncle John, on my mother's side, was a trialist for Arsenal."

Though her international allegiance lay elsewhere, his mother Rosie became a familiar figure as one of the more audible supporters at the Greenyards. "She's a Londoner and very proud of it, which created some interesting and funny situations in the household when watching Scotland-England encounters before I got my first cap. I haven't asked where her allegiance lies now!

"But both parents gave me tremendous support throughout my career. My father was always ready to praise or criticise my performances and my mother's English accent among the more vocal on the touchline.

"Dad's interest grew with my involvement and he was always helpful with his advice. I could always count on him to be level-headed about it."

The local rugby hero, Jim Blacklock of Melrose and the South, lived next door and "was always at me to go to the rugby," which was what started Robertson's involvement "He was always speaking about the rugby to me and messing about with a rugby ball on the back green. He got me thinking about the game."

Blacklock it was who persuaded the youngster to play in the famous Crichton's youth sevens tournament for the first time, aged seven and a half. He was to win a couple of Crichton's medals and would play further competitive rugby when his local school in St Boswells started playing the game when he was in primary six.

Age 13 he reckoned he joined the Melrose Colts, at a time when Andy Irvine was at the Greenyards club, but couldn't get a game. "They wouldn't let me play because I was too small so, age 14, I went back to St Boswells and played for the senior team there. I was just desperate to play rugby at that stage."

Having demonstrated that indomitable spirit Robertson returned to Melrose to learn from two of the club's all-time greats. "Eck Hastie and Davie Chisholm coached the Colts all the time I was there. I was very lucky, they were great coaches. They instilled the right attitude. You always had to have clean gear, clean boots, oh - and short hair.

"Eck was the jovial one. Davie was solid, always there every week." The pair set a record with their 13 appearances together at half-back for Scotland, surpassed of course during Robertson's time by his South team-mates John Rutherford and Roy Laidlaw.

"The youth scene was so good it attracted players like Andy to the club," Robertson notes.

Robertson's legendary touch was honed on the village green, through long summers of playing rugby and football. "Any game you can create handling a ball is good to develop skills in youngsters. We have to look for activities to keep them playing games during the summer."

Of course no amount of hard work, or even coaching, could develop what many commentators described as incredible poise and balance, allied to a conjurer's sleight of hand and a ballroom dancer's lightness of foot, or what the player himself modestly rates: "a reasonable level of natural ability!"

He is not given to false modesty, however and is well aware that he had God given gifts which allowed him to play the game a very special way. "It comes from a feel, knowing what's round about you and how to use the ball. A lot depends on the situations you find yourself in. Sometimes risks come off, more often than not they don't."

On that score he considers himself strangely lucky to have played first his early club rugby, then his early international rugby, with sides which were struggling. "In the early days at Melrose we didn't have a big pack so had to take risks. People at the club tended not to get after me too much for taking risks. Creamy (Jim Telfer) eventually did mind when we had a bit of control up front.

"It sounds strange but I found it quite easy playing international rugby. There was very little immediate pressure on the wing compared with playing at centre week-in, week-out. Also I came into a side which was struggling and we only got the odd chance to work with the ball, so had to try things when we did get it. I used to come off my wing a lot looking for the ball.

Pundit: His playing days over, Keith Robertson now enjoys being one of the few people in the Melrose Press box who knows what he is talking about.

"In the early days when you got a bit of shrapnel you looked to counter-attack all the time. We created a lot more space in the backs then. We were up against less organised defences because at that time wing forwards did not break off scrums at all. "It was a long time before defences got to grips with miss twos, even miss ones. Good direct running caused a lot more problems then."

If there was something of a cavalier attitude in that approach it was to change with the return of Robertson's club-mate Jim Telfer to the international scene. Having captained his country to what remained in 1994 Scotland's last win in Paris, among other things, Telfer's coaching career was to take him to new heights and, as mentioned earlier, Robertson had already discovered that the growling, grey eminence preferred discipline and strategy to undisciplined flair.

Against England in 1980 Scotland's backs played with dash, almost French elan, yet they were never close to preventing Bill Beaumont 's men from completing their Grand Slam, overpowered up front and with harem scarem defence allowing John Carleton to run amok, picking up a hat-trick of tries, though perhaps fortunately for Robertson he was over on Bruce Hay's wing.

Something had to change and Telfer's appointment provided the necessary direction. The Murrayfield stronghold was immediately rebuilt with wins over Wales and Ireland in 1981 and defeats in Paris and London were both very respectable. That summer Telfer began to place the importance on touring which has become central to Scotland's development since.

"Tours are great development grounds. I missed the New Zealand tour because our daughter Nicky was due to be born, but the tour of Australia the following year was tremendous. The atmosphere and comradeship on the Australia tour was incredible. After winning our first ever international on tour in Australia we felt we could do really well in 1983."

Robertson played a fairly substantial part in ensuring the success of that tour. He it was who finished off the move which produced the only try of the opening Test which was a historic moment for Scottish rugby. It was the first time Scotland had won an official Test match whilst on tour and although the Wallabies roared back in the second Test, running in three tries to none in handing out a salutary thrashing, Scotland's win at Ballymore laid the foundation for the successes of the mid-eighties.

He was part of a squad which was on its way towards making an even bigger place for itself in history, although the final match of the following season's Five Nations Championship approached a few of them might have needed convincing of that.

"During that championship when we hadn't won until the England game it was looking like a whitewash. We were playing well yet wondering where the results were coming from," says Robertson, for whom that Calcutta Cup match allowed him to re-establish himself as a centre.

Without that victory at Twickenham one can only ponder on the consequences for the administration of the time. As it was a magnificent win, inspired by the return of Rutherford, with Robertson popping over a drop goal to add to his try in Paris a month earlier, provided the team with the proof they themselves needed to convince them that they had the ability to do great things.

"That was probably the most enjoyable game of rugby I played for Scotland. Personally it was the best all-round game I ever played for Scotland and the most involved I've been both in attack and defence. Winning at Twickenham was the spark for 1984. That and our Lions players coming back and saying 'Look, we can beat these guys.' "

Like David Leslie, Robertson can perhaps look ruefully back on that Lions tour, wondering whether he might have been one of those to suffer in the bartering which goes on between the Home Unions to sort out the make-up of Lions parties. With so many Scots in contention for places, an unusual phenomenon prior to the eighties, one or two of those on the border-line for selection were going to miss out.

Certainly the 1983 tour was the best chance he had of going on a Lions tour, out of the three which took place during his representative career. In the event he would have missed out through injury, but he had been left out by that time.

"I think I definitely played better rugby after 1983, but that was certainly my best chance. We had beaten England down there in '83 and I had a couple of good games for the Barbarians."

Any other critic would be described as brutal if they were as frank in assessing Robertson's game. "I think, quite honestly, I wasn't a good enough centre and there were better wingers," is Robertson's stark summary. Again he dismisses any suggestion that his versatility worked against him. "The only way I would have gone would have been as a utility back," is his own opinion. "It would be right to say I was disappointed, but I didn't feel I had the right to be there. If I was being really honest I would say I wasn't among the best players."

However he does admit that he was let down that time, if only because of the way the newspapers built up his chances. "The biggest thing was that the papers built me up even in the English papers, so I was a wee bit disappointed. It's something I have missed in my career, but I never felt I had the right to be there."

In the event he couldn't even take on a stand-by role because he injured his shoulder at the end of the season playing for Scotland against the Barbarians.

To some extent over his career Robertson occasionally had something of a tendency to be in the wrong place at the wrong time. He missed out on the classic wins in Cardiff in 1982 because of tonsillitis and in London in 1986 as Matt Duncan charged onto the international scene, while he retired in 1989, just missing out on a second Grand Slam.

In 1984, however, everything came together nicely as Scotland achieved the first Triple Crown in 46 years, not to mention the first Grand Slam in 59 and this time Robertson was the beneficiary of someone else's misfortune.

"I was lucky. Initially I had been injured so was not selected for the trial. Steve Munro went down ill, though, so I came in on the wing for the trial. I played reasonably well so got in on the bench. Then Steve got injured or ill again so I got in for the England game on the Wednesday before the match."

Wales had already been beaten in Cardiff, for the second time in two visits and when England were swept aside history was there for the taking. "Euan Kennedy scored in that win over England, but he also got injured so I was pulled into the centre for the rest of the championship."

Robertson's performances in playing a full part as Scotland turned it on, allowed him to embark on a first extended run in the centre, which lasted until the end of the 1985 season.

"I scored a try against Ireland in the Triple Crown game. It was a great performance. We went off at such a rate. The Irish made a big mistake, winning the toss and giving us the wind. Roy got his two tries to set us up and Peter Dods and I finished off great tries in the later stages." Oh the celebrations!

"I remember getting told pre-dinner that we were going out live on Sportscene and Creamy coming round and telling us not to get too drunk.

"When we went on the programme and sang a song which starts 'Let the Irish sing of the Emerald Isle', which then goes on to a chorus which had no relevance to the day whatsoever. Creamy was standing in the background going 'Cut, cut' - but he never stopped us from finishing the song. It was possibly the only instruction he'd given us that season which we hadn't carried out, although I'm sure he wouldn't say so...

"After we'd won the Irish arranged for us to go to a club and when we got there they ushered us to a corner which had a banner above us - 'Scotland's Triple Crown'. It was almost like winning at home. We had about a week of celebrations."

The mood of euphoria amongst Scotland supporters was tempered by the knowledge that the French were also bringing a 100% record to Murrayfield for the first-ever Grand Slam decider - and with a squad which read like a roll of honour, men like Serge Blanco, Philippe Sella, Patrice Lagisquet, Jean-Pierre Lescarboura, Jerome Gallion, Jean-Luc Joinel and Laurent Rodriguez, led by their magnificent captain Jean-Pierre Rives, there was a feeling that the Scots had achieved as much as could be expected.

This was not a mood which found its way into the Scotland camp.

Fortunately after said week of celebrations there was another week in which to regain their condition and concentration. "There was real focus going into that French game. We knew there were certain things we had to do. Man for man there was no doubt they had more quality than us, but we went out there and pulled it all together. By the time Saturday came round there was a real simple plan, dependent on making no mistakes.

"That game in particular we had to work to the game plan, so while we played some good rugby the only thing we were really looking to do was to keep the ball in front of the forwards. If we'd tried to play them at the same game as they wanted to play we would have had no chance."

Robertson happily acknowledges that the Scots knew the game was effectively over from the moment Jim Calder latched onto a loose ball to claim the decisive try: "As far as we were concerned that was it." But he is not alone in reckoning that the telling moment had perhaps come earlier in David Leslie's bone-juddering collision with the brilliant Gallion.

"I think we knew we had a really good chance after that," says Robertson. "I was close to him when he went down and Rives was in there with his fingers down Gallion's throat because he'd swallowed his tongue. It really did shake the French...took their focus away from them."

This time around there was no TV bow - no need to hold back and, consequently, little to remember of the post-match fun and games. "I honestly can't remember much

Scottish rugby immortal: Royal Bank group employee Keith Robertson is captured in the painting they commissioned to commemorate the 1984 Grand Slam moment.

about the celebrations - the dinner's just a blur. When it was over though I have to admit the feeling after the Triple Crown was possibly greater. There wasn't that same feeling of elation.

"From time to time I look at the video now. If someone's round and pulls it out of the rack of I just look at it myself and when you listen to the singing of the crowd in the last 15 minutes it's little wonder that sides say now you have to be 10 points better than Scotland to win at Murrayfield."

On a personal level Robertson doesn't believe he reached his peak until after the Grand Slam and he brought his influence to bear in 1987 when, having watched from the bench as Scotland were being "cuffed right, left and centre" he came on as a replacement for the injured Doug Wyllie.

"I was probably at my best and confident at around the age of 30/31. You gradually develop so much confidence about the game and know so much about what to do in game situations. It helped that I had never put on weight and never lost any pace."

In the final match of that championship Robertson had the satisfaction of scoring a try, even although England once again denied Scotland. Yet that summer it was only a hamstring injury to Scott Hastings which got him into the World Cup side alongside Alan Tait, the future Rugby League star who came into the side for his first cap after John Rutherford's early exit against France and Doug Wyllie's subsequent switch to stand-off.

"I think we learned a lot from that World Cup," he says. "By the time the second World Cup came around we realised we had to rest players during the tournament. In 1987 we felt that we couldn't afford to play anything below our full-strength side in the group matches."

Robertson recognises that such a view was virtually unavoidable given the make-up of the group. Scotland opened against France, who were fresh from winning a Grand Slam and after a magnificent fighting draw had to face something of an unknown quantity, as they were then, in Zimbabwe before having to beat Romania to be sure of a place in the quarter-finals. Having lost to Romania immediately after winning the 1984 Grand Slam, the Scots were only too well aware of the dangers of taking that match lightly. But in retrospect and since they met them at the same stage in 1991, it was a valuable lesson, since Scotland were far more aware of being able to rest first string players the next time around.

"The net result was that we went into the New Zealand game with far too many players less than fully fit," is Robertson's recollection of Scotland's exit.

Two more appearances at centre, alongside Tait against England and Australia in 1988 would follow before the sudden arrival of Sean Lineen from New Zealand to partner Scott Hastings in the Edinburgh and Scotland sides meant that he was destined to go full circle, ending his international career back on the wing.

Despite finishing with yet another defeat in Paris a year before the Grand Slam win over England, Robertson has no regrets about the timing of his departure at the age of 34. "No that was me in more ways than one," he reckons. "I had a wee boy who was beginning to hate the sound of the word rugby."

Keith had always been keen on training: "I loved proving that I was fitter than anybody else. Nobody could out-do me. I enjoyed training." But even he recognised that the demands were becoming too great for a family man.

"Alison and I got married pretty young and I don't think she had any idea of the lifestyle ahead of her. An athlete at the top level in any sport can be self-centred and she had to suffer some pretty serious changes in mood depending on my performances on the park and battles for fitness. Thanks for hanging in there, Ali! Unless you're single you have to have a very tolerant wife to play top level rugby these days.

"We had the improvements from the people before us, but the game's continued to evolve. The players require to be paid."

He is, however, candid enough to admit that last tango had found him out a little, just as he had got away with things the first time out - identifying two moments of truth.

"There was one situation where I got one on one with Lagisquet. I've never been so glad the whistle went. It was right in front of the stand with the press in it. There were only a couple of yards outside me to the line. He came hurtling down, feinted inside, then went outside me and he was past me. I never laid a hand on him - and I knew I couldn't have done that to him. The other bad one was when I let him in to score. I went in to tackle Sella, which I shouldn't have done. If I'd stayed on my wing Lagisquet wouldn't have scored." At least retirement meant that he no longer had to keep his nose clean.

As the squad descended the stairs in their Paris hotel, bound for the dinner, Robertson, suitably attired in dickie bow and dinner suit, was with them. However as they mounted the bus he was hiding behind a parapet, set for dinner with Alison and some friends. "I actually got a reprimand for that," he laughs. "Although I think it was a joke. One of the committee men came up and said 'If you do that again you're in trouble.'"

His international career over there was one last, hugely controversial appearance on the global stage. At the end of the 1988/89 season Robertson was the only Scot who agreed to join the World Select which toured South Africa as part of the SARU centenary celebrations. He was heavily criticised in sections of the media and although he does not delude himself into thinking that the tour played a part in breaking down apartheid, with Nelson Mandela still in prison at that time, he has no problem with his conscience.

"I don't think we helped the situation at all because it was already in the process of coming along. But as for fuelling apartheid which some suggested we would be doing, I am positive we didn't. I have absolutely no regrets whatsoever. I would have done if we had got there and discovered we were being used for propaganda purposes, but that wasn't the case."

He admits that his decision was based on an overwhelming desire to visit the one great rugby nation he had not visited, but there was nothing naive in his approach and he sought wise counsel. "I had a lot of discussions with people I greatly respect and they all felt I should go." In the event it all ended in pain, if not tears!

"I was injured in injury time in the first game," he says. The damage was so severe, in fact, that he spent the rest of the tour, after an operation in South Africa, encased in

Career highlight: Lifting the championship trophy at last as Melrose captain in 1990.

plaster. "I think I would have been picked for the Test side and that would have been a nice way to go out of international rugby. But after being operated on out there I was in plaster from hip to ankle for eight weeks."

He still hirpled around pretty effectively on his return. So much so that with the double responsibility of being club captain and backs coach he ended his last league season holding the trophy aloft as the first Melrose skipper to lead a Championship winning side.

Of course no record of the career of this particular son of the home of sevens, the Melrose club, would be complete without a mention of sevens rugby.

"Sevens was always the thing for me. All that open space - a chance to play. Well I did win a Melrose medal. Aye, nice and recently - 1975. All those years and one runners-up medal and one winners medal, although there were a number of occasions we got close."

Never closer than at the end of his last full season in 1990 having already led the team to that first national Championship, there could have been no more appropriate climax than if Keith had lifted the famous trophy. "That was a bit sad for me - it would have been a grand finale."

Once again though he was upstaged by an out and out winger, although once again it had to be a truly world class performer to do it as Wallabies star David Campese stole the show.

As he looks back it is warming to hear this great sevens specialist keep thoughts of the abbreviated game in context as he considers what is required to keep Scotland at the top in the world game.

"I think it has to keep its place alongside XV-a-side rugby in April. There are few enough days of rugby in decent conditions as things stand at the moment. We play far too much rugby in bad conditions."

What is also good to know is that while he is now managing to spend a bit more time at home, the Edinburgh-based Royal Bank of Scotland senior business manager is still managing to pass on, first hand, the secret of those silky skills to the next generation.

Going into the 1994/95 season he took on his first representative coaching job, assisting South coach Eric Paxton by taking the district's backs.

A man of strong views he believes that the SRU must move to ensure that terms and conditions for players and coaches are such that the rugby "bran drain" south of the Border is stopped.

He took on the district job because he felt he could give it the necessary commitment without spending the entire winter away from his family, either working or indulging his "hobby".

Prior to agreeing to work with the South he had undertaken to work with his club's developing talent and encouraging youngsters to learn the basic skills of the game is high on his list of rugby priorities. He also believes the environment must be right for them to gain a rounded rugby education.

"It's an important part of the process at Melrose. When we were kids we rubbed shoulders with the star players and the kids at the club know all the first team players now.

"I think there are usually a few open mouths when visiting youngsters hear our lot calling Craig Chalmers 'Chic', but that's the way Melrose is."

Career statistics: K. W. Robertson

1978 Scotland 9 New Zealand 18.

1979 Scotland 13 Wales 19; England 7 Scotland 7; Scotland 11 Ireland 11 (1Try); France 21 Scotland 17 (1Try); Scotland 6 New Zealand 20.

1980 Wales 17 Scotland 6; Scotland 18 England 30.

1981 France 16 Scotland 9 +; Scotland 15 Wales 6 +; England 23 Scotland 17 +; Scotland 10 Ireland 9 +; Scotland 12 Romania 6; Scotland 24 Australia 15.

1982 Scotland 9 England 9; Ireland 21 Scotland 12; Scotland 16 France 7; Australia 7 Scotland 12(1Try); Australia 33 Scotland 9.

1983 Scotland 13 Ireland 15; France 19 Scotland 15 (1Try); Scotland 15 Wales 19; England 12 Scotland 22 (1DG).

1984 Scotland 18 England 6; Ireland 9 Scotland 32 (1Try)+; Scotland 21 France 12 +; Romania 28 Scotland 22 (1DG); Scotland 12 Australia 37+.

1985 Scotland 15 Ireland 18 (1DG)+; France 11 Scotland 3; Scotland 21 Wales 25 +; England 10 Scotland 7 (1Try)+.

1986 Ireland 9 Scotland 10.

1987 France 28 Scotland 22+ [1]; Scotland 21 Wales 15+; England 21 Scotland 12 (1Try)+; World Cup - France 20 Scotland 20+; Scotland 60 Zimbabwe 21; New Zealand 30 Scotland 3.

1988 Scotland 6 England 9+; Scotland 13 Australia 32 (1Try).

1989 England 12 Scotland 12; Scotland 37 Ireland 21; France 19 Scotland 3.

All appearances on wing except + at centre. [1] Replacement for Doug Wyllie.

Unanimous Choice

10 - J. Y. Rutherford

John Rutherford first encountered his lifelong partner at one of the world's most famous rugby grounds in 1976. No, it wasn't Roy Laidlaw he met at Cardiff Arms Park. It was his wife Alison. He'd already known Roy for years by then.

Alison may not be too happy about it, although she's probably got used to the idea, but when rugby fans think of her husband's partner they will always tend to visualise him not with her, certainly not with another woman, but with that other man.

Rutherford and Laidlaw. Their world record half-back partnership may have been well and truly broken by Nick Farr-Jones and Michael Lynagh, but it is appropriate that such a great pairing should only have been overtaken by true world champions.

Symbiosis is a word which has been popularised within a sporting context since the end of their careers. The way the two tended to be characterised one might have reckoned that even by the occasion of the 1984 Grand Slam John would be the only one to have a decent shot at the meaning of the word - for all that he now teases Roy over the posh accent adopted in his role as South youth development officer - since the classic image of Laidlaw is of the then "sparky" rewiring the public toilets in Jedburgh the day after that historic winner-take-all victory over France at Murrayfield.

For all the similarity of their upbringing John, after all, was the one who was eulogised as an example of classy, elegant sophistication on the sporting field. Roy, as he alluded to in their joint autobiography, had to put up with words like busy, tireless and comparisons with burrowing animals and Border terriers as he battled to provide an armchair ride for his stand-off.

Whatever! Symbiosis is the word which best describes the coming together of two great Border-bred footballing talents who cannot be separated when the career of either is recalled. They were born to play together, albeit they both reckon that their fellow Borders legend Bill McLaren went just a bit far in attempting to sum up the depth of their understanding. "I think he said 'These fellows could find one another in a darkened room,'" says John. "As Roy said, I'd be the last person he'd want to find in a darkened room."

69

But it would be understandable if people were to read into their relationship rather more than a well practised ability for bringing the best out of one another at rugby, as John acknowledges.

"The coincidences are quite remarkable. We were both brought up in the Borders, but we both have parents who come from Glasgow — my dad and Roy's mum. We're both Librans, in fact our birthdays are on consecutive days. We always got on well. Our styles complemented one another," says John.

"But the most remarkable one of all has happened since we stopped playing. We both had two sons for quite some time and Roy had told me more than once that they weren't planning on having any more. Well I phoned Roy to tell him that Ali was pregnant again. Two days later he phoned me back to say that Joy was pregnant."

It really was quite some time before hockey player Alison and promising rugby player John, met at the Welsh national stadium in the mid-seventies that the Rutherford and Laidlaw paths crossed. "We were both at school when we met for the first time, but Roy left early," recalls the then college-bound John of his "labourer", the man whose graft did so much to help Rutherford be acknowledged as the most influential pivot in Scottish rugby history.

They actually started playing together at Under-21 level for both the South and Scotland, but by modern standards at least, both were late developers. John was 23 when he finally found his way into the national side in 1979. Roy got in a year later.

That first Rutherford appearance in the no.10 shirt is fondly remembered and there is still a trace of awe in his tone as he remembers the occasion, another international against Wales, but this time in Edinburgh. "You never see the opposition until you are on the pitch, but the Welsh were so famous. They were in every mag-azine, every paper, on TV... The Pontypool front-row, Derek Quinnell, Geoff Squire, Terry Holmes, Gareth Davies, Steve Fenwick, Ray Gravell, JPR. But I will always remember this, that when I ran out it was like looking at card-board cut-outs because they were so famous."

The young Rutherford grew up quickly as Selkirk struggled in Division 2, with Roy Laidlaw's Jed.

But not for long. Soon they were a force in Scottish rugby with the likes of Iain Paxton's power, here testing the Calder twins and a Brewster or two of Stewart's Melville.

Almost inevitably, since Scotland were in the midst of an all-time slump having lost the previ-ous seven matches and had six more to go before a win would be recorded, the Welsh won the day

19-13. Yet it was not a game-turning moment of brilliance which imprinted itself on the Rutherford memory on his debut, but the decidedly rude welcome he received to the game at the top level.

"They had a nutcase called Paul Ringer playing off the back of the line-out. From the back of the first line-out he shouted across to me 'I'm going to break your f——ing legs today. Since then attention to detail has become such in terms of preparation that new-comers to Test rugby can expect to have been primed for every eventuality as they enter the scene, but it was not so in 1979.

"I couldn't believe it! Here I was suddenly in front of 70,000 people with a guy telling me he was going to break my legs." Naturally a slightly rattled Rutherford looked to the veteran outside him for some sort of backing. In 1979 they reckoned you had to find out the hard way! "The ref couldn't speak any English, he was French, so I turned around to look for support and Jim Renwick was just laughing at me." At this distance Rutherford sees it all as having been a valuable lesson. "After the game it turned out Ringer was a really good bloke and that's how I discovered that a lot of inter-national rugby is just intimidation."

He also discovered, albeit Scotland had been in fairly desperate straits at the time, or what we prefer to call a transitional phase, that this was a level of rugby at which he could compete. "We lost in the last minute to a push-over try. I scored a try in my second game against Ireland, played fairly badly against England (Scotland drew both matches), but the game against France was a cracker, three tries all at The Parc."

At the relatively advanced age of 23 the hard work was just about to begin. Just as it is wrong to present Roy Laidlaw as essentially a hard working player whose game was based on industry rather than inspiration, then the image which persists of John Rutherford being a player of vast natural talent who simply glided onto the international stage, is largely erroneous. As with all great players he had to hone that talent, but the odd thing, looking at it from the perspective of the modern, highly professional approach, was that it wasn't until he had tasted Test rugby that his appetite was stimulated sufficiently to get down to making the very best of himself. "I felt I really started to work on my game after that championship," he says.

Things took a while to turn around for Scotland at Test level, but strangely enough Rutherford doesn't pinpoint the famous 1980 game against France, when Andy Irvine followed a nightmarish first hour with 20 amazing minutes of play to record Scotland's first win in 14 matches, as the point at which things really began to turn around.

"Creamy (Jim) Telfer joined us in my third year. He gave me the mental hardness. He was tough on us, but everything he told us was true. It's right that the truth often

Rutherford's international career had a shaky start in the middle of a run of 14 Scotland games without a win five of them in his first season, culminating in the customary defeat by the touring All Blacks.

hurts. Roy had arrived in my second season and we obviously knew each other pretty well by then, after the Under-21s and playing for the South together."

In terms of a moment when things began to come together the Welsh were once again involved in establishing a Rutherford milestone. "I felt everything changed when we played Wales in 1981."

There was a single incident in that match which several members of the side have subsequently recounted as a key point in the maturing of this Scottish side, albeit the incident itself was a bit unpalatable. It came when the first scrummage collapsed and Bill Cuthbertson emerged from the bodies to land a substantial blow on Pontypool front-row man Graham Price. The Scots froze for an instant waiting for the assembled Welsh legends to exact wholesale retribution, but nothing happened and psychologically the Scots grew in stature. Having lost, as ever, at the Parc des Princes in that season's opener, this was Telfer's first win as coach and was perhaps the start of the Fortress Murrayfield image which was firmly established by the latter part of the decade.

"I thought that at Murrayfield the team became almost unbeatable. Creamy's record was magnificent and 1981 was the start of it." In fact Telfer didn't lose a match at Murrayfield in his time as Scotland coach between 1980 and 1984, the only blemishes preventing a perfect record being the drawn matches against England (1982) and the All Blacks (1983). To put that in some kind of perspective when he took a year out in coaching the Lions in 1983 they lost both Murrayfield matches and on his departure, again under Colin Telfer, they were whitewashed in 1985.

Colin was not helped, however, by the fact that of the six matches John Rutherford missed between his debut and departure from the international scene four of them were among the nine matches for which he was coach.

Come 1982, back at what was becoming a home from home in Cardiff, Rutherford took part in what was the standard-setting performance from a Scotland side which was building towards a permanent place in the history books. Oddly enough there were parallels with the way the 1990 team was to produce its most spectacular play ahead of the year in which they achieved most.

"The 1982 game with Wales was probably the best game I ever played in and yet I remember Jim Renwick saying to me during the first 20 minutes that we were going to have to keep concentrating or we were going to get stuffed. There was him, David Johnston and me in midfield. I don't think we ever tackled as well.

"It all turned on that situation where they had four on two and Gareth Davies chipped ahead. It was gathered by Roger Baird and he launched the attack which changed the game." The left winger produced an electrifying burst down the touchline to take Scotland out of their 22, before finding support from his pack as the visitors swept from end to end for Jim Calder to score the first of five tries in a sensational 34-18 win. Quite a way to record a first win in Cardiff for 20 years.

"Gareth Davies was their captain and it was the first time they had been beaten at Cardiff in a Five Nations match for a decade, which is an amazing record. At the post match dinner he got up to speak and he said in many ways it was a relief that the record had gone and to lose it to such a side playing so well. He then said there was only one way they felt they could respond and the entire Welsh team got up and sang Flower of Scotland. It's hard to believe the way things are nowadays that that was only 12 years ago."

Davies, incidentally, never captained Wales again and played only three more matches for his country when he made a brief comeback in 1985. It was, indeed, the sort of match which could make, or break, an international career.

The remarkable thing is that 1982 was the first year Rutherford, who will always be remembered as one of Scotland's finest ever kicking half-backs, began to develop real confidence in putting boot to ball. "I was a terrible kicker when I came into the Scotland side. I used to throw the ball into the air goalkeeper fashion. We've got a new type of player nowadays who is well coached right through, in fact the flare is maybe coached out of them in some cases. But that certainly wasn't the case with me. I used to use Jim Renwick to do all the kicking when I first got into the national team."

Any tardiness in his rate of improvement was by no means down to a lack of dedication. "I had a fear of being dropped and that's what made me work so hard. When I started I worked with Scottish Mutual and they were great employers. I used to go to Murrayfield four lunchtimes a week and kick between 100 and 200 balls. I used to get Dougie Arneil and John Roxburgh out of the SRU offices and sometimes get Gordon Hunter to catch for me.

"It got to the stage I could stand on the 22-metre line on either side and put nine out of ten kicks between the posts right footed and left footed. I also hit hundreds of drop goals and drop-outs. Jim Telfer always felt they were an opportunity to get the ball back."

The biggest technical breakthrough, though, perhaps came during Scotland's 1982 summer tour of Australia, almost three years after Rutherford had established himself in the Scotland XV.

"I got a lot of help from Paul McLean, the great Wallabies half-back. I couldn't believe how high he kicked the ball. I went to him after the Queensland game and he showed me the technique of almost hitting the ball directly on the bottom.

"Craig Chalmers now uses the same technique. When you're told about it you would think the ball might go anywhere off your foot, but the first time I tried it the ball just went for miles. Gregor Townsend's now working on it as well."

Rutherford's opinion of McLean was reinforced during the Test series when, after Scotland had beaten the Wallabies with the legendary Mark Ella at stand-off in the opening Test of the 1982 series, McLean returned to dominate proceedings, scoring 21 points in Australia's comprehensive second Test win, remarkably his last ever Test appearance. Quite a way to go out!

Entering the 1983 championship season, Rutherford could be considered the finished article, yet things didn't turn out too well. "It was a difficult year for me. I suffered a fractured shoulder bone and didn't come in till the England game at the end of the season, which we won. I think I got on the Lions tour on the basis of that."

From this distance it is hard to believe that a player's of Rutherford's class was not an automatic choice for what was to be a very difficult tour of New Zealand yet that's how it was. Nor was there much chance of him getting the Test stand-off berth with Ireland's Ollie Campbell then at the peak of his powers.

"It was a good tour for me, though. I felt I was putting pressure on Ollie all the way through, but they needed him as a place-kicker. However halfway through the tour Creamy asked if I'd consider playing at centre and I realised I had my chance."

No-one could have been better placed to realise that Rutherford, who had played almost no rugby at centre, had the versatility to make the switch. Little wonder that Rutherford has no hesitation in naming that summer's Lions coach as the biggest influence on his career and in his one Test appearance for the Lions, before he dropped out of contention with a groin injury, Rutherford vindicated Telfer's faith by scoring a try in a match which also saw 27-times capped Scotland winger Roger Baird register his only international touch-down.

Telfer himself had a very difficult tour with the Lions being whitewashed in a Test series for only the second time in history, amidst suggestions (never substantiated by Telfer himself), that the Irish tour captain Ciaran Fitzgerald and Irish tour manager Willie John McBride, tied the Scot's hands. Telfer's troubles provided the spur for the great events of the following season.

"That was when all the Scots got together on the flight home. We had always had an inferiority complex, particularly against England and Wales, but that changed on tour." says Rutherford. "The first training session we were doing sprints and I was winning a few of them against these guys who were supposed to be flying machines... By mid-tour I think we realised we were every bit as good. There were eight of us on tour. The biggest ever Scottish contingent and they were the nucleus of the Grand Slam team - plus David Leslie. It was ridiculous he wasn't there, especially when you saw the other flankers. He was the hardest player I ever played with - a crazy man.

"I would say we felt we had to do something for Creamy. At the end of the last Test I think he was depressed. We had faith in him, both as a person and as a coach. It must have been difficult for him at selection when Scots names came up because they were his boys, but Colin Deans and The Bear (Iain Milne) were especially hard done by. Roy played more games than anybody on tour and had a really hard time, but acquitted himself well."

All in all it was a hugely motivated group of Scots which made that trip home and did they do something for Creamy in 1984?"It was a great year. Our critics said we just kicked the ball up in the air and chased it. We did kick the ball a lot, but our play was geared towards what to do when the ball came down," Rutherford explains.

Indeed that was to be the template for much of the best Scottish play over the next decade...and much of the carping from elsewhere. "We scored 10 tries in that campaign," Rutherford points out. "It was a very aware team. We would use every scrap of possession as well as we could. The rucking was excellent. But you've got to kick the ball! People who think you can just run from anywhere and win internationals are naive. I do think, though, we had more variety of kicking than more recent Scottish sides."

Yet again a meeting with Wales proved a major landmark in the Rutherford career and it's worth noting that from 1968, right through the seventies Scotland beat Wales just twice, by a point in 1973 and by two in 1975. Though perhaps lacking the style of two years earlier Scotland were again worthy winners at The Arms Park, with the supremacy of their forwards demonstrated by tries from skipper Jim Aitken and no.8 Iain Paxton, while Wales subsequently overhauled their pack.

"When we beat Wales in Cardiff it was really on then."

Again there were shades of things to come as England turned up at Murrayfield a fortnight later as odds-on favourites. "Lucky Jim" Pollock had scored a match-saving try and Peter Dods given notice of his form as Scotland had earned a draw with the All Blacks in November 1983. But a week later England had beaten New Zealand 15-9.

"England were massive favourites," says Rutherford. The bookies doubtless reckoned that was all the more so when the rain poured down on the day of the game, forcing the Scots into a late change of game plan. We felt their pack was slow and intended to move the ball a lot to outside centre, but the rain was so bad... One pass was all that was on." That theory was proved right when England tried to move the ball wide on two or three occasions and, in Rutherford's words, "we blitzed them."

The stand-off's exhaustively rehearsed precision with the boot was put to good effect as Scotland found an alternative way of keeping the the big English pack on the move. "Their wings were Mike Slemen and John Carleton, both great wingers, but we had looked at a lot of videos and they sat very flat. There was acres of space behind them."

The rest, as they say, is history, with Roy going on to establish Laidlaw's corner at Lansdowne Road, before suffering a head knock which allowed Gordon Hunter to join his Selkirk clubmate at halfback in sealing the Triple Crown celebrations on a day in Dublin which ended with more than the scrum-half seeing stars. Laidlaw had made a full recovery from his "footballer's migraine" a fortnight later so that the old firm were reunited in the epic win over the French, sealed by Jim Calder's "Turning Point" try.

A veil is best drawn over the following year, Scotland's last "whitewash" season, but there were a number of serious injury problems, perhaps a hangover from the efforts of 1984 and indeed the strain had begun to show at the end of the 1983/84 season when the Grand Slam Scots were beaten 28-22 by Rumania in Bucharest. At that time it was, perhaps, not just the place to go for a relaxing trip to ponder a season of heady success.

The 1986 season, though, was a hugely different story and in what proved to be the twilight of his career, Rutherford was part of what he considers to be, at least potentially, the best Scottish side of them all. It saw the arrival of the irrepressible Hastings brothers, while Finlay Calder effectively replaced brother Jim in the squad.

"I felt sorry that side didn't have two or three years together. It could have been the best of all time. We had the five number eights, Packie (Iain Paxton), Derek White, John Beattie, John Jeffrey and Finlay, the experience of myself and Roy with Scott, Davie Johnston, Matt Duncan, Iwan Tukalo and Gavin in the back-line." All that without mentioning a front-row comprising David Sole, Colin Deans and The Bear. "If we'd had one 6'8" giant that would have been the perfect side," is the Rutherford verdict.

During that campaign Scotland played some exhilarating rugby with six debutants in for the opener against France, though that one was admittedly won by the boot of Gavin Hastings, one of those making a first appearance, who created a new Scottish record for points in an international with 18 (six penalties). This time a trip to Wales provided a less happy memory for Rutherford as they provided the Scots with their only championship defeat. But even then Scotland scored three tries to one at The Arms, Paul Thorburn out-kicking an off-form Gavin, including sending over a penalty from some 70 yards out.

However the coup de grace came in the visit of England to Murrayfield, Rutherford scoring the last of his six international tries against the country he had opened his account against, in the midst of a magnificent 33-6 record Calcutta Cup win.

"Scotland were brilliant. The big win against England was very special. The performance was right up there with the 1982 win over Wales, but because it was England it added something to it. Some of the passing before the last try, scored by Scott Hastings, was incredible."

And so to 1987 and the occasion of the only, or at least best documented case of a rugby victim of the Bermuda Triangle. Scotland might have won another Triple Crown that season, but this time wet conditions for the meeting with England worked against them and the pack was out-played at Twickenham. Nonetheless Scotland looked to be in excellent shape for the first-ever World Cup with a young man who has gone on to make a huge name for himself in rugby league, Alan Tait, joining the aforementioned list of legends.

Between the Five Nations Championship and the World Cup, however, an illicit trip to the Caribbean was to effectively cost Scotland its playmaker. "In the World Cup we had a side which could have scored from anywhere, but we had to beat France in the group match because you had to avoid New Zealand to get anywhere. I think they were always going to win it.

"Of course my World Cup lasted six minutes! My knee wasn't right. It was a gamble which didn't pay off, although to be fair to the coaches they put me through a hard session the week before to check my fitness and I came through it. It's a different story in

OVERLEAF
Left: Much hard work went into the development of Rutherford's now legendary punting ability.
Right: A long line of partnerships could be on its way — Rutherford and Laidlaw each has three sons.

a game though and the first tackle I took that was me. I thought my leg was broken the crack was so loud, but I'd damaged my cruciate ligament."

The gamble had been brought about by an injury suffered in an invitation tournament, really just a bit of fun, for players of international standard. "The only problem with Bermuda is that it happened there," Rutherford now reckons. "We were all invited to play over there and we'd agreed to go. Then, after the last championship game, we were suddenly told we were not allowed to play until the next squad session prior to the World Cup. I don't actually think they would have bothered if I had not got hurt. We would have just got a rap over the knuckles.

"Anyway we were coming back on the plane and we saw all these guys in light blue blazers and realised they must be a team of some sort. We made some investigations and they turned out to be a Spanish rugby side coming to Scotland so we realised there would be SRU men everywhere at the airport and here I was about to be helped off the plane all bandaged up. So we explained the situation to the captain of the plane and asked if we could stay on for half an hour after everybody else to try to hide and he agreed. We thought we'd got away with it, then five minutes after I got in the door at home Bill Hogg (SRU secretary) was on the phone and he and the late Bob Munro, the tour manager, were at my house right away."

Even with the benefit of hindsight, though, one suspects the only regret Rutherford has about the trip was not that it upset officialdom, but that it ended his career a bit prematurely. It should be remembered that, particularly for Scots, trips were the only real perks for rugby players even as recently as the late Eighties.

As he looks forward to a future in the game, his foot already on the representative coaching ladder with the national under-18 squad, Rutherford is still closely involved with the two men his name will always be linked with. He is a partner in the insurance firm James R.Glass, based in Roy's home town, Jedburgh.

"We will be remembered as a partnership rather than as individuals. It's nice now, the families still keep in touch and Roy will be in at the office a couple of times a month just for a chat."

As for Jim Telfer, there is always the impression that there is minimal time for small-talk when there are life and death matters of rugby to be discussed, but he and Rutherford will work together, for sure. "Creamy will be good at using the knowledge of former players," reckons one of the first Telfer prodigies.

And there's always John's beloved Selkirk, the side he played for even when it meant travelling to and from Glasgow, when he was studying at Jordanhill in the seventies, the college then being one of the powers in the Scottish game. Going into the 1994/95 season he was faced with the difficult task of re-establishing his lightweight side in the upper echelons following relegation from division I.

"I'm Selkirk through and through. I was put under pressure to play for Jordanhill, but there was never any chance. Mum made the teas, Dad was a committee man and my brothers both played for Selkirk. I think they would have thrown me out of the family if I'd played for Jordanhill."

Even in those days playing for Selkirk, a town of just 5000, was a difficult business, yet Rutherford believes it stood him in good stead. The size of the town may have helped in as much as a talent like Rutherford's was always going to stand out.

The love of the sport kindled by his first coach at school John Torrie, grew as former British Lion and Leeds rugby league star Ronnie Cowan attempted to eradicate mistakes from the young Rutherford's play, never offering compliments, always homing in on errors, however good the performance.

"In many ways it was good for me because I had to get stuck in, so when it came to internationals it couldn't be that much tougher. Roy was the same, because at that time Jed were similar in the second division."

That message is doubtless being passed on to three young men, only one of whom, the oldest Michael (8), is showing a real interest in the game so far, having won his first rugby medal at the Musselburgh mini tournament just a few days before we spoke. The Selkirk youngsters are in good hands, learning the game under another of Rutherford's close friends and 1984 Grand Slam colleagues, Gordon Hunter, whose own son plays

In elite company with the Barbarians the Scotland star displays his running skills

scrum-half to Michael's stand-off in the primary four team, just as the old men did for Selkirk, the South and Scotland.

Grant (5) and Stuart (3) may be "more into Transformers" at the moment, but with three wee Laidlaws on the way through as well the South selectors may have a rich vein of talent to tap into as we move into the next millennium.

Career Statistics: John Rutherford

1979 Scotland 13 Wales 19; England 7 Scotland 7 (1Try); Scotland 11 Ireland 11; France 21 Scotland 17; Scotland 6 New Zealand 20.

1980 Ireland 22 Scotland 15; Scotland 22 France 14 (1Try); Scotland 18 England 30 (1Try).

1981 France 16 Scotland 9 (1Try); Scotland 15 Wales 6; England 17 Scotland 23; Scotland 10 Ireland 9 (1DG); New Zealand 11 Scotland 4; New Zealand 40 Scotland 15; Scotland 24 Australia 15 (1DG).

1982 Scotland 9 England 9 (1DG); Ireland 21 Scotland 12 (1Try); Scotland 16 France 7 (1Try); Wales 18 Scotland 34 (1DG); Australia 7 Scotland 12 (1DG); Australia 33 Scotland 9.

1983 England 12 Scotland 22; Scotland 25 New Zealand 25 (2DG).

   New Zealand 15 British Lions 8 (1Try);

1984 Wales 9 Scotland 15; Scotland 18 England 6; Ireland 9 Scotland 32; Scotland 21 France 12; Romania 28 Scotland 22.

1985 Scotland 15 Ireland 18; France 11 Scotland 3; Scotland 21 Wales 25 (2DG); England 10 Scotland 7.

1986 Scotland 18 France 17; Wales 22 Scotland 15; Scotland 33 England 6 (1Try); Ireland 9 Scotland 10; Scotland 33 Romania 18.

1987 Scotland 16 Ireland 12 (2DG); France 28 Scotland 22; Scotland 21 Wales 15 (1DG); England 21 Scotland 12; World Cup - France 20 Scotland 20.

All appearances at stand off.

CAPTAIN'S COMMENT:
On the certs: "I think most of the players who were involved in the past 30 years would have sat down and selected what they thought the team would be before it came out. There's only player out of that whole team who would have been selected by all those players - that's John Rutherford. Rutherford was just magic. The other one for me was The Bear (Iain Milne). The Bear missed the Grand Slam in 1990, but he came back for the tour of New Zealand that summer and proved he could do it. Then he could go, relax and prop up the bar.

Inspiration

9 - G. Armstrong

It was a pretty inexperienced bunch John Rutherford was asked to coach when a Scottish Districts Select faced Auckland in November, 1993...with one major exception. Rousing words were needed to ensure that the youngsters involved knew what was required.

"You're playing against Auckland," Rutherford told his charges. "They are a top New Zealand province. They are ruthless. You might be the nicest guy in the world off the pitch, you might be a great sportsman on it, but against these people you have to be an out and out git."

His captain, shortly to be named his half-back partner in the Famous XV, was one Gary Armstrong, making a comeback at scrum-half after opting out of both playing the position in which he had made a global reputation and playing for Scotland.

Eager to drum home the message Gary added a few choice phrases of his own, summing up by reiterating, as he thought, the coach's words. "And just remember what Rudd told you," he stressed. "When you go out against boys like these you've got to play like gits."

Rutherford recounted the tale to demonstrate the esteem in which Armstrong is held by his peers, or those who would be his peers. "There wasn't a murmur," the great stand-off recalls. "Nobody was going to laugh . . . because it was Gary."

The man himself remembers the day well. "Aye," he says. "I made a bit of a mess of that. The heads just went down at the time, but I got some stick after the game." Whether or not that slip of the tongue by the skipper, just about his only error on an inspirational day, helped relax his men, the District Select rose to the occasion, Armstrong scoring a try in a memorable win.

"We were the only team to beat Auckland on their British tour. That was something since we only trained together twice. The boys played bloody well. The forwards were tremendous and the backs tackled like demons." The important thing as far as anyone interested in Scottish rugby was concerned was not that result, remarkable though it was, but that Gary was back...

"Once you've learned the position it doesn't take long to get back into it. I took about 10 minutes to feel comfortable. It was just a one-off select game. I was approached and asked if I'd be available to help out."

Gary was not naive enough not to realise that his appearance there would prompt considerable speculation about his plans. Efforts to persuade him to make himself available again for Scotland were redoubled after two humiliating defeats for the national side at the hands of New Zealand and Wales.

In between times he had indicated that his resolve was wavering when he appeared for the Barbarians, at scrum-half, against the Kiwis. "The invitation to play for the Barbarians had come just before Scotland played the All Blacks. Once Scotland got that hammering at Murrayfield I accepted. I just wanted a crack at them. I was quite pleased with the way it went."

The rib injury he collected confused the issue, however and in any event with Andy Nicol in the no.9 jersey scrum-half was by no means the biggest of Scotland's problems in the wake of the All Blacks defeat.

"The pressure didn't really start, from the management or the media, until after the Wales defeat," says Gary. "But after Andy got hurt in the Wales game and they knew he would be missing the next game it really started."

It was not an easy decision, but one over which he had had time to agonise at some length, particularly since the 51-15 drubbing Scotland suffered at the hands of the All Blacks.

"When I decided at the beginning of that season not to make myself available that was me! I was quite happy to play out my career with Jed in another position. The commitment was too much.

"There were a lot of reasons for coming back. When I announced my original decision Duncan Paterson asked me if they could approach me if they needed me. My work said they'd give me time to get fit as well. And another thing was after the Scotland - All Blacks match I was coming down the stairs and someone shouted 'It's your fault Armstrong.' I think it was light-hearted enough, but it's the sort of thing you go home and think about."

The agonising was typical of a man who is, in so many ways, a reluctant hero. Once he had made his decision to return, however, the time for hesitation was over. Following record back to back defeats by New Zealand and Wales the difference one man can make was demonstrated in spectacular style over the next two internationals.

He was unprepared to commit himself, though, until sure he could make such a difference. The injury suffered playing for the Barbarians meant he was out of the game

Family man with wife Shona, Darren and Nicole.

altogether for six weeks, making his first appearance for Jed only on the morning of Scotland's defeat by Wales. Even although no-one was in the least doubt who they had in mind, he would not allow the selectors to list him for the game until convinced he could contribute, leading to the rare sight of a Scotland side for a Test match being issued incomplete. "I had to be sure I was fit. I only finally made the decision to play a week before the England game. That's why I asked if they wouldn't name me."

His employers, Mainetti, took the opportunity to add their weight to the national cause by agreeing to permit their lorry driver time off work in order to work on his fitness. After Nicol quickly confirmed there was no way he could play there was little doubt as to the true identity of "A.N.Other".

With England in pursuit of a third successive Grand Slam, eager to intimidate the rest on their first Championship outing of 1994 and Scotland in such appalling form the portents were not good. Yet Armstrong's presence was a huge factor in an inspired performance as the Scots raised their game magnificently to come within seconds of creating a major upset. Only a hugely controversial penalty score by English full-back Jonathan Callard deep in injury time prevented Scotland from beating the Auld Enemy for the first time since the Grand Slam match of 1990.

A month later Armstrong produced perhaps his finest ever display for Scotland in a match which was very one-sided, yet somehow ended drawn against Ireland, the only time Scotland avoided defeat in the 1993/94 season. He puts his virtuoso performance down to the weather. "We went over there with a game plan to move the ball a lot against Ireland, everybody knew what was happening. But then we got there and it was a howling gale so we realised we had to keep the ball in our hands.

"The way that match went, though, with that great effort by the forwards in the first half, it was maybe a bit unfortunate that we were into the wind first, because we thought we had the game won with the wind advantage to come in the second half.

"I didn't feel in myself I was there for the England game. I was just a yard or so off it," he says, demonstrating his own incredibly high standards, since most observers considered his showing almost super-human.

Perhaps the "yard or so" reference related more to the specific moment in which he broke from the back of a close range scrummage and was held back by John Hall just millimetres short of scoring the try which would have won the game for Scotland.

Armstrong had shed some 10 pounds in the run up to the game, such was his single-mindedness once committed to return. "I didn't feel weak that day," he says of the weight loss. "I just felt I could do with another game. It was only in Ireland I really felt I was right back again."

One man may not make a team but with Armstrong having picked up a serious thumb injury, still troubling him months later even although he played most of the second half against Ireland after taking that blow, the Scots wilted again in allowing France to end their 16 year run of never having won at Murrayfield.

It is typical of the man that following an international season in which he confirmed his own status in terms of his importance to the side, he regards 1993/94 as having been a time of utter frustration at that level. "It really was disappointing the way the season went, especially with France coming across and beating us and getting over the barrier of coming to Murrayfield."

The ultimate team man, he also had a hard time of things at club level over the same period, again because of the pressure applied to come back to scrum-half. Armstrong had given his word to his former understudy at Jed-Forest, Grant Farquharson, that he would not play at scrum-half that season as he helped persuade his Jedburgh townsman to return to the club from Gala. The season was not half-way through before he was forced to succumb to intense pressure to return to his international berth, with the club struggling for form and under threat of relegation. The views of the two players sum up why Armstrong is regarded with such affection by his peers.

Following his return to Gala, Farquharson has, on several occasions, made it clear that while less than happy with the conduct of some Jed officials who, effectively, emotionally blackmailed Armstrong into returning to scrum-half, he has absolutely no complaint about the way in which his team-mate behaved.

"I was gutted for Grant, but I was under a lot of pressure," is Armstrong's feeling. "I was happy enough to play at stand-off, in fact I told the club I would be happy to play in the seconds for a year and learn my trade in another position, but they wanted me in the firsts. I actually never had more than two or three games in any one position. They kept asking me if I would play other places. Then they wanted me to move back to scrum-half because we were in trouble."

Again typically he underplays his own role in the Jed revival which saw them surge up the first division. "The forwards didn't function in the early part of the season. I don't know why they struggled so much, but that made it very difficult for Grant to do anything."

Armstrong only went back because of his devotion to Jed-Forest. "I badly want to win something with the club. I missed the play-off game with Kelso for the Border League a few years ago because of a broken kneecap. We were unlucky another year when Melrose won the national league. If we'd beaten them on the final day we would have taken the title."

If anything that is what motivates him more than anything else now, rather than Test rugby. "I've made it to the top, made it to a Lions tour, won the Grand Slam. I've done everything I really wanted to do in international rugby," Gary explains.

Paradoxically it is clear that he will keep playing for as long as possible to try to ensure that Jed-Forest does fulfil all of its potential. He is the ultimate home town boy, leading to the joking suggestion from one observer that if he was to succumb to one of the many rugby league offers put his way it would not be to a major club like Wigan or Leeds, but to second division Carlisle: "Because he can get home for his tea." Armstrong laughs at the suggestion, but recognises the truth in it."I'm not the sort of person who gets excited about going abroad. I like to be at home. I'm quite happy just to come home and watch the telly all night.

"I was away in Lisbon recently to play rugby, but that was all right because Shona and the kids came with me. Don't get me wrong — touring is great. You're fed well, then you do your training or play a match, then relax."

He bridles at the suggestion that his closeness to his family is any sort of impediment to his international career. "A lot of people say 'Oh you're not playing because of your wife.' That's rubbish. I have to think about it any time I'm going to be away for a long time. It is down to the family, but it's me much more than Shona. She doesn't mind at all. We were together for four years before we got married in 1989. She knew I played rugby long before I married her.

"I love my rugby, but I don't like to miss the family," he explains. "I've spoken to a lot of rugby players who've missed out on their kids growing up." Family is everything to him, which also goes a long way towards explaining the devotion to Jed-Forest.

"I used to go down to watch my father play. He was a wing forward and centre for Jed. I think he played one game for the Co-Optimists, but as long as he could pull on a blue jersey that was him."

Father, Lawrence and mother, Margaret, are cited as the two main influences on the Armstrong career and it was probably no coincidence that Lawrence was one of the prime movers behind the introduction of mini rugby in the town just as his two sons Gary and Kevin, a year younger and a rugged flanker who has toured with Scotland, were getting big enough to think about playing the game.

"My father and some of his mates got the mini rugby started. I would have been about six years old, a bit young to play. When Kevin and I first went down I used to go in my ordinary clothes, but we joined in and the clothes got a big manky so my mother soon got fed up of that and started sending us down kitted up."

That was in the mid-seventies and it was not surprising that with Roy Laidlaw established as the local hero and set to establish himself in the national squad for a run which would eventually see him replaced by Armstrong, this promising little lad should choose to play at scrum-half. Yet, Armstrong reveals, Laidlaw's presence was not a factor in his decision to play scrum-half, albeit he helped him develop later on.

"I played scrum-half all the way through. It wasn't even to do with size or anything, it just seemed to suit me. Of course Roy was an inspiration. I was playing scrum-half anyway, but it's the same with all wee boys. When you go out onto a field you try to be like who's playing for Scotland.

"Once I started playing senior rugby Roy showed me a few things to do. He pointed out one or two ways of doing things. But he always stressed that you're your own player and you have to develop your own game."

It is fair to say that while the backgrounds of the Jed pair may be very similar their playing styles are quite different. However it should be noted that Laidlaw made sure he accommodated the prodigious talent on its way through.

"I spent a season in the seconds under Roy, then he switched to stand-off the following season, his last in international rugby, to help bring me on, by letting me play some first division games."

By doing so Laidlaw paved the way for his successor at international level since Armstrong - who had in fact played his first match for the first XV on the wing at Gateshead in 1986 - made such an impression in that first full season that he was picked for the international B side at the beginning of the 1988/89 season.

He would play only two B games, in the second scoring three tries against Italy, an effort which was quite enough to edge him in front of Hawick's Greig Oliver, already an

Grand Slam heroes: in the tunnel at Murrayfield, 1990.

established internationalist, in the eyes of the selectors. "When Roy retired it was between Greig and myself. There's always been a bit of rivalry between Hawick and Jed and that just added to it."

Armstrong made his debut against the mighty Wallabies who had been stung with a defeat by England the previous week and responded with a magnificent display to thrash Scotland 37-13. The 21-year-old debutant at scrum-half more than coped with the job in hand.

"It was a hard game and it was that quick...Farr-Jones was good," is Armstrong's summary. "You come off and reporters are asking you what you saw and how you did this and that. It was the same with the Grand Slam game. You can't really assess it yourself until you see it again."

Even with the benefit of hindsight he is unwilling to take much in the way of credit for what was an outstanding debut against one of the finest scrum-halves in the world. "It's a team game and we were well beaten that day," he says.

In the thick of World Cup action versus Ireland

That same day a new stand-off emerged, though not in the senior side itself. As a curtain-raiser to the Test the Scotland under-21 side met a New Zealand Rugby News Youth XV at Murrayfield and although the Scots were narrowly beaten a youngster by the name of Craig Chalmers oozed authority. Scotland had just lost the Rutherford-Laidlaw world record breaking half-back partnership, yet the new combination would, within a few years, be well within sight of their mark.

"I'd come right through the Grades with Craig, eventually into the Scottish team. I played alongside him for the South District Union junior sides when I was in the Jed seconds. I'm not sure if we played together at under-18 level but I do remember playing alongside him in a South District Union game against Glasgow at Hughenden."

The pair could not be more different in outlook. Chalmers worldly, outwardly self-confident and swaggering, Armstrong an unassuming man of relatively few words. "We phone each other up a fair bit. We're very friendly," Armstrong says of the relationship. A lot of people don't like Craig but when you speak to him one to one he's nothing like the way he sometimes comes across."

Armstrong believes the traits often diagnosed as arrogance in his most frequent Scotland partner are, in some ways, necessary towards making the Melrose man the player he is. "The stand-off is the man who controls the game. He has to be confident."

In tandem they made a huge contribution to Scotland's 1989 championship season which, under new skipper Finlay Calder, began with a comprehensive defeat of Wales, saw them dubbed "scavengers" when drawing at Twickenham, then win a Murrayfield spectacular against the Irish before losing their chance to win the championship by losing heavily in Paris.

"The 12-12 draw at Twickenham is the best I've ever done down there. A lot of folk were tipping us to get a hammering. I learned a lot in Paris. Things had gone well but Craig and myself were just boys among men when we went over there."

He acknowledges a one to one rugby lesson received from future French coach Pierre Berbizier. "He just took a loan of me. He was up to everything. Standing on my feet, knocking the ball out of my hands and grabbing my jersey at scrums.

"It was the first time I'd ever come across that in a top game. The next year again I did the same thing to him and he didn't like like it. But it's the only way to earn respect at that level and he came over to me after that match and shook my hand."

However well things had gone in the championship Scotland's new half-backs were hardly prepared for what came next. "We certainly weren't expecting to be getting into a Lions tour at the end of our first season. It shows you how well the Scots were playing, though, that there were nine of us there."

In the event the pair took the opportunity to do some more maturing, Armstrong as a regular in the unbeaten dirt-trackers side, Chalmers, after Irishman Paul Dean was injured, actually finding himself thrown into the first Test against Australia, which the

Lions lost before late arrival Rob Andrew established himself to guide them to victory in the second and third Tests.

As well as useful experience Armstrong gained a close friend in the man he understudied, Welshman Robert Jones. Contrary to his general outlook he enjoyed the tour, even if it was a bit long. "Everybody mingled in and got on well. Everyone was very impressed by Ian McGeechan as coach," says Armstrong of the man whose first match as Scotland coach coincided with the scrum-half's international debut.

"We did our bit." he says of the midweek regulars. "It's important for any touring party to get wins, on Wednesdays or Saturdays. It was a good trip to be on. But it was the first time I'd been away. It was my first time on tour and, to be honest, I was glad when we got on the plane home. I'd been involved in every game as scrum-half. Either playing or on the bench. It was hard work and I did miss home."

He returned to a real family occasion - his wedding. "The best thing was I was able to leave Shona to do most of the arrangements," he smiles.

The Scots on that tour returned battle-hardened, not least their young half-backs. Places in history beckoned. "We'd had all those players on the Lions trip giving us the right sort of experience, but we did struggle through the other games to get into a position to win the Grand Slam, particularly in Wales and Ireland," Armstrong recalls of the build-up to the 1990 epic match.

"Then we got to Murrayfield for that decider... The English wives were getting interviewed on television, they were so confident. We got into the dressing room and decided to walk out. The crowd just erupted. It was an amazing atmosphere."

It was only at the second time of asking that Armstrong correctly instigated the move which was to win the game, breaking from the back of a scrum on halfway, making ground and committing defenders before feeding his full-back Gavin Hastings. "We'd had a similar situation in the first half and I released the ball a bit early and got a bollocking off Gavin because Rob Andrew managed to get him.

"It was a move we'd practised and when we got the chance to do it again I was determined to do it properly. It was Gavin's vision that created the score though. He chipped it over perfectly for Tony Stanger to score the try."

As an occasion nothing would, surely, ever match that day - but, like many of his colleagues, Armstrong felt that greater Scottish performances were produced even that year. "The most satisfying rugby I've ever played was on the tour of New Zealand, team wise. Those were hard games. Not just the Tests but all the way through. Midweek and on Saturday. It says a lot about the Tests that they only won because Fox kicked everything."

That year was, indeed, the best of times. "That New Zealand tour was perfect for me, as much as anything else because it was only a month long. When you go there you just have to get into their way of play. We learned our lesson in the first two games. It was back to the same thing. You have to win the respect of these people," he says almost euphemistically.

New Zealand were in the middle of an eight year spell in which they were not to lose a Test series at home. Scotland pushed them as close as anyone in that period.

By now Armstrong was, if not exactly a veteran, certainly a senior member of the side. "The longer you're in the team the more pressure there is on you," he believes. Once you've been in that wee while you start to get a lot more press. I must admit I don't like being splattered all over the papers."

As preparations for the World Cup gathered momentum Armstrong took the opportunity to demonstrate to his teacher how well he had learned his lesson from Pierre Berbizier in Paris. Indeed he was keen to show he was, by now, worthy of taking the field with anyone. A lengthy altercation with the great full-back Serge Blanco, which left the pair entangled, sorting out their differences some 60 yards from the action, left

Back after intense pressure to return to scrum half, Armstrong transformed Scotland after their dismal start to season 1993/94 and almost, but not quite, capped it with what might have been a winning try against England.

little doubt that he would treat all-comers equally, without undue respect for reputations.

"He put up a high ball and, talking about showing that you're streetwise, I just put
my arms up and ushered him towards touch. He didn't like it and grabbed hold of me.
But he wouldn't let go. I only hit him once." Blanco sported a fairly spectacular cheek
wound at the post-match dinner that evening. "He's a player like anyone else,"
Armstrong explains. "I'd have expected the same thing if I'd grabbed hold of someone
else in that way. Mind you, the Parc was a funny place to be after that — a fight with
Blanco in front of 60,000 Frenchmen."

Nor was the hostility confined to the field of play as he discovered when indulging in
one of the less formal post-match traditions. "In Paris that evening, as always, we had
to change hotels to go to the official dinner and you get a backie on the police motor-
bikes that give the team bus an escort.

"I got on one of them and suddenly realised I had to tell the policeman to get moving
quickly. There were three old women standing on the corner holding brollies and they
started coming towards me shouting 'You the man who hit Blanco...'"

The World Cup ultimately proving disappointing Armstrong was to be given respite
from the limelight the following year. "The World Cup was frustrating. We just about
beat England. It was a bit sad. England played a far different game than their previous
visit to Murrayfield, but we were only beaten by a drop goal. Those matches at
Murrayfield summed up how much it means for Scottish players to play there.

"Just about right after the World Cup we lost the whole back-row which made it difficult.." What the selectors were not counting on was that they might lose their scrum-
half, however, Armstrong suffering his first really serious mid-season injury just the
week before the 1992 Five Nations Championship began, knee ligament damage being
inflicted during his club's league meeting with Currie.

He missed the entire championship and the summer tour of Australia, during which
time Scotland's invincible Five Nations run at Fortress Murrayfield was ended in some
style by the English and the international side lost a total of four of six matches, their
worst run for several seasons. It was a huge tribute to Armstrong's new deputy Andy
Nicol that he should catch the eye sufficiently to be selected for a World XV at the end
of the summer, producing some doubt as to who would be Scotland's first choice scrum-
half for 1993.

One appearance close to home at Melrose against Italy for the Scotland A side, a near
full strength national side, soon sorted that out. Nicol had arguably been the best in
Europe in the absence of the Borderer, but there was only one Gary Armstrong. He was,
however, now finding that age was catching up on him a little. Injuries were by no means
new to him, for example he had gone through much of the 1990/91 season with what had
to be a real problem for a player in his position.

"I played all season with a piece of bone floating about in my arm. I couldn't straighten the arm. I got an X-Ray and it was like a piece of cartilage that had come away. SRU doctor Donald McLeod knew about it and said it wouldn't do any damage in the short term so I just played with it till I could get it fixed. I had the operation to remove it before the World Cup. I've still got the piece of bone somewhere."

That sort of effort contributing to his previous image of indestructibility, the knee problem in 1992 was the first of a string of debilitating injuries. These reminders of his own mortality doubtless contributed to the decision, after missing the British Lions tour of New Zealand due to a severe groin problem, to opt out of international rugby.

"People are playing far more rugby now. They're going to come into the international scene much earlier, but go out much quicker. As soon as I decide I'm packing in Test rugby altogether I'll change position permanently."

"I enjoy playing scrum-half, but you take a lot of batterings. I don't mind that now, but I sometimes wonder how it will affect me later. I've always done everything the same way. It's just catching up on me. Roy did the right thing ending his playing career in another position. I am getting older. I don't mind training, when the weather's good! I used to like the mud, but I am 28 now..."

As the game continues to move increasingly towards professionalism this elder statesman had no added incentive to extend his stay at the top. "I try to keep my rugby as a hobby. If the switch of position had worked out I'd probably never have been back," he says,

"As long as I've got enough money to feed the family I'm all right. I've got a nice lifestyle.We're buying a horse just now. It's something Shona and I always wanted to do. I lived on a farm with my grandparents Jim (sadly missed following his death after taking ill on Father's Day 1993) and Bet for seven and a half years. I always used to exercise horses before that. We've got a stable and a field sorted out so we thought the time was right. It would be nice to make lots of money in some ways, but I really wouldn't know what to do with it. I've never had lots of money."

The demands already placed upon players are also completely at odds with the philosophy of a man much more intimidated by the prospect of sitting the CPC examination required to allow him to run his own business than by any All Black, Springbok or Wallaby.

"They're talking about fitness schedules and diet sheets for months up to the World Cup in South Africa. Some players maybe do need that, but I don't," he says without a trace of arrogance. He is merely a man stating a fact.

"I've never been on a preparation schedule to get fit, except for the England game last season (1994), when I had to do some because I really didn't know if I would be fit - and that was two weeks. It's all about mental attitude."

Career Statistics: Gary Armstrong

1988 Scotland 13 Australia 32.

1989 Scotland 23 Wales 9 (1Try); England 12 Scotland 12; Scotland 37 Ireland 21; France 19 Scotland 3; Scotland 38 Fiji 17; Scotland 32 Romania 0.

1990 Ireland 10 Scotland 13; Scotland 21 France 0; Wales 9 Scotland 13; Scotland 13 England 7; New Zealand 31 Scotland 16; New Zealand 21 Scotland 18 [1]; Scotland 49 Argentina 3 (1Try).

1991 France 15 Scotland 9; Scotland 32 Wales 12 (1Try); England 21 Scotland 12; Scotland 28 Ireland 25; Romania 18 Scotland 12.

World Cup - Scotland 47; Japan 9; Scotland 24 Ireland 15 (1Try); Scotland 28 Western Samoa 6; Scotland 6 England 9; Scotland 6 New Zealand 13.

1993 Scotland 15 Ireland 3; France 14 Scotland 3; Scotland 20 Wales 0; England 26 Scotland 12.

1994 Scotland 14 England 5 Ireland 6 Scotland 6.

All appearances at scrum-half. [1]Replaced by Greig Oliver.

FOOTNOTE: On Thursday August 25, 1994, Gary Armstrong was training for the new season. Those who had seen him in action in a practice match against Peebles the previous night had never seen him so fit at that time of year, so hungry for the start of the season. "He was really buzzing," says Jed-Forest coach Donald Millar.

With the Selkirk Sevens due to start the season a couple of days later and at Armstrong's prompting, a practice sevens match was taking place. The scrum-half made a typical break and unselfishly looked to pass rather than beat the last man. The challenge looked innocuous but as Armstrong twisted, his studs caught in the turf. The seriousness of the incident was immediately apparent as he screamed "It's the same knee!" on crashing to the ground. He had shattered the same left knee which was so badly injured in 1992.

Five days later Armstrong was told by a specialist that he was out of the game for a year. He would miss the World Cup. As this book went to press he was still awaiting an operation. Bruising and swelling alone were so bad that surgery was not possible for six weeks.

Once again, Scottish rugby had lost the most inspirational player of his generation.

The Walk

1 - D. M. B. Sole

He was the man out in front and he was the man behind THE WALK. As sporting declarations of intent go it has become one of the great symbols. The image of David Michael Barclay Sole moving slowly, yet so powerfully onto the Murrayfield turf will long remain with those of us lucky enough to be there, not to mention the millions who watched on television.

"I think part of the effect was that it took everyone by surprise," he says now. "I must admit it got an even better reaction than I had anticipated." That said it had achieved exactly the shift in momentum that the man who was on course to break fellow loose-head prop Ian McLauchlan's record number of appearances as captain had been looking for. "It was pure gamesmanship. It was just a case of thinking how we could get one up on them and fully capitalise on the fact we were playing at Murrayfield."

The change of status experienced that day by someone who idolised McLauchlan as a youngster - "We all need our heroes and the Lions tours of '71 and '74 were the big rugby events when I was growing up" - is something he treats philosophically. "I think that would have happened to whoever had been captain that particular day."

In three more meetings with England before his retirement in 1992, widely regarded as premature, Sole never got the better of the English. In fact it was the only time he tasted victory over them in seven meetings. But if ever there was a time to win...

There are those who would like to claim that David Sole was on the wrong side that day. Certainly he was born and spent his earliest years in the South of England and father Tommy was an Englishman. However from the moment his maternal grandfather died, vacating his estate in Aberdeenshire which the family moved North to take up, perhaps before, the man was a deeply patriotic Scot.

"I did play for English Universities, but that was different. We had Welshmen and all sorts. It just depended on where you were studying. I always wanted to play for Scotland. I played in the England Under-23...Students v Under-23s, but I wrote to the secretary of the SRU at the time - I think it was John Law - seeking clarification as to when I burnt my boats for Scotland. I got a letter back saying that if I was picked for their Under-23s that was it. So I played in the trial just to get experience of playing at that level."

97

As for the accent, which his first Scotland skipper thought was English, but now carries a very subdued Edinburgh twang: "I suppose I had just got used to the accent in the South West by the time I first played for Scotland. After all you've got to communicate with people like Gareth Chilcott!"

Nationality in rugby terms is a subject on which he feels strongly. "It is the burning question. What do you want to do? Play for Scotland or just play international rugby. It's up to the individual to sort that out," he says using diplomatic words, but his tone perhaps suggesting otherwise. "I could easily have gone through the English set-up."

His first experience of the game had also been a little before, at the age of eight, that family move to Glenbuchat in Aberdeenshire. He played scrum-half at school there, but his real rugby education began at Blairmore Prep School, where they knew a loosehead prop when they saw one. So much so that he was given the no.1 jersey for the school under-11s team when he was just eight "and a half".

There were only 60 or 70 youngsters at the school so it was a limited pool to choose from and he was a natural. "I was always pretty keen on sport in general...reasonable at most things I turned my hand to." The school has only produced one other internationalist - oddly enough a direct predecessor of Sole's in the in the eighties, Gregor Mackenzie. "I think it's pure coincidence that we are both loosehead props," he reckons.

From Blairmore to the "sporting paradise" of Glenalmond with its magnificent cricket square, delightful little golf course and powerful rugby tradition. "We always seemed to have one or two in the Varsity match and they were playing in front of huge crowds at Twickenham." From that stemmed a rare unfulfilled Sole ambition, to win an Oxbridge Blue. His father had played hockey-for Cambridge after his rugby career was curtailed in his late teens by injury.

His second choice University, after three years of first XV rugby and first XI cricket, was St Luke's College, Exeter. His rugby coach at Glenalmond was a St Luke's man and it showed where Sole's priorities lay that his application followed an appearance by the College on "Rugby Special" followed by a successful run in the Middlesex Sevens, shown on the same programme. When the College merged with Exeter University it only served to prove that Sole had made the right decision, rugby-wise at least.

"The rugby there was probably a better proving ground than playing at Cambridge with their fixture list and getting gubbed by 60 points all the time. Obviously we lacked size and had to play to our strengths and basic skills, trying to run people off the park. But we did have some quality fixtures against the likes of Plymouth Albion, Bath, Gloucester, Bristol and Rosslyn Park.

"In my last season there we had a really good record. We lost to Gloucester 17-10, and were beaten by 20 points by Bristol, but we drew 6-6 with Bath late on and they had been going well, undefeated since the turn of the year." That was a Wednesday night and it was where Bath spotted...Richard Hill.

In terms of attitude the man Sole would get the better of some years later in the biggest match ever played, taught him a great deal about attitude. "Hill was an incredibly dedicated guy. Not in the same league ability-wise as, say, Gary Armstrong, but he just worked at his game all the time. We had a couple of gyms at St Luke's and every day for about an hour or so he would be in one of them practising his passing against a crash pad."

Not that Sole was any slouch himself in that department. "I did a lot of training. I always enjoyed it - and not just for the results. I never wanted to be shown up in training. "When we did two minute runs at squad sessions someone like Alan Watt is just prepared to do enough. I always wanted to be right up at the front."

Rugby had become a major factor in his life at senior schoolboy level when he was selected for the Scottish Schools team. "We had a reasonable side, were narrowly beaten by France and Wales, but beat England in England for the first time. I suppose that was my first big taste of the big time.

"I think at every level you think being selected means you have a chance of going on, but until it hits you between the eyes you never really believe you are going to play for Scotland."

A lengthy apprenticeship towards that target had begun on going up to University. Indeed international honours came a little bit more easily than top class rugby in the tough breeding ground which is England's South West corner.

The third sending off in the career of Chilcott — an individual, nonetheless, of whom Sole will hear nothing bad spoken — provided a vacancy for Sole which gave him the opportunity to step up. "At the time Bath hadn't won anything. I joined at the start of that era."

In typically understated fashion he offers an interesting insight into the man credited with much of that success in the late eighties and early nineties, Jack Rowell, who has gone on to take over as England manager.

"He's a great manager of people...gets the best out of them, without necessarily being the most astute tactician in the world. He is a very successful businessman and a very nice guy, but you do have to have a certain ruthlessness to get on in that world." (Since retiring from international rugby David Sole is doing rather well for United Distillers in the world of grain buying, incidentally.) Others, such as John Horton, John Palmer and captain Roger Spurrell accelerated the rugby development of the young Sole.

"What I learned at University and before I broke into the Bath first team was probably the most valuable time in that I learned to look after myself. I learned a lot in terms of technique as well as discovering that you have to be totally focussed and fairly ruthless."

"In my formative years at Bath we seemed to be going up the Valleys into Wales every week. You were either up against some guy who had been a top notch player and was on the way down or against some young back eager to prove a point.

"Some of the games were brutal. When you went to ground you got some real kickings and one of the closest times I ever went to a sending off was during that period at Mountain Ash in Wales. We had driven over a ruck and a Welsh guy just hoofed one of our players. I came running from 10 yards away and decked him. I was by no means the only person involved but when I knocked the guy down the referee gave a really loud blast on the whistle and I thought 'That's it.' But all he did was turn to the guy I'd hit and said - 'You deserved that'."

A hard school indeed and one which has contributed to forming in Sole some strong views on what it takes to make a top rugby player. "I'm not terribly comfortable with the way the game is going," he admits. A strong advocate of professionalism he does not, however, want to see the rewards come too easily.

"I think it is very important that the players do get their just rewards, but people also have to earn respect. I always remember Ian McGeechan's words when we arrived in New Zealand in 1990, that you'll get given nothing out here except from what you do on the field. A lot of players have a fair bit to go to understand that. We had hard times, as well. We lost three games on the trot in 1991/92 - to England twice at Murrayfield and to New Zealand, but we came back and won the next two. It can be very difficult to turn things around and losing is a hard habit to get out of...but that can apply to winning as well."

For the 1994/95 season Sole, like Finlay Calder, was getting involved in the national scene at management level with the youth squads - a challenge he was looking forward to hugely.

"I would hope we get these jobs for more than a year so we can have time with them to instill the awareness of what you need to

Left: Plotting the 1990 Grand Slam.

Right: Captain Sole leads the walk that became part of Murrayfield legend.

become a top player. It's an excellent stage to be working with players. I think one of the major factors in the revival of Wales has been putting Bob Norster in charge of the national squad, someone whose playing days weren't that long ago. He instilled the right philosophy.

"For us Ian McGeechan was a superb coach. Not only did he have the methodical preparation from being a teacher, but he had been there and done it. If you are looking to build a good coach I believe you need to have that combination of a teaching background combined with having played international rugby."

The McGeechan influence had first been felt by Sole in 1983 when the great centre made a one-off emergency comeback for the Anglo-Scots in a victory over the North & Midlands at Dunfermline. They almost shadowed one another in progressing through the ranks as player and coach thereafter.

Having made his presence known to the Scottish selectors Sole found progress a bit easier to make north of the border. He won five B caps, two each in 1983/84 and 1984/85 and one in the 1985/86 season, yet it was only after New Year 1986, around the same time as he was first selected for Scotland, that he properly established himself as a first team regular - and then only thanks to the vision of Jack Rowell who did not want to see talent drifting away from the club.

"My breakthrough was down to Jack's management. We had three quality props. "Cooch" Chilcott could play on both sides, Richard Lee could only play tighthead and I could only play loosehead. Jack struck on the idea of a rota system and with the other one on the bench it meant no-one had to go to places like Cwmbran and Mountain Ash..."

There had been disappointments at international level, however, after winning his first B cap in that 1983/84 Grand Slam season. With Jim Aitken not making the trip he had been optimistic about his chances of going on the 1985 summer tour of North America, but with only three props making the trip he missed out. Come the 1986 trial he had something of a point to prove to convince the selectors.

"It was a good day to be in the Reds," says a man who was never on the losing side in a trial. "You are on a hiding to nothing in the trial. I was lucky with them, but being in the Blues was just the worst." That day, though, few would have relished the prospect of playing loosehead for the Possibles against the Probables. "I had to prove myself scrummaging against The Bear. That was never easy, but I did all right."

He was deeply conscious of the fact that doubts lingered over his scrummaging. "I was about 16 stone when I went to Bath so I wasn't small, but I had the reputation of not being able to scrummage. It was the old thing that if he's running about like that he can't be doing his job in the tight." Sole acknowledges there might have been a trace of truth in that early on, although there is no doubt that in that context his fitness worked against him. The doubters were given ammunition in one of his early appearances for Bath, however.

"I remember playing one match against Austin Sheppard of Bristol, who had played a couple of games for England, just as I was breaking into the first team. It was midweek under lights and I spent most of the night eating grass. I must admit there wasn't a lot of running about that night," he laughs. "I spent a lot of time working on my scrummaging, but I took a long time to live that down."

Yet he can look back contentedly and allow his record in that department speak for itself at the highest level. "I'll maybe go to my grave with people doubting whether I could scrummage. But in my time playing for Scotland we scored four push-over tries and conceded NONE."

A particularly sweet memory is the pushover score against an England pack in which he faced Jeff Probyn, with whom he had been conducting something of a war of words through the media throughout the previous few months after Scotland's World Cup semi-final defeat, in the 1992 Calcutta Cup clash at Murrayfield. Scotland lost heavily that day, yet the match remains more memorable for the way Scotland shunted the much-vaunted England pack. "That score made up for a great deal," he says, with passion.

The clashes with Probyn also resulted in Sole introducing a new fashion for loosehead props when he cut the left sleeve off his jersey. That ploy backfired on one occasion when a well-meaning attendant cut off the wrong sleeve — the mistake was remedied before he took the pitch

The Scottish selectors took a bit less convincing on the matter of scrummaging than the English media, fortunately and the fleet-footed Sole was introduced for the meeting with France in 1986. He was part of a new, rather laid-back sort of rugby star - part of a new generation altogether as five other new boys, including the Hastings brothers and Finlay Calder, made their debuts that day.

"I was sharing a room with Roy Laidlaw before the game and I think I drove him crazy. He was trying to wind me up, giving me a countdown - saying things like '30 hours to go' and I was just telling him to get lost. To be honest the way I saw it if I just won one cap it would still be fantastic."

He believes that ignorance is bliss as far as international rugby is concerned. "You are pretty relaxed before the first cap because you have no idea what the hell is going to happen. I just wanted to savour every moment. It gets worse from the first cap on because you then know what's going to happen."

Not that he didn't have the odd anxious moment during the run-up to the game - that sense of anxiety building in the early moments of that particular match. "At kick-off you are psyching yourself up and I was up against Jean-Pierre Garuet who had been sent off the previous season for gouging. Gavin kicked it directly into touch and I was thinking that he might at least have forced them to run about for a bit before I was forced to get into a scrum with this guy. So then I was getting ready for the scrummage back at the centre and they ran away and scored a try."

In the foreword to Sole's autobiography "Heart and Sole", Ian McGeechan recounts "the look of bemused amusement" on Sole's face at that moment as one of the outstanding personal memories of this star pupil. He would rarely be bemused again during an international match - or for that matter amused in any way by an opposition score!

He admits that his detailed recollections of his thought process during that passage of play are relative rarities. When it is put to him that a glaze of almost other-worldly intensity seemed to come over his face at the start of an international and remain there throughout he is once again amused, but accepts that it may well be the case that the adrenalin engaged a part of his brain only required under the most severe pressure.

There would be only one more appearance for Scotland that season, in the only Championship defeat of the year suffered at the hands of Wales courtesy of Paul Thorburn's 70 yard penalty, before an incident which did nothing for his rugby prospects, but, he believes, improved his looks - long-term at least.

The week before the Calcutta Cup match which saw a record victory by Scotland, Sole was playing in a Cup match for Bath against Moseley when at a line-out, his nose came into direct contact with the elbow of former England lock Steve Boyle.

"I could hear the crunch and I put my hand up to try to feel my nose. The bottom half of it was spread across my face. Tears were streaming down. I went off and people didn't think there was much wrong with me. But when I went into the shower room my sinuses just suddenly exploded. It was a real elephant man job. As well as the nose, the bones surrounding the orbit of my eye were damaged. They said it would be extremely stupid to play again that season."

The incident cost him his chance of establishing himself in the Scotland side and postponed an English Cup winners medal for a year. He was in the Bath side which lifted the trophy just before setting off for the 1987 World Cup, however and indeed just before returning to set up home in Scotland.

Between February 1986 and the summer of 1987 a bit of lost ground had to be made up, however. "Alex Brewster had come in and helped Scotland get a share of the Championship, so I didn't know whether I would get my place back."

In the event he would return as soon as he was available and would be a permanent fixture in the Scotland side from that point until his premature retirement in 1992. "The second season is supposed to be harder, but I had only played two games in my first international season. I had quite a reasonable second season - had a really good game in Paris in a great match and played well as we beat the Welsh easily. I was just glad to be involved as we put ourselves in a position to win the Triple Crown, but we played so awfully at Twickenham. We had a new centre partnership with Keith Robertson and Roger Baird and we got it all wrong...trying to do miss moves in appalling weather."

The stick at his home club in that wake of that defeat was not what drove him away, however. "It was always very good-natured whether you were winning or losing. There was a fair bit of needle, but it was very much a family type atmosphere. At a successful club like that people respect one another."

From a personal point of view, however, his time with Bath ending in such style with the Cup win, he was on a real high entering the first-ever World Cup. "Playing all four matches in the Championship was a real vote of confidence." An established internationalist, then, he was to find himself and indeed his sport, moving on to another plane that summer.

"The World Cup was very much a festival of rugby. I wouldn't say it was friendly exactly, but it was a wonderful event to be involved in. At the time it exemplified the gap between some of the emerging countries and the established ones. It's narrowed a lot since then and the World Cup has had a lot to do with that."

More importantly he was visiting a country full of like-minded rugby people. "It was my first trip to New Zealand and I picked up a strong sense of the intensity of the feeling for rugby there. They were a very good side," is the verdict of one who found out how good in the quarter-finals.

Scotland, though, learned a great deal from that and, indeed, Sole believes they went on to emulate the development of that All Black side. "They had spent a year in the embryonic stage in 1986 and from then they were undefeated until 1990. They developed in the same way that our 1990 side came together in 1987 and 1988. We reached our pinnacle in 1989 and 1990."

Sole is unsentimental in his diagnosis of the strengths of the Scottish side which began to develop in 1987 with the ones which have performed so disappointingly since his departure from the scene. "The problem with some of the players now is that they don't appreciate what you have to go through to get there. They are getting star status too quickly and they've all got huge profiles. It takes a lot of physical and mental hardness. Then you had players who were determined and ruthless when the going got tough. Now there are not so many people who will ignite things."

If 1987 saw the right ingredients being identified, 1989 was where the blend was refined. "The draw at Twickenham was a very good away result and then on the Lions tour we got the chance to see the players we were up against close up. You go out there with enormous respect for them, but by the time you've worked closely with them and have seen them in training and under pressure, you also start to respect that they are only human as well.

The Lions tour saw the end of Finlay Calder's brief, but hugely successful and inspirational, time as a captain. "Personally I think he had a pretty tough time of it. A lot of us were fairly oblivious to it, but you got to see some things which obviously disgusted you quite a bit. However, had Finlay come in and said after the first Test that he should drop himself, as was being suggested in some quarters, I think the players would have been absolutely unanimous that he should not - and I think I can say that even includes his rival for his position, Andy Robinson."

"We all felt none of us had done ourselves justice in the first Test. But Geech had been on countless Lions tours and was especially good at keeping the pressure off the players. Then when we got back into the Test series Finlay showed his strength of character and he was immense."

Nonetheless enough was enough and when Calder missed Scotland's first match of the new season, against Fiji at Murrayfield, a new captain had to be found. From the effervescent Calder the selectors turned down the volume at press conferences quite dramatically by introducing a man whose every word merited full attention, if for no other reason than that he was so soft-spoken."I can't remember why Fin missed the game, but I was quite happy to take up the reins," Sole says, admitting that it was an ambition "but nothing like the sort of goal that playing for Scotland was."

As for his own selection as skipper:"You know that you are in with a shout, but it was still a pleasant surprise to be asked." The style might have changed - "Everybody goes about the captaincy in his own way" - but the results were similar. Scotland remained winners.

"We had a nucleus of good players coming from '89 and I have to admit the games fell well for us, having the two hardest nations at home was good and so was having all our matches on a straight fortnightly basis. England had far too long to think about the decider. We hadn't really thought about the Grand Slam game until after the Welsh match."

Sole is realistic about the comparative performances of the two nations in the build-up to the 1990 decider. He shares the view held by several of his team-mates, that following England in the rotation made each individual match harder, but he is also very conscious of the relative limitations of his side that season.

"We'd been written off because we weren't putting 30 or 40 points past everyone like England, but the sides we faced were on the rebound. Basically, though, we don't have the players to put on those sort of scores, but when it was there for the taking we had people who could take it. In a one-off game like the Grand Slam decider it's the side that wants to win most."

Calder may have stepped down from the captaincy that season, but, as Sole happily recounts, he was to have his most senior pro to thank for relaxing the side perfectly with a prank which has gone into Scotland squad legend.

"Finlay set up the whole thing with a girl who cut his hair. Everybody was party to it except John Jeffrey. There was a senior pros meeting held in the Golf Tavern on the Thursday night before the game. In comes this blonde girls and she rushes up to Finlay and said she had to see him, right away, adding - 'It's positive'. Finlay puts his pint down and went off with her. We were sitting there dead pan saying 'What was all that about?' JJ was shocked. We went back to the hotel and on the way back we discussed it and decided we had to keep it quiet. Finlay had primed Craig Chalmers, though, to ask what was wrong with Finlay because he'd just come in and gone rushing up the stairs without saying anything. JJ said 'There's nothing wrong, there's nothing wrong' and we all clammed up. Scott Hastings was sharing a room with Finlay and next morning he purposely sat at JJ's breakfast table. He sat there and told the general company that he didn't get a wink of sleep - 'Because some stupid bitch kept phoning every hour to speak to Finlay.'

"JJ said nothing and when Fin came down he asked him 'OK?' and Fin just nodded. We got on the bus to the public session at Meggetland and it was customary for everyone to read everyone else's mail. Finlay was always reading Sean's out so Sean lifted this letter which was addressed to Finlay and said 'Ah...marked private! He then held it to his nose and said 'Perfume...smells like a woman'.

"By this stage Finlay is trying to get over the seats at him and JJ was just sitting there in shock. Sean started reading out the letter which began 'My darling Fin are you going to leave your wife and children or do you want me to have an abortion. It went on in that vein with lots of sweet-talking stuff then at the bottom Sean said 'PS - Got you this time JJ, hook line and sinker.'

"It had worked perfectly for everyone, except maybe JJ who'd lost a night's sleep. But we got off the bus in a tremendous frame of mind, did a light session, maybe 35 minutes tops, but we knew the work had been done."

By this time the decision to walk onto the pitch had been made. Sole had discussed it with his lieutenants and they were in agreement, with just one suggestion of dissent. "Finlay said we'd done it before we lost in Australia, but to be honest I couldn't remember running out that day. I think the tunnel was so long that by the end of it the rest of us were just running."

In any event it was bound to be a much more successful ploy in front of 50,000 near-hysterical supporters, rather than in front of the opposition fans on the other side of the world. And the match itself?

"Usually internationals are frenetic for 15 minutes then settle down, but it was maintained for the whole game that day. To be honest, my biggest memory of the game is just the desperate defence and the fear of giving away stupid penalties. But England had not done their homework and of course there remains the great debate as to who was their captain on the field that day."

He plays down any suggestion that there had been personal points to prove, however. "I think it was the media hype that put the intensity into the match, it wasn't personal. We had been on tour with so many of them and respected them for the rugby they played."

If Sole's assessment had been right, in that Scotland had built up to that point in time in the manner of the All Blacks side of the late eighties, then that summer's tour of New Zealand could not have been better timed. So it proved as the champions of two hemispheres clashed.

"That tour of New Zealand was the highlight of my rugby career for all sorts of different reasons. It wasn't just in the Test matches that we performed well. It was throughout the tour. Not winning the second Test was desperately disappointing, incredibly frustrating. There were one or two things that didn't go our way, like when Finlay was judged offside and for once he didn't deserve to be," Sole laughs. "But it was a magnificent performance."

There was no real sense of anti-climax, however, with another World Cup on the way...this time on home soil with the qualifying matches, quarter-final and semi-final all due to be played at Murrayfield. "It wasn't too hard to keep motivated with that around the corner. That tournament moved rugby on to a whole new level of interest."

Thereafter, though, as he moved past McLauchlan's captaincy record, he was finding it harder to maintain the necessary enthusiasm. "I have no regrets whatsoever about opting out when I did," he says of his departure after Scotland's tour of Australia in 1992 at the age of 30. The only thing I miss is the international rugby itself, but not the work you have to do to prepare for it. And all the reasons I packed in for are justifying my decision, especially in terms of career. Anyway, I always wanted to go out at the top. I didn't want to be forced out."

He has progressed much more quickly with his company than he would have expected to had he still been spending so much time on the training ground. Furthermore there is rather more time to spend with wife Jane, children Jamie, Gemma and the latest arrival in 1994 - Christopher.

David Sole at The Palace with wife, Jane, and mother to receive his MBE.

Even in defeat, he ensured that happened in some style in Australia as his inexperienced Test side was well beaten in the second Test, having already lost the first to the
Wallabies. "It was nice to score the last ever four point try in international rugby and
finish with a landmark." As ever, an impeccable sense of timing, since it was one of
only three he scored in his 44 appearances for his country.

Career Statistics: David Sole

1986 Scotland 18 France 17; Wales 22 Scotland 15.

1987 Scotland 16 Ireland 12; France 28 Scotland 22; Scotland 21 Wales 15; England 21 Scotland 12;

World Cup - Scotland 20 France 20; Scotland 60 Zimbabwe 21; Scotland 55 Romania 28; New
Zealand 30 Scotland 3.

1988 Ireland 22 Scotland 18; Scotland 23 France 12; Wales 25 Scotland 20; Scotland 6 England 9;
Scotland 13 Australia 32.

1989 Scotland 23 Wales 9; England 12 Scotland 12; Scotland 37 Ireland 21; France 19 Scotland 3;

Australia 30 British Lions 12; Australia 12 British Lions 19; Australia 18 British Lions 19;
Scotland 38 Fiji 17*; Scotland 32 Romania 0*(1Try).

1990 Ireland 10 Scotland 13*; Scotland 21 France 0*; Wales 9 Scotland 13*; Scotland 13 England
7*; New Zealand 31 Scotland 16* (1 Try); New Zealand 21 Scotland 18*; Scotland 49
Argentina 3*.

1991 France 15 Scotland 9*; Scotland 32 Wales 12 *; England 21 Scotland 12*; Scotland 28 Ireland
25*; Romania 18 Scotland 12

World Cup - Scotland 47 Japan 9*[1]; Scotland 24 Ireland 15*; Scotland 28 Western Samoa
6*; Scotland 6 England 9*; Scotland 6 New Zealand 13*.

1992 Scotland 7 England 25*; Ireland 10 Scotland 18*; Scotland 10 France 6*; Wales 15 Scotland
9*; Australia 27 Scotland 12*; Australia 37 Scotland 13* (1 Try).

All appearances at loosehead prop. [1] Replaced by David Milne. *Captain

CAPTAIN'S COMMENT:
*On his own captaincy: "I took over through
default more than anything else, both Scotland
and the British Lions. The key to being a good
captain is having good players around you, you
have to have a solid spine - good players at no.8,
scrum-half, stand-off and full-back, with a good
front-row. If the spine is in line you're all right. I
was the caretaker captain for David Sole."*

Hooker

2 - C. T. Deans

Whisper it, but Colin Deans is living in Gala. At least he has been planning to. "I'm waiting for my passport to come through before I break the ceremonial sword over my knee," he laughs. Joking apart, however, the man whose place in Hawick history, at least, looks safe for many a year to come as a joint record cap holder, appreciates he can expect few days to go by without some sort of verbal bullet to be fired his way deep in enemy territory. "But I've got a thick skin."

There is a certain symbolism in the defection of Scotland's first World Cup captain, albeit the passion for his beloved Hawick remains. The Greens have come on relatively hard times since Deans' departure from the game.

As a youngster he entered first class rugby in season 1973/74, the inaugural national league season and was a central figure in a side which dominated the first six championships. In 1987 his last league season with the club saw Hawick lift their 10th title in 14 years of campaigning. They have not won it since.

Those of a superstitious nature with activities at Mansfield Park close to their hearts might well have been concerned at the timing of Deans' move across the Borders, just ahead of the 1994/95 season which would see six sides relegated from division I to reduce the top flight to eight in the new Premier League.

Deans, however, having had a spell coaching The Greens in 1993/94, was not among those who believed that the club's proud record of never having been relegated, was under threat. "The players are there. Once we were streets ahead of the others in terms of preparation and they've caught up, but that special feeling still exists in the town. If they pick the youngsters and let them play they'll be all right," he reckons.

Deans knows all about that and it's something he had to fight for throughout his career. On first being selected for Hawick the powerful, classically rugged Borderer Derrick Grant wouldn't let him demonstrate the art which would, almost a decade later, be the focal point for those arguing in favour of the de-selection of a British Lions captain. It didn't take Deans long to persuade Grant that he could do rather more for the side throwing the ball in rather than blocking at line-outs as a damage limitation exer-

111

cise, since his opinion of the throwing ability of the club's wingers of that era was not high. A natural propensity for hard work was evident as he honed the technique which would provide pin-point accuracy and skillful variety in finding Hawick's jumpers. Deans always wanted to maximise his role within the team.

"I never wanted to be just a hooker as such. I wanted to bring a new dimension to the position," he says. In seeking to redefine his own role, Derrick Grant's opposition to him throwing in at the line-out was by no stretch of the imagination the greatest discouragement Deans had suffered.

"I didn't play at High School because my PE teacher Ernie Murray told me I would never make a player. I think he still cringes every time he sees me." In mitigation it should be noted that Ernie was a referee!

Always eager to learn Deans was aware from an early age of the importance of being seen, however. "My father told me always to be first to every line-out. It's advice I still pass on to youngsters."

These were the words of one who knew. Peter Deans was Hawick's hooker for many years and until the very end of his international career Colin would still be told 'Yer no' as guid as yer faither'. "It was just the old worthies winding you up," he says. But it had its effect. "I think the first real spur for me was to do at least as well as my father had."

Something else he learned from his father was not to be too pushy. While Roddy and Ross Deans can expect every support from the old man, they won't find him driving them to work on elements of the game. "My father never pushed me. He always took an active interest in my career, but there were no great expectations."

What he did was help his son develop a love of the game initially, a love developed at a very early age on the sidelines watching Hawick Wanderers, where Peter was President. "I always had the ambition to play the game. Not really to play for Hawick so much as just to play the game."

More of an influence was another of the grand old men of Hawick rugby, that legend of the microphone Bill McLaren. It was McLaren who simplified a nine-year-old's difficult decision over which would be his best decision, an exchange immortalised in the title of Deans' autobiography.

> McLaren: "Hey you, tubby, what's your name?"
> Small boy: "Colin Deans, sir."
> McL: "Is your faither Peter?"
> CD: "Yes, sir."
> MCL: "You're a hooker, then."

That decision, at the town's Trinity School, would shape almost a quarter of a century of the youngster's life. McLaren, an itinerant PE teacher, roamed the Border town's primary schools identifying and encouraging talent. He took great pride in the achievements of any Hawick boy.

"Bill used to take us for country dancing as well as cricket and rugby. In fact anything except athletics," says Deans, who discovered the importance of sprint work elsewhere in later years - "the great thing about that is that you see a big improvement very quickly" - sharpening his famous pace and reactions on the Border Sprint circuit.

"Bill was a god to us. He wasn't as well known as the voice of rugby at that time because he only covered the four international matches a year plus tour games. There was no "Rugby Special" at that time. I remember once, during an international, Bill said: 'There's Colin Deans, an old school pupil of mine. If you look closely you can still see the belt marks. Someone wrote to The Scotsman complaining about that and Bill phoned me to apologise. He's funny like that, Bill," Deans says fondly.

Others than Bill McLaren, though, took a bit more convincing. Beyond Ernie Murray's assessment and the difficulties of getting the chance to show all his talents for Hawick, Deans still had to persuade men of influence, such as The Scotsman's rugby correspondent Norman Mair, no mean judge having won four caps as a hooker in the fifties.

"I think Norman always had reservations about my size," Deans believes. "He always referred to me as 'the slight but swift Deans'. I couldn't put weight on because I was training too hard," he now, a little more portly but still in great shape, explains.

At Hawick he was by no means considered even the outstanding prospect of his generation in his position, right up the point of selection for the club.

"Come the start of the 1973/74 season I got into the Hawick trial. I was up against Billy Murray who was the boy. He was going places. He'd played for Hawick in the sevens when he was 17 and he was the heir to Derek Deans (no relation). At the second trial I cleaned Billy out. I took something like 17 against the head."

Never in the frame for schoolboy caps Deans managed to impress sufficiently to be involved in the embryonic international under-21 set-up, with matches against the likes of the Post Office and minor tours and he acknowledges the major part playing in such a dominant side as Hawick played in that.

"I came into the Green Machine, which it really was then. That meant being in the shop window all the time."

Playing where he was opportunities would never be long in coming and in 1977, with four national championship winning medals behind him, Deans got his first big chance on the development tour of the Far East, where he could size up the challenge ahead of him. Duncan Madsen, recently turned 30, had earned 14 caps as part of a magnificent front five in the mid-seventies, but was beginning to wind down and didn't go to Japan. Colin Fisher had, in the previous couple of seasons, picked up five caps and did travel, but Deans played in the spectacular 74-9 unofficial Test win in which a number of youngsters shone.

"I think Colin Fisher had too good a time in Japan. He was maybe a wee bit compla-
cent as well," says Deans. Despite that big win the selectors showed real reluctance to
blood the youngsters who had done so well come the Five Nations Championship.
Fisher would never play for his country again, but Deans found himself on the bench as

Deans, McGuinness, Rowan and Jim Calder wait to renew the tight battle versus Ireland in 1985

Scotland lost by a single score to Ireland at Lansdowne Road, Madsen enjoying, as it turned out, his swansong.

A flood of thoughts went through Deans' mind when the long-awaited invitation arrived ahead of the visit of France to Murrayfield. "I remember being delighted then realising that it said that I was to pick up a white jersey. Beforehand I would have been quite happy just to be capped once. But when I saw that I knew I had to keep my place. I wanted that blue jersey."

Self doubt also lurked, as so often when a player first gets the call. "I always had this inferiority complex. I never thought I was as good as the papers said. Scottish players have this perception — I think it's the nation in general, not just rugby players — that we're not as good.

"Anyway it said on the invitation that I had to indicate if I was unavailable or unfit to play and I remember wondering if this was a get out clause if you didn't think you were worthy to represent your country. I thought 'Am I really fit to play for Scotland'. Then I thought 'Aye, give it a go'."

A debut against France, the defending Grand Slam champions, could hardly have been tougher, particularly with the career of the great Sandy Carmichael having ended with that Irish match. In opposition were Gerard Cholley, Alain Paco and Robert Paparemborde, a trio who would collectively earn 120 caps and had already operated in concert 15 times.

"Cholley had chopped Donald MacDonald in Paris the previous year, but before the match Ian McLauchlan, who was our pack leader, took us into the shower area. He pointed to the soles of his boots and said 'See these silver things. These aren't for holding the ground. These are for standing on Frenchmen'."

The approach didn't altogether surprise the new boy. "Ian played for Jordanhill and they were a very physical side. We could mix it if we had to at Hawick, but Jordanhill was one side you didn't mix it with. You beat them playing rugby"

If Deans' head was reeling at least he was among friends, with Norman Pender at tighthead prop and Alan Tomes locking in behind. Indeed Hawick very much provided Scotland's nucleus in his early days. To the quintet which played in Deans' first match, flanker Brian Hegarty and Jim Renwick were the others, was added Renwick's midfield partner Alistair Cranston for Deans' second match, against Wales. Graham Hogg, by then with Boroughmuir but a Hawick native, had to replace Dave Shedden on the wing during both matches.

The attempt to tap into the Hawick winning formula wasn't that successful for the majority, though. The careers of Hegarty, Pender and Hogg did not extend beyond 1978 with Scotland in the middle of a run which saw them go 13 matches without a win. Cranston would play only twice more for his country, in the defeats in New Zealand in 1981 and even Renwick, though he set the 52-cap record, would win only twice away from Murrayfield in a career spanning 12 years. Deans' place was never threatened as he went on to victories at home and abroad, only injury, in 1980 and his own decision not to go to Romania in 1984, costing him three caps as he was chosen for every other match over the next nine years. "I was lucky because during that winning run I always had a decent game. I was fortunate with the line-out play."

To his benefit was that, with international referees rarely supervising more than a couple of the same nation's matches and with video examination less prevalent than it would become, one of his innovations as he helped transform the image of hookers, an essentially illegal manoeuvre, went unnoticed.

"I was always thinking about how to get to the ball quicker and it was just a case of, after throwing the ball in, heading directly to the opposition side. I was always first to the ball on their side. I was offside, but it took them 10 years to notice. Once they did I got sorted out a bit, but until then nine times out of ten the ball would break for you and you'd get a boot on it or something. I never had much time for hookers who just threw the ball in then waited to see what happened."

His first two matches as a squad member in different ways summed up the bad luck which dogged a stylish Scotland side in the late seventies. At Lansdowne Road he watched from the sidelines as Dougie Morgan opted to run a very kickable penalty which would have tied the game. "I admire Dougie Morgan for the decision he made. You have to support the captain's decision. You don't get anywhere kicking penalties. Dougie always wanted to play an open game and he sticks to that now."

In the meeting with France Morgan had a drop goal disallowed because, it was reckoned, he didn't tap a penalty before dropping the goal and again Scotland lost by a score. Deans, though, admits that while disappointed with defeat, that was not his principal emotion on leaving the pitch.

"I was relieved that I had done all right. At the end I was so pumped up with adrenalin I could have had another game, although when I got back to the hotel room I collapsed and the next morning I couldn't move. Right up to my last game that was always the same."

Deans experienced the highs and lows of international rugby in double quick time that afternoon, not once but twice. First he had the satisfaction of playing a major part in setting up a Scottish try, winning ruck ball which was rapidly propelled to Andy Irvine, but Deans never saw his team-mate touch down. "I stuck my head up to see what was happening and gave Cholley a target. He just came right through me." Lesson one: keep your head down. Lesson two: keep the noise down.

"My most vivid recollection was taking one against the head and letting out a yell of enjoyment. One of their locks came through at me from the second row and for five seconds I was on my hands and knees wondering where I was."

Successive draws against England and Ireland in 1979 and the epic win over France in 1980 were all Scotland had to show for Deans' first three seasons. Then came the change. "In 1980 we went on a development tour to France and got beaten in the first game. The next day we went to hell and back. Four hours training in the morning. Four hours in the afternoon. Two hours in the evening. Jim Telfer is here," is the way Deans sums up the entrance of the new coach. "We played the French Barbarians on that tour. It might have been their first ever game and it was their 1975 Grand Slam team. George Mackie was playing, a lovely guy. Real gentleman. But Creamy pushed him to his limit before the match and George was swinging at him in the changing room. When we came off the pitch at the end George was worried because he'd swung punches at the coach, but Creamy was quite pleased."

Scotland were effectively refereed out of a match they could and should have won, but a team which had become accustomed to losing, was learning to win or at least go down with all guns blazing. Scotland never lacked fight, but now there was a collective sense of purpose. In many ways cavalier days were gone, reflecting the times and a new spirit was comically summed up by another moment involving the dreaded Cholley, a former boxer and Scotland prop Gerry McGuinness.

"Gerry had tackled Cholley as he went over the line and Gerry was on his back as as they went over with his arms wrapped round Cholley. He couldn't ground the ball, but the referee Francis Palmade, awarded the try. Later on Cholley took a massive dunt at somebody and Gerry went after him. He caught up with him and Cholley just put his hand on Gerry's head. Gerry was swinging away and couldn't lay a glove on him. It was like something out of a cartoon.

"In the last match Davie Gray was warned seven times for punching. Davie Gray of all people." Gray otherwise tended to be known as 'the Gentle Giant'. Meet fire with fire was Creamy's belief. He wanted to get the big guys in the team to throw themselves about."

The attitude required to allow Scotland to beat nations with far greater playing resources was emerging and following the respectability of two wins at Murrayfield in the next championship, the toughening up process was completed in New Zealand the next summer. Not that getting there was a meticulously planned process, as Deans notes.

"It wasn't on the schedule originally. South Africa had been due to go to New Zealand for 12 weeks, but they cut it six weeks short because of all the protests. So it was a late booking...half price. The SRU bit their hand off. Creamy was delighted to get the chance."

The coach again showed his tendency to be over-zealous from the off. "The first day of the tour we all went down and had a nice big breakfast. We were told to report for training at 9.30 am and we all walked down to the training pitch. By 9.45 am everyone had seen his breakfast again. We went right through to 1.30 pm and at last he said 'OK lunch!'. Roy Laidlaw had torn his groin. Andy Irvine did his hamstring. Neither was really right again all tour.'

Had Telfer learned his lesson? "We were heading off for lunch and he said - 'Don't bother getting changed. You're coming back again in an hour.' - We then did two hours scrummaging." In the short-term the methods were slightly counter-productive.

"I remember Andy Haden saying after the second Test that Scotland had left their fitness on the training ground and he was right. We could have won the first Test and the thing is we could have won the second Test as well." Two crucial moments counted against the Scots. Steve Munro, not fully fit, was caught by Bernie Fraser in a situation where he would normally have been unstoppable. Jim Calder put a foot in touch just before going over for a 'try'.

"Then we blew up and they ran away with it in the last 20 minutes, but the scoreline never reflected the match. That was the start of us growing up, though. We were never dirty, but we had learned to be more physical."

That Scotland could win whilst retaining some of the style of the late seventies was underlined spectacularly the following season with a famous win at Cardiff Arms Park, the first there for 20 years and the first anywhere outside of Edinburgh for six years. Yet Deans has slight regrets about that one and has yet to forgive a clubmate who denied him his chance of touching down a historic try.

"I should have scored the try in Cardiff that started things rolling. I was on Toomba's (Alan Tomes) inside when he gave the scoring pass and that was the natural way for him to pass. But when he was tackled he twisted his body really awkwardly to give the ball to Jim Calder who went over." Deans smiles ruefully as he ponders what might have been, taking no consolation from the fact that the try is remembered by most as Iain Paxton's. "Maybe nobody else remembers it was Jim Calder's try...but I do!"

Given his eagerness always to be in support Deans' Test tally is remarkable. "Playing for Hawick if I didn't score there was something wrong. But I only got three tries for Scotland. One against New Zealand, one against Spain (no cap was awarded) and one against Romania. I set hundreds up, though.

"And...I must hold the record as the most consistent at being the first man up to congratulate the try scorer," by way of illustration pointing to a photograph on his office wall of him hauling a triumphant John Rutherford to his feet. "Support play was very important to me. I always drove myself to get beside the ball carrier."

The high of being part of the first Scotland touring side to win a Test overseas, the opener in Australia, was followed by the low not only of heavily losing the second Test, but of then, inexplicably, losing the first three matches of the 1983 championship, before the return to form with the Calcutta Cup win over England.

Then at his absolute peak, aged 28 with 29 caps to his name, no-one could doubt Deans was on his way to New Zealand with the British Lions. It was an ill-fated trip - for the Lions, in general, for Colin Deans, in particular.

Give Deans his due, he was resigned, in advance, to making the trip as second choice hooker behind the Lions captain, confident though that in the course of the trip he would prove himself the better man. The only thing was he identified the challenge wrongly and a rival he regarded as a lesser player proved a harder man to shift. For all the wrong reasons!

"I was disappointed that they took Ciaran Fitzgerald. My own personal choice as captain was Peter Wheeler. I'd have picked him as a leader. He had the necessary respect. Fitzgerald was pretty new. Respect was the key. Don't get me wrong Fitzgerald was obviously a good player for Ireland. The players obviously responded to him and he had to be a good player, but I knew I was better.

"It didn't bother me at all personally if I'd gone with Peter Wheeler. I'd have been happy with that. I had a load of respect for the guy, but maybe he was on the way down by then. Again I knew I was better."

He also knew that Jim Telfer, who was coach, had close personal knowledge of circumstances in which a British Lions captain had stood down for the good of the side when a better man was available. Telfer was in the British Lions Test side on the 1966 tour of New Zealand when Scot Mike Campbell-Lamerton showed great courage in dropping himself. I believed in Jim Telfer. I was sure I'd get my chance if he had the power."

However as Deans shone in provincial match after provincial match and Fitzgerald reached the stage where he couldn't throw the ball in straight at line-outs, nothing was happening. Deans sought out Telfer and was assured that if he played better he would make the Test side.

Telfer had one voice on selection. The Irish, in the shape of Fitzgerald himself and that greatest of all Lions Willie John McBride, who was manager, had two. In fairness to Fitzgerald, Ireland had retained the Five Nations Championship in 1983, having won a Triple Crown in his first year as captain and after the army captain missed the second half of the 1984 Championship they collected another Triple Crown under him in 1985. In New Zealand in 1983, however, his form deserted him.

"Creamy was undoubtedly out-voted," is Deans' opinion, shared by fellow Scots on the trip. "I never discussed it with him at the time or since and he would never say anyway. There was no point in speaking to Jim about it. What's the use. But you caught the looks and glances and you knew what was going on. I wish I'd been a fly on the wall when the Test sides were picked, though."

He is keen to note that he was by no means the only Scot to suffer, describing his long-standing front-row ally Iain Milne as "really hard done by", while adding that the selectors simply had to find a place for John Rutherford, because he was playing so well, albeit he eventually only got one Test out of position at centre.

"I think they even thought about putting The Bear at loose-head at one stage. I worked with him on getting his feet right and they would have done better even putting him on that side," Deans reckons.

On a personal level the wrong was put right when he captained the Lions against the Rest of the World at Cardiff in 1986, but there are regrets since those 1983 All Blacks were, in Deans words, "there for the taking", yet were allowed to complete a whitewash. "Our selection was a wee bit off," he understates. "I don't think I'd have made the difference to the way the series went, but if I'd played the first Test I think we'd have won. Fitzgerald put in something like 15 squint throws and the referee, it might have been Francis Palmade again, even warned him that he might have to send him off for persistent infringement. More importantly it was giving 15 pieces of possession to the All Blacks that should have been ours."

He is strong in his condemnation of the disheartened effort from some of those involved in the fourth Test debacle. "That last Test was lost the minute we walked off the park in Dunedin having lost the third. I lost respect for some of the other players on that tour. That helped a lot the next year though, because you wanted to kill them for playing like that."

Deans adheres to the common theme that the ground-work for Scotland's Grand Slam was done in New Zealand. "We went there thinking the players from other countries were supermen, but we were the only ones still standing after training sessions wanting to do more. Jim Calder was always a hard-worker, Johnny Beattie would come along for the extra work for something to do, but the only non-Scot who really got involved in the extra training was Terry Holmes.

"We started to really believe in ourselves. Jim Telfer really pushed us and there were some of the Welsh boys in particular who weren't too keen on doing all the work he wanted done. But they did it."

The Scottish squad really came together during that time, refusing to be distracted by outside influences. "It was at the time that David Lord was trying to do his Kerry Packer style thing with rugby. The English boys were all signed up, in fact I think everyone else was. We didn't even talk to anyone. They were talking funny money."

Of the 1984 campaign Deans selects neither the Triple Crown nor the Grand Slam as the most satisfying moment. "We knew that if we got off to a good start in Wales, which we did, then something was achievable. You feel sorry for the Irish when you beat them, but the English... Beating them was my highlight of 1984," he grins. "It always would be. They were pretty confident, as usual, but we kept scoring at the right times."

A highlight of the season was the magnificent understanding Deans struck up with David Leslie as the line-out tail-gunner. "Leslie and I really plugged into one another's thinking that season. He would do whatever was required to get to the ball - think, push, shove, fake. But he often took the ball two-handed, which gave us a great platform. We could even play to the tail in bad weather."

If that served to underline Deans' value as a thrower, ironically two of Scotland's tries in that campaign came from wayward efforts. "Against England we had one which went over the top, was a bit lucky and found David Johnston who scored. The other one was the famous try against France. It was a long middle ball to Toomba, but it went too far. Joinel knocked it back and there was Jim Calder. "I can't really describe what happened when Jim touched down. There was just this feeling of self-confidence, as if somebody had injected you with something. This self-belief was suddenly there.

"You could hear the French yipping at each other and that was always a good sign. They had a go at The Bear. The worst thing you could do to The Bear was punch him. I never saw him throw a punch. His retaliation was just to destroy you in the scrum. By that time we felt super-human, had this inner-strength. The scrum broke up. Dintrans and Rives yipped at the referee after he gave a penalty. That was 10 yards closer, Peter Dods put it over and that was it."

Deans pays tribute both to his coach and captain that year. "Before the Irish game Jim Telfer's psychology was brilliant. He played the game down that much, telling us

The captain appears to comfort Derek White after John Jeffrey scores a try in Wales, 1987.

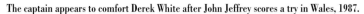

how useless we were. He did that a lot. We started to believe him. We were so wound up for that game."

The Scottish team probably contained the only 15 people in Lansdowne Road who didn't regard themselves as favourites that day. That wasn't the case come the Grand Slam clash.

"We'd never been in that position before, but Jim Aitken was very good at helping Creamy take the pressure off. You knew their backs were so good that if they put it together we were in trouble and they did for the first 15 minutes, but we slowly clawed our way back."

There was no way back the following year as Scotland slumped to a whitewash under first Roy Laidlaw and then David Leslie. Come 1986 they hit on Deans. "I actually thought they might have given me a chance the previous year, but maybe it worked out well." He would captain his country in each of his last 13 internationals, revelling in the responsibility.

"I only really started to enjoy international rugby on my 40th cap when I was given the captaincy. It's just hard work in the front-row." His baptism could hardly have been tougher, with six new recruits watching bewildered as France scored a try from a quickly taken line-out after Gavin Hastings kicked off directly into touch.

"I couldn't help them. I was standing wondering what to do, but fortunately Gavin had his kicking boots on." The babies clearly required little nursing and with The Bear still alongside, Deans was now joined by David Sole.

"I wondered if he spoke to begin with," he says. "He couldn't understand my Border accent, and when he did try to say something I couldn't understand his English accent. But he was dynamite, possibly even better then than when he finished. A prop that han-dled...and you could say what you liked to him and he would just nod."

"Having the captaincy was great, although I was lucky that alongside the new play-ers I had guys of the calibre of The Bear, Toomba, Packie (Iain Paxton) and John Beattie in the pack with John Rutherford and Roy Laidlaw at half-back. The blend of youth and experience was perfect and the pace we had in that pack... We were all 11.6 second men - well, except The Bear. It was just as well we had him to push the average pace up to that of a real pack." Five wins in eight Championship matches preceded the first World Cup.

"Losing Rudd (Rutherford) was the killer blow. it took a lot of guts for the side to come back from that the way they did. Dougie Wyllie was a good player, but I do wish we'd had the Doug Wyllie with the confidence he showed last season (1993/94)." Again a sucker punch from the French proved crucial as they took a quick penalty with two players lying injured and scored a vital try.

"Matt Duncan had blood running from his mouth and I was trying to get referee Fred Howard's attention. Berbizier was injured as well, but he crawled off the pitch to let play continue. It was a very controversial moment."

Again Scotland fought back well, but this time they could only earn a draw. "We had the beating of them fair and square that day," Deans says of the side which went on to the final, losing as Scotland did in the last eight, to the All Blacks.

For those who believe in going out at the top Deans timed his retirement perfectly, opting to go after that first World Cup. "The tournament was a strange experience. Playing France that day it was like an international and yet it wasn't. Scotland v France on the other side of the world in front of a smallish crowd. It was a slightly unreal situation to be in. Completely different from anything we'd experienced before.

"I always planned to go out at that point. I was 32. I could have gone on and I often wonder if I could have made the next Lions tour, but I realised that the Hastings were starting to beat me at training. I ran out of excuses for myself and realised I was just getting old.

"The quarter-final put the last nail in the coffin. I had never played against a side which was so physical. I tried everything to turn it around and we didn't cave in. They said we were the best side they played against and they were right, but they still beat us 30-3."

The decision made Deans continued to show his leadership qualities, writing an autobiography and choosing to keep the proceeds. The Scots had become increasingly aware, at that antipodean World Cup, of the money being earned by players in other countries from off-field activities.

Deans was, inevitably, banned from the game, a decision which cost him five years involvement in the sport. The only surprise was that it took so long for matters to come to a head. "The turning point was when I wanted to play in a gash Golden Oldies game and asked what would happen if I played. I was told that all the players would be banned and the SRU would take action against the referee, touch judges and the club whose pitch the match was played on. "I didn't mind taking them on myself, but I couldn't be responsible for all those people so I decided not to play, but then I was invited to play for Scotland in a Classics game against Wales I was speaking at a dinner with Jamie Salmon and he said I should play. I decided that I was prepared to go to the European Court of Human Rights over it.

"I spoke to Bill Lothian of the Edinburgh Evening News and told him that. He called me back a few days later and told me that six players had been reinstated by New Zealand and Australia to play in the Classic tournament in Bermuda. I repeated that I intended to play and would go to the Court of Human Rights. Bill said he would call the SRU. That same afternoon I got a call from SRU secretary Bill Hogg. He asked me how I was doing and I thought - 'You didn't call me to ask me that'. Then he said 'We had a meeting the other night and we wondered if you would like to be reinstated.' I asked if this was actually the result of a call from Bill Lothian, but he said it hadn't been. He told me if I wanted to be reinstated I would have to write to them requesting it. He then asked me if I knew of anyone else who would like to be reinstated and I pointed out that as far as I knew they'd only banned four others.

"I never actually felt I was in the wilderness and I would have had no hesitation about playing sooner had it not been for the implications for other people. I must admit there is something strange about the fact that they always say you're an amateur player 'But you have to wear these boots'."

A leader on and off the pitch it is little wonder that this intense man, who once made a double glazing sales pitch to the Queen at a garden party and who at the age of 39 was still greeting the morning with 100 sit-ups every day, is managing director of a double-glazing firm.

Yet the thing he relishes most has not been the winning but the friendships and, now back in the fold these continue to develop. "I've played quite a bit since I got back and in the summer of 1993 Jim Renwick and I were over in Australia for a special celebration. We had a great time with Jacques Fouroux, who was surprisingly good fun.

"I got spotted out training on Sydney Harbour Bridge and was asked to play in a Classics match between Australia and New Zealand. I didn't even know which I'd be playing for till we got there, but the New Zealand lads hauled me in right away. I never expected to be an All Black but — I'm trying to keep it quiet from Jim, — I'm now claiming 53 caps!"

Career Statistics: Colin Deans

1978 Scotland 16 France 19; Wales 22 Scotland 14; Scotland 0 England 15; Scotland 9 New Zealand 18.

1979 Scotland 13 Wales 19; England 7 Scotland 7; Scotland 11 Ireland 11; France 21 Scotland 17; Scotland 6 New Zealand 20.

1980 Ireland 22 Scotland 15; Scotland 22 France 14 [1].

1981 France 16 Scotland 9; Scotland 15 Wales 6; England 23 Scotland 17; Scotland 10 Ireland 9; New Zealand 11 Scotland 4 (1Try); New Zealand 40 Scotland 15; Scotland 12 Romania 6; Scotland 24 Australia 15.

1982 Scotland 9 England 9; Ireland 21 Scotland 12; Scotland 16 France 7; Wales 18 Scotland 34; Australia 7 Scotland 12; Australia 33 Scotland 9.

1983 Scotland 13 Ireland 15; France 19 Scotland 15; Scotland 15 Wales 19; England 12 Scotland 22; Scotland 25 New Zealand 25.

1984 Wales 9 Scotland 15; Scotland 18 England 6; Ireland 9 Scotland 32; Scotland 21 France 12; Scotland 37 Australia 12.

1985 Scotland 15 Ireland 18; France 11 Scotland 3; Scotland 21 Wales 25; England 10 Scotland 7.

1986 Scotland 18 France 17*; Wales 22 Scotland 15*; Scotland 33 England 6*; Ireland 9 Scotland 10 *; Scotland 33 Romania 18* (1Try).

1987 Scotland 16 Ireland 12*; France 28 Scotland 22*; Scotland 21 Wales 15*; England 21 Scotland 12*;

World Cup - Scotland 20 France 20*; Scotland 60 Zimbabwe 21*; Scotland 55 Romania 28*; New Zealand 30 Scotland 3*.

All appearances at hooker. [1] Replaced by Ken Lawrie. *captain.

The Bear

3 - I. G. Milne

People like bears. As dangerous animals go they get easily the best press. A process of indoctrination begins in the earliest of our formative years with the teddy and continues through the influence of the small and large screen with the likes of Winnie the Pooh, Yogi, Barney and Baloo.

Mentioned alongside those cartoon characters there was nothing comical, for opponents in particular, about The Bear who graced Scotland's navy blue during each of the past three decades. Yet the nickname is even appropriate in these terms, in as much as few players are regarded with greater affection by their peers than Iain Milne.

Few nicknames have ever fitted a rugby player better. Milne's frame hung from a broad pair of shoulders and huge haunches. Though soft-spoken his on-field body language came over as a menacing growl. Within that, though, there always seemed to be an innate decency. There was nothing vicious about The Bear. His ability to strike fear into the hearts of opponents lay in sheer physical strength, rather than through the threat of violence. A certain mysticism about his powers was added to by his unpreparedness to be provoked.

"I've never felt intimidated by anyone. Foul play was never going to affect the way I was going to perform. I'm not a violent person myself," he explains. He has strong views on the subject. "The Unions at the moment have to get their act together.The ban on Johann Le Roux for biting Sean Fitzpatrick was one thing, but only a year ago Richard Loe got a much shorter ban for gouging someone's eye and for New Zealand even to consider picking a man who did that is wrong. And then there's the Tim Rodber situation in South Africa. I know he was being provoked, but he still reacted. It's becoming a laughing stock. I've got a very strong attitude on this and there's no need for that sort of thing. The Unions have to take real steps to stamp it out. I would give a penalty in front of the posts for any instance of foul play.

"The SRU within their own house are keeping it in order, but they cannot let other Unions get away with it. It's destroying the image of the whole game, although having

said that I think the game at club level is cleaner than when I first started to play. There used to be a lot of people going around standing on heads."

It would be wrong to regard Iain Gordon Milne as some sort of shrinking violet. However, his retaliation to would be bear-baiters was to crank up the pressure in the next scrummage. Several of his 1984 Grand Slam colleagues speak enthusiastically of the way he reacted to punches from the second-row in the decider by letting out a roar, then reeking havoc at the next set-piece, simply by legitimately driving through the French front-row.

Iain Milne was not, you see, a man obsessed by an all-consuming passion to play Test rugby. The word "enjoy" is never far from his lips. He enjoyed playing rugby, enjoyed

Two faces of 'The Bear' — today's affable businessman, yesterday's fearsome rivalry with Graham Price.

touring, enjoyed international rugby and has a simple philosophy that the important thing is to enjoy life.

It would be wrong to think that life as a cub was devoted to the rough and tumble of learning to play rugby, despite the fact that both his brothers, David and Kenny, would follow him into the Scotland side. "No-one in the family played rugby until I went to secondary school. It was a choice between cross country and rugby at Heriot's." He baulks a little at the assumption that the choice was that obvious. "I did run in the athletics team at one stage." Indeed the characteristic shape was not to develop until after his schooldays. "My first few games were at scrum-half," is the amazing revelation. "But I wouldn't give anyone else the ball."

It is stretching things a little to suggest that there was a complete role reversal once he made it to the top, but he isn't afraid to poke a bit of fun at his own reputation as a handler. "In later years I never got the ball very often."

They know a thing or two about rugby at George Heriot's School, however and they didn't take too long to sort out the right sort of position for the first of the Milnes. He soon graced their front-row and played in the first team at each age group through secondary school.

"I was never any sort of star, but I enjoyed it," that word again. "It was only when I got to fifth or sixth year I began to take it seriously though." However he was by no means an over-powering individual even at that stage. "I played for Edinburgh Schools but was told I was too small to play for Scottish Schools."

Playing for Edinburgh against the international front-row he gave notice of what was to come - "I was obviously reasonably good. I played for Edinburgh against the Scottish Schools front-row and we took umpteen against the head" - and he didn't take too long to establish himself with the FPs where he was immediately given his chance.

"At FP level in the seconds I never found it too difficult. But I got a handful of games in the firsts and obviously at 18 in the first XV I got a few stuffings, but I just wasn't bothered about that. "I just felt I was lucky to be given the opportunity. It was around 1974 when Heriot's FP were all backs, no forwards, although Jim Burnett was there at the time and he went on to prop for Scotland. But I always enjoyed it."

There has been much agonising over the years about the pros and cons of the discovery of oil in Scottish waters, but one of the unseen benefits was its effect on the international rugby team. "Basically I started to put on bulk just after I left school when I did a fair amount of manual labour for a company involved in the North Sea industry," Milne says, before providing another, more startling revelation. "All my size is natural. I've never done weights. Done a lot of circuits from time to time, but I've never done weights. I probably would have been a better player if I had, but it was all a bit different in those days. The last five years there has been quite a dramatic change in the approach to rugby. I think I would have enjoyed it as much," (goes without saying really) "but I wouldn't have been involved as long." Loosehead props the world over may throw messages heavenward at the very thought.

Though he was developing into The Bear and indeed the nickname may even have been coined by that stage, Milne does not regard himself as having been a destructive performer in those early FP days. In fact, that is the case right up to his early appearances in the international side. "Scrummaging was what I was famed for, but it was actually loose play that got me into the national set-up. I was no great scrummager. As you get older and more experienced you develop that and as a prop that has to be your number one job."

Perhaps it isn't surprising, given that assessment of his own strengths and weaknesses at that stage, that the man he regards as having been the biggest influence on him was not another prop, but a clubmate whose style, Milne acknowledges, was not quite the same as his. "I got very friendly with Andy Irvine. He had infectious enthusiasm and we did a lot of training together in those days. I learned a lot from him. We may have played a bit differently, but we are very much on the same wavelength. Although I relied on self-motivation he was probably the biggest influence on me when he was at the peak of his career and winning the club championship with Heriot's FP under his captaincy in 1979 was very special."

So too was another day in 1979 for the Heriot's pair - March 3 to be precise, when Iain Milne made his international debut against Ireland at Murrayfield. He arrived towards the end of Scotland's sequence of 13 matches without a win, but the security he would provide was perhaps demonstrated early as Scotland avoided defeat, drawing 11-11, Irvine, as ever, on the scoreboard with a try and a penalty.

"My first game was against Phil Orr who was pretty experienced by then and I felt I did all right," Milne says. In fact Orr had been an ever present through 17 matches since 1976 to that point and battles between the pair would be a feature of Scotland-Ireland encounters for several years to come.

"I suppose you are just quite happy to survive. I had been at squad sessions for quite a long time and there was a lot of press coverage about me at the time. Looking back I wasn't really ready for it," is Milne's modest view of his own introduction.

His next match was a rather different confrontation, a visit to the cauldron of the Parc Des Princes to go head to head with a man who had already gained something of a reputation amongst the Scots. "The French are pretty intimidating anyway and I was up against Gerard Cholley who had caused mayhem with the Scots two years earlier. It was all built up that way.

"He had one fling at me early on in a line-out. I kept a back seat at the line-out from then on." That statement, combined with the belief that he was no great scrummager could invite the impression that Milne is contradicting himself, having claimed he was never intimidated. However there is a euphemistic ring to the following words. "He wasn't a great prop though. I didn't find it too uncomfortable. I felt I did all right at that stage." The ability to strike fear into the hearts of opposing props through a reputation for applying sheer pressure applied in the set-piece was beginning to develop. "Intimidating opponents is a gradual process when you first come in. My scrummaging at club level was pretty solid by then," he concedes.

"People are not worried about you at first, but that began to change at club level where I was in a very good front-row with Calum Munro and Jim Burnett. Trying to think back it's hard to say where it changed internationally, but after a few matches I started to find it a bit easier, even playing against the likes of England."

Significantly he was missing, through injury, from the Scotland side which was over-powered as England secured their 1980 Grand Slam and he would not return to the Scotland side until the summer of the following year.

From Ian McLauchlan, through Jim Aitken and on to David Sole it's a safe bet that the great captains who wore Scotland's no.1 jersey throughout the seventies, eighties and nineties felt a lot more comfortable in the same scrummage as Iain Milne than their opposite numbers.

"It was after 1980 that things changed. Probably on the New Zealand tour." Milne was deeply conscious of a change in approach at that time and, indeed, is quite specific in identifying why he believes Scotland became the cavalier, stylish losers he joined in the late seventies. "I was involved in sessions with Bill Dickinson and they all talked about the great pack of the mid-70s. I felt that had a lot to do with Bill's coaching methods. It's just my observation, but I would say the backs were stronger than the forwards even then, but everything was concentrated on the pack.

"Remember, though, that side never won away from home. Then, in the late seventies, the backs had all the experience which is why we developed the way we did. Jim Telfer's introduction brought organisation." It is fair to say that, philosophically, the two men are by no means kindred spirits, but Milne has nothing but respect for the man who led Scotland to Grand Slam glory. "I remember Jim's introduction as a culture shock. He used to love me," The Bear chuckles, oozing sarcasm."Having said that he must have had a reasonable opinion of myself and some of the other Edinburgh boys like Jim Calder. It was pretty hard, gruelling work if you couldn't take it and some fell by the wayside, but you had to respect what he was trying to do." In fairness to Milne he was never by any means the happy-go-lucky, turn up for the game then put your feet up for a week, sort that some of his own comments might lead people to believe.

"People build up a picture of you, but it's wrong to think I didn't work at all. I did a lot of training on my own. I was never quick, but I always felt that scrummaging was what I was primarily there for."

In developing that theme he gives a real insight into his method, one he believes to be too rarely practised nowadays. "It's a mental process. You've got to keep working at the scrummaging from the first to the 80th minute. A lot now accept parity if they don't get anything from the scrummaging in the first 20 minutes. I was struggling to get on top all the time."

Though it was demanding he learned to love both New Zealand and touring on that 1981 trip. "Touring really is the easiest thing to do. It really would be a nice way to make a living. Apart from one trip to Canada all my tours were to Australia and New Zealand where the top rugby was played, with South Africa pretty well out of things at the time. I found touring so easy. You just switch into training and leave home behind. I had my wild moments as well, but I found it suited me to be honest. And the fact you are training all the time suited a heavy bloke like myself."

In terms of significance he is in no doubt about the place which should be allocated to that first journey with Scotland. "It was the biggest thing. We were unlucky to lose the first Test and did a lot better than the scoreline suggested in the second. Then a result away from home in Australia the following year and it was coming together. In terms of fitness we were much better too"

The Ballymore win on that tour Down Under in 1982 was Scotland's second in succession away from home, following the momentous win at Cardiff just over three months earlier, but it was also only the second since 1976 in Dublin. Belief was growing.

"It all started to build up in '82 with that game against Wales and then the Australia tour. For Scotland to win anything in rugby we have to pick the best available players and utilise their strength to the maximum. We did that in 1984, although we could probably have played a more expansive game than we did. But Jim Telfer had hit on a successful formula."

From a personal point of view Milne went into the opening game utterly confident that he could help provide a platform upon which the artists could perform. "I never really looked at that season in the sense of making a point, but I had played against Staff Jones in practise matches and was not bothered about playing against him," he says of the trip to Cardiff that year.

Like his front-row partner Colin Deans, Milne had suffered considerable frustration on the previous summers British Lions tour of New Zealand in which he had worked against Jones on the training ground. Unlike Deans, Milne had to play second fiddle to a man for whom he had the utmost respect, but he knew he was the better man.

"I think I was better than Graham Price — he was past it by then," Milne reckons, succinctly. "But I never get bitter about things like that." Price had played his last game for Wales by that point, but Milne takes solace from the fact that he knew he gave his best shot to winning a Test place on that tour.

"I probably played some of the best rugby of my life over there that time. Every game we were taking five, six or seven against the head. Even Canterbury, who beat us by a point, were fairly well destroyed up front. But I think the only way I would have got in was if Colin had got in as well. That was just the way things were going. In fact by the time the fourth Test came along I didn't particularly want to play. It would have been a sop."

As Deans noted there was consideration given to fielding The Bear on the loose-head side. "Yes," he shrugs. "Staff Jones and Ike Stephens got injured. It wasn't a serious possibility, but I would have taken the opportunity all right."

Lions Test recognition would evade him throughout a long career as the most damaging scrummager in British international rugby, spanning three Lions tours. In 1980 he missed the last two Five Nations games through injury, so didn't go to South Africa with the Lions and in 1989 he missed almost the entire Championship through injury ahead of the Lions visit to Australia. The only other opportunity was in 1986 when he was part of the Lions squad which played a couple of games in Wales, but was again left out for the Test against a World XV.

His place in legend was secure, however, within nine months of returning home from the 1983 Lions tour. "The Grand Slam tended to creep up on you," he says. After Wales we played England who at that stage really fancied themselves. My opponent was a bloke called White and I got on top of him. It was one of his early games. England had the players at least to match us but we got everything right in terms of preparation. I believe we were ahead of our time in terms of fitness and tactical awareness thanks to Jim Telfer."

The Triple Crown was on - a chance to win it for the first time in 46 years. "I always fancied our chances of winning in Ireland," says Milne. Yet he remains candid as ever in considering his own contribution. "I didn't actually play that well against Phil Orr that time, but they were in disarray having dropped a lot of people. We got scrums on their line, dominated them and Roy Laidlaw scored twice. The scores came pretty easily and we finished with two beautiful tries, but Phil Orr gave me as tough a game as any other time."

Milne does accept, though, that the Scottish scrummage was a huge factor in the Grand Slam triumph. "We worked a hell of a lot on the scrum from the point at which Telfer came in, onwards. The prop's first consideration has to be that. The laws in 1993/94 maybe took away a bit of the influence from the scrums but that is changing again with the return of the ruck law. "People have forgotten what damaging scrummaging can do," says the expert.

"In the 1991 World Cup I was very critical of our approach and we've picked sides in recent years to run teams off the pitch. But you have to get the platform right. If you are under pressure on your own ball you are struggling. At club level as well as international level we seem to have forgotten that. Even when we had five no.8s we always had a pretty solid front row and I maybe became more important then."

Right: The three bears — brothers
Iain, Kenny and Gordon Milne of
Heriot's, the Barbarians and Scotland.

In any event Milne, Deans and skipper Jim Aitken made a good job of demonstrating why the 1983 British Lions were wrong not to place the emphasis on Scottish power — but France, who had shared the title with Ireland a year earlier, presented a very different proposition.

Though they had lost on their two previous visits to Edinburgh, talk of a Murrayfield hoodoo to match Scotland's apparent jinx in Paris was not even beginning. France were, man for man, the best side in the Championship, but the Scots were by now growing ever more certain of themselves, particularly on home soil.

"Though we were delighted at winning the Triple Crown most of us would have been disappointed at that stage if we hadn't gone on to the Grand Slam," says Milne. "I don't remember the same jubilation after the Irish game as after the French match when we won a lot more accolades."

As to the match itself. "We were lucky in the first half. They dominated but our defence was superb. If they had got a couple of scores ahead we could have been in real trouble, but you always felt, particularly then, that if you could keep the French to one score they would feel the pressure and we did that — with a bit of help from the Welsh referee.

"I felt with about half an hour to go that I had a real advantage over my opposite number. There was one good scrum when we pushed them back and that was a big psychological moment. It was a great collective effort and we certainly got more control as the game went on. If the game had gone on another half hour we would have won by 20 points. We won going away!"

As ever The Bear partied in style. "It was a tremendous week for celebrating and enjoying it!" His only regret about that season is that the momentum was not properly maintained. Scotland were whitewashed in the next Championship, having lost to both Romania (no Milne) and Australia later in 1984 although in contrast to the '84 Irish match — "I felt I had one of my best games in terms of technique against the Wallabies. The score that day could have been much more."

It was remarkable how quickly the Grand Slam team broke up, but they can take great satisfaction for the way they transformed Scotland's international standing. "I never felt there was any extra pressure on us not having won anything before the Ireland game. But I think we did make it easier for subsequent Scottish sides. Yes, we did raise the level of expectation — but we should expect success. There are a lot of excuses made at the moment and even after '84 we never really built as we should have. Certainly we could have won another Triple Crown."

Instead, come 1986, he was part of a Scotland side to which John Beattie had been reintroduced, Iain Paxton embarking on a lengthy run in the second row, while six new caps began the Championship. That new Scottish side played a more entertaining brand of rugby, yet Milne sticks by the team of two years earlier when weighing up the respective units. "The 1986 team was certainly the most exciting to play in, but the '84 team would have just had the edge for me. That would have been a very difficult team to beat at any time."

The new team shaped up impressively towards the first-ever World Cup, winning every match at Murrayfield over two seasons as well as in Dublin and in Bucharest. As ever Milne "thoroughly enjoyed" most of the visit to New Zealand for the tournament, yet it ended with an episode which almost killed his appetite for Test rugby.

It is hard to imagine a man like Iain Milne being accused of feigning injury yet that, he now reveals, is exactly what happened. "Part of the problem with trying to play the same team right through, as we did, was the number of injuries picked up. I got a pretty bad leg injury...a torn calf muscle that happened in training.

"But there were accusations saying I wasn't injured and had been faking it from a couple of members of management. I was pretty upset at the whole thing. The pressure got to the management more than the players. Players go on tour after tour. Managers don't. In many cases the players are more experienced."

He chooses not to name names, but speaking within a few days of the death of one of the most respected officials in Scottish rugby over recent years he was anxious to clear that particular man's name. "I exonerate Bob Munro from making that accusation."

As to Scotland's performance Milne believes, quite simply, that no more could have been done. "Looking back I think that was the best ever team that has played for New Zealand," he says of the All Blacks who knocked Scotland out in the quarter-final."

He played in that match as much to prove a point as anything else. "But that incident probably got to me more than anything else. I had played between 30 and 40 games for my country and was shocked to be accused of that. That alone wouldn't be enough to make me pack in, but I wasn't enjoying the game just as much.

"Then came the realisation that Kenny was coming through and maybe I would get a game with him. In any case I still got a tremendous buzz out of international rugby and you always want to see if you can still do it. I would have had a wee regret if I'd packed in then."

Through the decade the Milne mythology had been added to by the emergence of not one, but three bears. By 1987 speculation was mounting as to whether they might all one day form the Scottish international front-row as they did for Heriot's FP. All three did play for Scotland, yet , like the Calder twins, they never all played in the same side, although Iain and Kenny did play a couple of matches together. Otherwise comparisons with the Calders are few.

"There was never any competitiveness between the brothers. We are all different personalities but I don't think my success drove them to want to match me by playing for Scotland. There was probably a greater desire on my behalf that they do well. I was always there for them if they needed advice, but there wasn't much I could help them with. They know as much about training as I do. We played a long time at club level together."

It was perhaps that personal motivation more than anything else that saw Milne make a big effort to regain fitness after missing the entire 1988 Championship. "After the World Cup till '89 I must say it didn't bother me as much, but in '89 I made quite a conscious effort against Wales and did well. We got a push-over try." That match was Kenny's first for his country after Gary Callander was forced out having led Scotland throughout the previous year.

"I had the Lions trip at the back of my mind, but then someone stood on my foot and tore the ligaments. It's even more frustrating to get an injury like that at that stage of your career when you've put so much into achieving a goal. That effectively finished that season, although I did play one other game."

That one game, for the Barbarians - a club which is very dear to Milne's heart - is what ensures that 1989 is remembered fondly rather than regretfully by Milne, even although he was by no means fit for it. "It was the one chance that the three brothers were going to get to play together at that level and I wasn't going to miss it. There's no doubt that was one of the highlights of our careers."

By now Milne was finding it harder and harder to get motivated, however and was never a contender for the Grand Slam of 1990. "I had no real ambition to play serious top rugby again and was never fit to be properly considered."

However the chance of a trip to New Zealand was always an attractive proposition and that's where Scotland were scheduled to visit in the summer of '90. "I'd only played about five or six games in the second half of the season, but there was no real automatic second choice to go on the tour. Once I made up my mind I just wanted to do my best. I can be reasonably strong-willed about these things when I do make up my mind. I felt quite rejuvenated then."

Milne's impact in New Zealand was such that he overtook Paul Burnell and played a huge part in two epic Test performances by Scotland, in the first of which they ran out of steam after a stirring early effort and in the second of which they really should have beaten the All Blacks.

Now thoroughly injury prone, however, he missed the 1991 Championship and was thought by most to be finished as Scotland went into intensive preparations for another World Cup. Yet the man whose attitude had been questioned four years earlier was prepared for one last big effort.

"Scotland played against Argentina at the beginning of the 1990/91 season and they said I wasn't fit to play, but in my own mind I was. I did spend a lot of that season injured, though, which was disappointing and with business and family life becoming more important it was harder to find time for training.

"When you are injury free it's easy, but it gets harder and harder to fight your way back to fitness. I was disappointed though, that after working my way back in '90 that was it. I didn't really expect to make the World Cup squad."

He did not enjoy being written off, however. "I didn't realistically think I would be considered and maybe still had that thought at the back of my mind and then I was told, can't remember by who, that I might be considered if I was fit. I also heard a lot of people saying I couldn't do it and it was maybe a bit of bloody-mindedness. There was also the chance that David and Kenneth would both be involved. When the squad sessions started I think I surprised everyone, but then I suffered an injury that put me out."

This time it was serious enough to convince even the most stoic of individuals that this was it. Maybe he pushed himself a bit too hard, but he believes too much was asked too soon. "It was what could have been quite a bad neck injury," he says. In fact it might have been little short of life threatening.

"I was fit for running, but not for scrummaging. I blame the training methods to some extent. Scrummaging is something you just can't go straight into. It was live work with the two World Cup packs against each other. As soon as we started into it I knew something was wrong. I was blacking out and getting tingling down my arms.

"I realised it could cause more permanent damage. I could have conned my way into the squad, but it was my decision to pull out. Subsequently I discovered that a main artery to the head was being pinched and the blood supply was being cut off. I went to one more training session and although I made the decision I think our doctor, Donald McLeod, was relieved as well. He didn't want to have to be the one to tell me to pull out."

This time he knew there would be no coming back and, quite contentedly, relaxed and watched the tournament. It was to be a frustrating tournament for the Milnes as Kenny was forced to under-study future Springbok John Allan, while David injured himself in his hurry to get out of the grandstand to make his debut, but at least the middle brother did finally match the other two in winning a Scotland cap.

"I think he was disappointed he never got a full game, but I was delighted for him. David was certainly a lot more dedicated than the two of us. A lot of players in Scottish rugby work very hard to get what they achieve. By his own admission David never had the physique so it was great to see him get his cap."

Since then time has finally become more available for family considerations and Iain and wife Marian had their first son, Ross, in 1992. Work, too, gets that bit more attention for the sales manager with East Kilbride-based Sun Chemicals and the old philosophy prevails. "Life is to be lived and although I wouldn't work if I had a choice I try to enjoy everything I do," he laughs.

Career Statistics: Iain Milne

1979 Scotland 11 Ireland 11; France 21 Scotland 17; Scotland 6 New Zealand 20.

1980 Ireland 22 Scotland 15; Scotland 22 France 14.

1981 New Zealand 11 Scotland 4; New Zealand 40 Scotland 15; Scotland 12 Romania 6; Scotland 24 Australia 15.

1982 Scotland 9 England 9; Ireland 21 Scotland 12; Scotland 16 France 7; Wales 18 Scotland 34; Australia 7 Scotland 12; Australia 33 Scotland 9.

1983 Scotland 13 Ireland 15; France 19 Scotland 15; Scotland 15 Wales 19; England 12 Scotland 22; Scotland 25 New Zealand 25.

1984 Wales 9 Scotland 15; Scotland 18 England 6; Ireland 32 Scotland 9; Scotland 21 France 12; Scotland 12 Australia 37.

1985 France 11 Scotland 3; Scotland 21 Wales 25; England 10 Scotland 7.

1986 Scotland 18 France 17; Wales 22 Scotland 15; Scotland 33 England 6; Ireland 9 Scotland 10; Romania 18 Scotland 33.

1987 Scotland 16 Ireland 12; France 28 Scotland 22; Scotland 21 Wales 15; England 21 Scotland 12; World Cup - Scotland 20 France 20; Scotland 60 Zimbabwe 21; New Zealand 30 Scotland 3.

1988 Scotland 13 Australia 32.

1989 Scotland 23 Wales 7.

1990 New Zealand 31 Scotland 16; New Zealand 21 Scotland 18.

All appearances at tighthead prop.

CAPTAIN'S COMMENT:
On his major influences: "I've taken a lot of advice from Jim Aitken . . . Big Daddy. He's a very good friend of mine. He's not a man who courts popularity, but I've always admired the fact that he is his own man and has achieved so much, in business, in sport and in life. You either love him or hate him...I think about 95% of people would opt for the latter. Ian McGeechan was a backs coach, never the forwards coach. Jim Telfer was the big influence on the forwards. But they were the men I owed, which is why I came back for the 1991 World Cup."

Cornish Cream
4 - A. I. Reed

Many a young sporting talent has been fatally distracted when smitten by love. Not Andrew Ian Reed, though. Since they first met, his wife Sarah has been only a positive influence in the remarkable development of his rugby career. His first highly successful time in the game was the second half of the 1989 season — immediately after they met. Then, following marriage in the summer of 1992, his career moved into overdrive. "Everything fell into place after we got married," Reed believes.

The big Cornishman, for that, unashamedly, is what he is "first and foremost", only really began to take his rugby seriously in the late eighties. It wasn't as if he didn't come from a background in the sport. Father Alec, a naval officer who met Andy's mother Marjory - a native of Edinburgh - while based at Rosyth, played during his time in the service.

Reed, himself, played regularly throughout his schooldays. "Rugby was fairly strong when I was at school in Bodmin. But I played all sports," he explains. "It was a good rugby school at the time, but I also played football."

What drove him to take rugby more seriously was becoming a professional sports-man. "I didn't play too much rugby until I got paid for playing football for Bodmin Town. That meant I couldn't play football for anyone else, so I had time to start playing rugby for Bodmin."

Always tall for his age he was a goalkeeper and was actually, at schoolboy level, too big to play lock. "I played at no.8 for three or four years because they couldn't find anyone big enough to partner me in the second row. I was about 6'2" when I was 12, 6'6" at 15. I was very thin, though," he notes. "Didn't have much bulk at all."

There was no trace of him being too soft, however, as revealed in his explanation for not having taken to basketball. "I tried it at college, but I just wanted to nail the flash gits," he jokes.

His two years with Bodmin rugby club proved critical to future Scotland selection - despite the fact that it could hardly have been further away, whilst still on mainland Britain. From Bodmin he moved on to the biggest club in the area, Camborne and thereafter for a brief spell with Plymouth Albion. Naturally, too, the English selectors took a keen interest as the giant line-out specialist developed.

"After a couple of seasons at Camborne I was picked for the English Colts. From the England Colts you automatically get promoted to the Under-21s training, but I never got in. I had all the trials, but I didn't progress. Rather glad I didn't now."

Reed is eager to kill some of the myths surrounding his selection for Scotland. By way of proving he has nothing to hide he refreshingly admits to having cheered on England during the 1990 Grand Slam decider. "It was a bit of family fun," he explains. "I automatically cheered for the opposite side from my mum who is very patriotic."

But he is irritated by the constant questioning of his qualifications. "I do get sick of people asking me about my qualifications," he says, wearily. "My mother's not the reason I'm playing for Scotland. I'm playing because I'm entitled to and I'm the best man for the job.

"I admit I'm a Cornishman born and bred, foremost, but I have never had any doubts about my commitment to Scotland. I'm not out to kid anyone. I don't think anyone who hasn't done it can imagine the feeling of playing for your country. It's just phenomenal. I have no words to describe that feeling."

He notes that it is the case that those born in his part of the world tend not to regard themselves as English but as Cornish, in any case, and so he identifies more with the Scots. "England's just a large stepping stone on the way to Scotland," he laughs, doubtless aware that the comment can also be taken as a metaphor for his involvement with English youth sides.

"I hadn't stayed in Scotland for any more than a couple of weeks at a time previously, but I remember surprising a few of the boys when I first went up to Edinburgh with the Exiles. They thought I would know nothing about Edinburgh, but as we drove in from the airport I was pointing out things like where I used to play football with my cousins."

However it is not the case, as legend has it to the extent that it is reported in at least one respected rugby text book as a statement of fact, that he was spotted by "Scottish spies" because he was wearing a Heart of Midlothian scarf.

Reed admits to being a Hearts supporter, as a consequence of frequent family trips to Edinburgh as a youngster, but that's as far as it goes. His involvement in the Scottish set-up dates back to a meeting with SRU committee man Fred McLeod at Reed's home town club in 1991.

"Fred had come down to speak at the club dinner, he had family connections down there. I was sitting next to him at the top table and told him about my Scottish connections. Within a week I'd heard from Scottish Exiles secretary Fulton Patterson." His progress, already impressive, was closely monitored thereafter.

Reed had, by that stage, already enjoyed a fair amount of big-time rugby, as part of the Cornwall side. His first season with them ended with the county championship final, though on a disappointing note, as they were beaten at Twickenham. He gained vital experience that day. "Cornwall took a big support up to London. We played in front of around 25-30,000." The then 20-year-old froze. "It was my first taste of the big time and I didn't really perform at all." Two years later Reed would return to the same setting to put in a rampaging display as Cornwall beat Yorkshire 29-20.

By that stage he had moved to Bath, the South West finishing school for champions. He had joined the club for the 1990 summer tour of Australia, but took time to establish himself. A combination of circumstances, marriage in the summer of 1992 and something of a snub from his club, provided the necessary impetus.

"Bath had beaten Harlequins in that epic Cup final at Twickenham the previous season when Stuart Barnes put over the drop goal in extra time. But Paul Ackford had come out of retirement and cleaned us out in the line-out. Instead of looking to develop things within the club we recruited Sean O'Leary. That really put my nose out of joint."

Reed does, though, revel in the family atmosphere at Bath - the team spirit illustrated when he played for Scotland against Ireland last year while his then regular travelling companion Graham Dawe was in the England squad facing Wales the same weekend. "I dropped him off at the hotel on my way to the airport," Reed points out.

Early in the 1992/93 season Reed hit top form, including some of his performances at that time as among his finest ever. "There was one game for the second team against Northampton where I even surprised myself with some of the things I did and I was also very pleased with my performance against Leicester, my last game for Bath before I was capped."

The alacrity with which first the Scottish Exiles, then the Scotland selectors reacted said something about the problems Scotland were experiencing in the second-row, as well as about the marked improvement in Reed's game.

"There hadn't previously been room even in the Exiles side with Damian Cronin, Chris Gray and Neil Edwards all contending for places. But as soon as I played my first game on merit for the Bath first team, against Orrell in a game that was televised, they were back on to me."

A big opportunity had arrived, yet Reed had reservations. He felt that by being greedy he could ruin everything. "The Scottish District matches clashed with the Divisional games in England, so to some extent I had to decide in my own mind whether I believed I would be picked for Scotland right away. It had taken so long to get into the Bath first team I wondered if I should be going away from the club for an extended period at that stage to play for the Exiles.

"But Alistair McHarg was coaching the Exiles at the time and he said: 'If you've got confidence in yourself you shouldn't have any problems.' I went and explained the situation to Jack Rowell. He's a funny guy, but he had no problem with it at all."

Things went from good to better as his amazing 1992/93 season gained momentum. "I got home one afternoon from training and my parents had a double message. They said 'First, you're playing for Scotland A v Ireland A on December 28, second you're playing for the Blues in the international trial.'

"I didn't play well against Ireland in the first hour," he admits. "But I came on to a game. Then at the trial I just enjoyed myself. Nobody knew much about me. Trials are a different story when you've got a reputation to defend but nobody knew me then so I did all right. Even so Shade Munro and I had played together in the A match and we'd been chatting about our strengths and weaknesses. Then he came on against me in the trial and he knew what I was trying to do. That's the trouble with trials. People know too much about the people they're playing with."

However Reed had done more than enough to convince the selectors that he was the man to fill the massive, almost perennial gap in the middle of the line-out for Scotland. Suddenly a team which had had to make do with quick-witted streetwise line-out play, had a genuine specialist.

Reed was not fazed, however, by the speed of his elevation through the ranks. The Cornwall experience had been a valuable one in more senses than one. For a start in the Cornish approach to the game he saw more of a parallel with Scotland than within the English set-up.

"There always seemed to be so much more about the Scottish game which was more enjoyable," he says. "The passion...that's much more like playing for Cornwall than England. It starts with the national anthem before the game and it's there throughout."

Cornwall's achievements in reaching three Twickenham finals in the previous four seasons, they had been beaten there again in 1992, was also highly valuable in preparing Reed for the big occasion. He had learned the importance of savouring every moment. Few Scottish-based players have any idea of what it is like to play in front of a really big crowd before their first cap. "I remember getting to the ground and the pipes were playing 'Scotland the Brave'. It was a wonderful sound - I've loved it since I was a young lad. I knew I was going to enjoy the game. I was determined to, having been in that situation in the first County final at Twickenham when it had all just passed me by and I felt I had done nothing.

"I went out onto the pitch, knew exactly where Sarah and the rest of my family were sitting and just went out to enjoy the atmosphere. I got into the game early on which helped," he adds.

Reed got into the game, all right. His first noticeable involvement was to produce the scoring pass which put fellow debutant Derek Stark into the corner for a try - just minutes after kick-off.

"So far for Scotland, in fact in rugby, my most enjoyable experience was that first cap." (Only one more win has followed at time time of writing.) "On a personal level I was reasonably pleased with that first season, though. I felt I played quite well in Paris when we really could have beaten France. It's always difficult to go there, but if you've got ambition in the game that's what it's all about. I draw on the atmosphere whether the crowd is cheering for you or against you. France was great because the crowd was so hostile, it was a great environment to play rugby in. You really want to stick it to them. I was also pleased with the way things went against Wales where I won a lot of line-out ball and even against England I did all right in the lineout, although I had picked up the first of my knee injuries playing for Bath the week after my first cap."

That knee trouble would prove more of a problem later in the year, forcing him out of Scotland's plans for the ill-fated Murrayfield meeting with the All Blacks. In the meantime, however, Reed received what, at the beginning of the season, would most certainly have been an unexpected call-up to face those same All Blacks - with the British Lions.

On the face of it this should have been one wonderful experience after another for a 24-year-old newcomer to international rugby. Twenty years earlier that would probably have been the case, but in the highly intense atmosphere of a Lions tour in the nineties, Reed found things difficult.

"I hadn't been on a major rugby tour before. Three and a half to four weeks in it was very tough. I had no idea how to prepare mentally for a trip like that." Yet on a tour which saw the Home Union administrators blunder horribly with their treatment of Reed's fellow lock Wade Dooley, refusing to allow him to rejoin the squad after his enforced return to England following his father's sudden death, Reed came through those first few weeks impressively. So much so that the international novice found himself in the side for the first Test - a game which saw victory snatched unjustly from the Lions. "I was picked for the Test side and I believe I deserved to be in, as did Paul Burnell, but we lost to that late kick by Grant Fox and that was it.

"I was injured so couldn't train for the next four or five days. Then I found myself in against Hawkes Bay for the midweek game before the second Test. I have to admit I was in the wrong frame of mind. I felt I should have been looking forward to the Test instead of fighting for a place. In many ways that was the end of the tour for a lot of guys and sadly that showed the following week against Waikato.

"It was difficult after the Hawkes Bay match, though, because there was no time to do anything about getting back in for the final Test. But I genuinely believed I deserved the place in the Test side."

The fact that he was left out has left questions over his relationship with the man who arrived late on tour to claim Reed's place in the Test side, Englishman Martin Johnson. Reed denies that there is anything personal to it, however. "Everyone thinks there's

OVERLEAF

Left: Andy Reed with the SRU's Fred MacLeod who 'discovered' him in deepest Cornwall.

Right: Demonstrating the gifts which have twice transformed Scotland's lineout performance

still some feeling between us, but it's more the case that we enjoy disliking each other on the park."

Having begun 1992/93 as a newcomer to the English first division, Reed returned from that tour as a relatively seasoned campaigner. Once the knee problems which delayed his Scotland return were over he felt he had a lot to draw upon. "I knew exactly what to expect when we I came back for the game against England," he said.

As with the return of Gary Armstrong for that game it was no coincidence that the national side's fortunes improved dramatically with Reed's substantial presence to lean on. Though only a draw with Ireland would be gleaned from a disappointing 1994 Five Nations campaign, Reed also having missed the match at the closest international ground to his home - Cardiff Arms Park - his increasing influence within the squad was recognised after Rob Wainwright's late withdrawal when set to captain Scotland on their summer tour of Argentina.

The man handed something of a poisoned chalice, but with the strength of character to take it on, was Reed. "The South American tour was far more enjoyable than the Lions trip. It was really amazing to get the call just before we left, asking me to captain the side. It's a great honour though, the greatest, being asked to captain your country on tour. The only real disappointment was that we should have won both Tests. No-one remembers the district games, but everyone remembers the Test scores.

"In international terms we did have a weak side on paper with so many people choosing not to go. But we missed 27 points in kicks in the first game and another 18 in the second."

For Reed himself the emergence of a number of young players as contenders for international places was an eye-opener. "A lot of good youngsters were on the tour, although it was a bit awkward being captain, turning up and not even knowing some of their names," he reveals. "The second night, though, we went to the pub and I had a drink with the guys I didn't know and things went really well from there."

He accepted that without even having reached double figures for Scotland caps, but with a Lions tour and a tour leading his country behind him, he was going into the 1994/95 international season with something approaching senior status. That being the case he realises that he and players from the likes of Melrose who are used to winning, must bring their experience to bear on the others. "I suppose what I'd say to anyone is that you have to forget about the pressure and just go out and relax and enjoy games. That's what I've realised above all else. If you make up your mind to do something, just do it. If you get caught in two minds that spells trouble both for yourself and the players supporting you. It's been a difficult year for Scotland, but anyone who takes us as an easy option is in for a surprise."

He is eager for Scotland to shake of the perennial underdog tag, though. "We need to get used to going in as favourites and still producing the goods. That's what we're used to at Bath - being favourites and still winning. People make excuses because we're losing by the odd point, but at Bath, whenever it's close, Bath always win. For Scotland there's so much pressure on us to win but we've forgotten how to at the moment."

Such observations have the ring of a veteran about them and in forming his views on the game he acknowledges that he has benefited from working with some of the sharpest minds in the sport, particularly his first bath coach Jack Rowell, who has gone on to become England manager and his first Scotland coach Ian McGeechan.

"Jack is a very hard taskmaster. I think David Sole is right about him that he is more of a motivator than a tactician, but his methods haven't failed. He's like Jim Telfer...shouts and bawls a lot. He used to give me a very hard time. I got nothing but stick really, nothing was ever good enough, but I would just try harder. McGeechan has been a great influence - the guy's a legend. His coaching was just so refreshing...he had so many ideas. He's the master tactician. If you came up against a flawless side he'd find some sort of weakness."

As for McGeechan's successors as Scotland coaches, Reed is clear about his own responsibilities and those of his team-mates. "The coaches having been having a hard time of it, but we've let them down - at least that's how I feel. There are no excuses. It's up to us and we owe it to ourselves to turn things around."

As the historic visit of the Springboks, returning to Scotland after a quarter of a century approached, Reed seemed in the frame of mind to play a major part in doing just that. "My knees are good, touch wood and I'm still only 25. I just want to improve every aspect of my game and with that in mind, having moved up from Cornwall to Bath to a new job with haulage firm Western Freights, I've increased my training by 200% to 300%. I've got a lot more time available now that I'm not doing 12 hours travelling a week to and from training sessions. I've been a home bird for 24 years, so the move is taking a bit of getting used to, but the one thing I'm not missing is that travelling. Graham Dawe's welcome to stick with it.

"It's a bit alien to me, right enough, having to fit in the training after work. And Sarah pointed out that although I'm doing less travelling and she's not working full-time, she still won't see any more of me. But I think she can put up with me for a bit longer."

That said Scottish clubs should monitor the situation closely. Reed is determined to have a couple more seasons with England's leading club, but thereafter a move North has not been ruled out. He's getting to quite like it up here!

Career Statistics: Andy Reed

1993 Scotland 15 Ireland 3; France 14 Scotland 3; Scotland 20 Wales 0; England 26 Scotland 12;
New Zealand 20 British Lions 18.

1994 Scotland 14 England 15; Ireland 6 Scotland 6; Scotland 12 France 20;
Argentina 16 Scotland 15*; Argentina 19 Scotland 17*.

All appearances at lock. * captain.

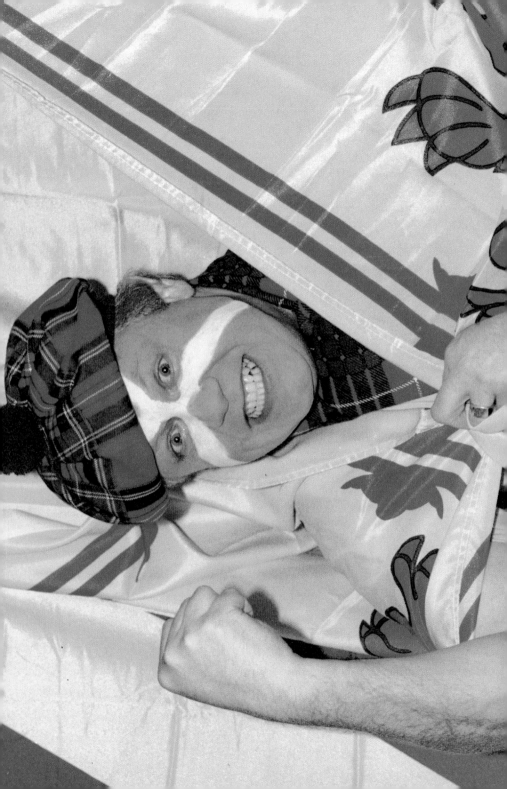

Broon frae Troon

5 - G. L. Brown

Rugby's boiler-house has been home to some of the sport's most imposing exponents and even within that company Gordon Brown - Broon frae Troon - was among the most formidable. It is something of a back-handed compliment to the followers of Ayrshire Junior football, then - and they are a breed who would certainly treat it that way - that they frightened this big man into opting for a career in rugby.

There was little doubt that it was in Gordon Lamont Brown's genes to have the capability toplay either sport to an exceptionally high standard. Father Jock, a Scottish Cup winner with Clyde in 1938, had played in goal for his country. Older brother Peter would precede Gordon into Scotland's second-row, going on to captain the national side.

Surrounded by brilliant sportsmen and women, since his mother Margaret was a quality hockey player, the Bairn of the Broons - "The family still call me the Wee Yin" - was bound to pursue a sporting career.

"I was football daft as a kid," says Brown, who at that stage supported the nearest of his father's clubs Kilmarnock although he only saw Jock play once, in a Junior match in Troon. Only the fact that rugby was compulsory at Marr College, led the Brown boys into rugby.

Peter was first of the three brothers to go to secondary school to learn the way of the oval ball and he set a fearsome pace. "Peter played in the first XV in third year. He was 15, the first person ever to do that," Gordon recalls.

Six years younger, four years younger than John, Gordon was in awe of the oldest brother's achievements. "You know I once wrote to The Wizard comic. They had a column 'My Hero' that you wrote in to. Most people wrote about their sporting heroes. I wrote to them telling them about Peter, saying how good he was at rugby and how he'd won six of the seven events at the school sports - and that was before he was capped. John didn't speak to me for about a month."

The Browns revelled in natural competitiveness, Peter regularly identifying the warning signs to protect his future Scotland team-mate.

"Peter saved my life 50 times...that was the number of times John was going to kill me!" From hero worship evolved a desperate desire to match Peter's success. "Our gym teacher at school was a guy called Keir Hardie, grandson of the Keir Hardie, and he said 'If you're half as good as your brother you'll do damn well.' So that was my target. To do half as well as Peter."

Hardie it was who realised that Brown, for all the footballing skill which would, in future years, be most brilliantly demonstrated on the other side of the planet, was not cut out for the role of play-maker. Obvious though it may seem now, it was not so when Brown was a 12-year-old setting out in the game.

"I was always bigger than average, but when I was picked to play stand-off at primary I was the fastest in the class, could handle and could kick with both feet. I had only played two games at primary school, both at stand-off and scored the winning try both times against Dalry High School. I only lasted 20 minutes at stand-off after moving to Marr, though, before he moved me to the second row." No mean judge the grandson of the founder of the Labour Party!

As he pursued the milestones set by Peter the youngest member of the family received a massive confidence boost just before the end of his third year. "In the second last game of the season I played for the firsts. By that time only Peter and a guy called Victor Dobbs, who went on to play for Saracens and London Scottish, had done it."

Other targets proved harder to attain. Though naturally the taller of the two Gordon never did convince his hero that he managed to achieve one of them. "Every time he left the cottage in Troon and stepped onto the pavement Peter would do this thing where he would lick his fingertips and jump up to leave a mark on the guttering. He said to me 'When you can do that you'll be getting somewhere.'"

The gauntlet having been thrown down Gordon became almost obsessive. "Every time you jumped and missed your fingers hit the roughcast and tore your fingers. Some nights I would keep jumping till my mouth was so dry that I wouldn't have left a mark anyway.

"But I remember the first time I left a mark on that gutter. I rushed in and Peter was slumped in front of the TV, hands in his pockets, really low down in the chair so he was nearly lying there. By the time I managed to drag him up and get him out there the wet mark had dried. He left home not long afterwrds and I never did it again before he left. He doesn't believe me to this day that I did it. I was 17!"

Another of Peter's feats in that cottage, which the family had moved to from a council estate courtesy not of pro football, but of Jock's chiropody and physiotherapy practice, led to more damaged fingers as wee brother tried to emulate him.

"We had a hatch in the hallway. Peter could leap up, push the hatch on its hinge, then pull himself up into the loft. He was only 6'3", but he got himself into great shape in his final year at school. He was a tremendous natural athlete, but he worked hard at it as well."

Another benefit of Jock's post-football career was that he got a closer view of his sons' international career than almost any parent in history. He was the Scotland physion while both were playing for their country.

Peter, who shared a bed with his baby brother as they grew up - "Nobody could sleep with John" - inspired by example and by a willingness to help Gordon work on his skills, many an hour being spent on Troon beach punting sand-covered rugby balls in bare feet, battling past each other to score tries and playing "shootie-in" with a rugby ball.

Even so Gordon was undecided on which sport to play when he left school in 1964, aged 16 - "School didn't thrill me" - to join the British Linen Bank and, with the football season starting first, in early August, he followed his father between the sticks with an Ayrshire Junior side - Troon Juniors.

An early Cup tie sealed his future! The game wasn't exactly close, six goals had been rammed past Troon's new goalie, when Irvine Meadow's star man 'Hooky' Walker homed in on his goal. He hadn't scored and the faithful were, to say the least, keen that he add his name to the roll of honour. To rhythmic chants of "Hooky! Hooky!" he mesmerised the Troon defence until there was only one man to beat. One more sidestep, the goal wide open and then...he was rugby tackled from behind! "It was pure instinct," Gordon protests to this day. A successful penalty strike by the Irvine captain - "He could have saved a lot of trouble by letting Hooky take it" - soothed few of the dissenters and coins reigned down on Gordon. The relief felt as the final whistle blew was brief. Though accompanied from the pitch by two members of the local constabulary, Brown got the message loud and clear as word was passed: 'We'll get the bastard when he comes out.' "I ran in picked up my shoes and ran the half mile to my house." A rugby player was born.

"On the Tuesday night I turned up at Marr FP and asked if they would PLEASE give me a game." Four years there behind "two great props" Arthur Dunsmuir and Tony McGuffie, provided an excellent grounding. Then, a change in banking hours meaning they no longer opened on a Saturday morning, meant he could, as many had advised, move to a senior club. "To go to Ayr or Kilmarnock would have been treated like Mo Johnston going to Rangers down in Ayrshire, but I got great support from the club when I went to West of Scotland."

His timing couldn't have been better. "It was purely coincidental but as I moved to West Peter moved from West to Gala. Alistair McHarg had been capped out of West as well after moving from Irvine and he went off to London at the same time. So I played my first game for the seconds then moved straight into the firsts because these two had left a huge hole.

"I started in a side containing Sandy Carmichael, Quintin Dunlop, Chris Rea and Ian Murchie - guys who had been heroes of mine when I'd gone on the team bus with Peter if Marr didn't have a game." Honours arrived rapidly.

"I'd played for the Glasgow Junior side when I was with Marr, alongside John McHarg, little knowing that his brother would become like a brother of my own in years to come. In fact the only thing that had really upset me in my Marr days was when I played for the Glasgow Juniors against the senior side in what was the final trial before the side for the district championship was selected. I gave Peter a torrid time in the line-out that day - I was more fired up than ever - and was really disappointed because people said I was bound to make the team."

Certainly there were indications from an early age that he had the advantage over big brother in that department, as Gordon has subsequently confirmed. "Peter's girlfriend, now wife, Jill used to get dragged down to Troon beach to throw line-out balls for us to jump at. It was only recently she admitted she sometimes threw it a bit squint to Peter's side," Gordon reveals.

With Peter playing for the South, district honours arrived almost automatically with the change of club, however and so, too, more surprisingly perhaps, came the international call. Though he was very much the baby of the party and played in only two of six matches, Brown made his mark on the tour of Argentina at the beginning of the 1969 season.

"I probably had Peter's absence to thank again, because he'd declared himself unavailable. They picked the squad in April, but the tour wasn't until September, so I had the whole summer to prepare. I got help from Walter Calderwood, the former Ibrox Sports winner who had helped Peter with his fitness."

Back on Troon beach Brown got into the sort of shape which was to make him a consistently outstanding performer. "You know, living in Troon I couldn't be luckier," he waxes lyrical. "Growing up I'd often be out there at 6.30 am, the sea like a mill pond as you looked across to Arran, with the seagulls flying around. The golf course just along the road."

Though accepting the criticism that he did not consistently make fullest possible use of that superb natural training ground during domestic seasons, Brown makes the same observation as Iain Milne that for heavily built men it is difficult to get into peak condition without tour conditions and the rare opportunity for amateur sportsmen to be treated as professional athletes.

In the summer of '69, though, Brown achieved the condition which would earn him a first Test cap against the nation in which he would earn legendary status, South Africa. Scotland won 6-3 at Murrayfield that day and, in three subsequent meetings with the Springboks Brown would go on to boast a 100% record against them at Test level - a remarkable claim to fame.

Discarded by Scotland, but Brown was still in the thick of the action for the British Lions v New Zealand, 1977.

Brown would go on to play in 28 of Scotland's next 33 matches at a curious time for Scottish rugby. Throughout that period, which also saw Bill Dickinson in charge as "adviser to the captain" as the SRU called it, the power source emanated from Glasgow district. The props were Sandy Carmichael and the 'Mighty Mouse' Ian McLauchlan, the locks were Brown and fellow Ayrshireman Al McHarg and among the hookers, the only position which varied much over the first half of the seventies, were Quintin Dunlop, of West. Yet Brown, not a man given to false modesty, is disparaging about his own contribution. "I was a donkey for Scotland," he says. "I hardly ever got the ball in my hands."

Every player of that era is deeply aware of Scotland's dreadful record away from home in that period. The gulf between performances at and away from Murrayfield was even more pronounced than has traditionally been the case. Though frank about his own efforts, Brown believes that much of that had to do with the way the Scotland backs retreated into their shell on less familiar ground. "From 1971 in particular, through to 1975/76 we got great respect from the other Home Unions, especially because of those forwards. But we never played well away from home. The backs never performed with the style they showed at Murrayfield. It was pure confidence - or lack of it."

He does, though, accept the criticism that Bill Dickinson tended to place an over-emphasis on his Glasgow-based pack, neglecting a star-studded back division which contained some of the most celebrated Scottish three-quarters of all time. He accepts it...with one reservation!

"There was always a philosophy of 'Get the ball to Andy.' When we played for West against Heriot's FP we used to put three men on Andy Irvine. There were certain members of the Scotland side who would have had Bruce Hay in because he was more reliable defensively. But I'm one of Andy's biggest fans."

After the Springboks game Brown was actually on the losing side at Murrayfield in three of his next four appearances. But after the home and away double over England in 1971 Scotland lost just twice more at home in the course of his career. Yet throughout his career that Calcutta Cup win over England in 1971 was joined by just one more victory celebration outside Edinburgh - the match which marked the premature end to Brown's career in 1976 at Lansdowne Road.

There can be little doubt that where Brown revelled in the freedom from day to day responsibility which went with touring, he was not at his best under the strictures of the SRU. He appreciates the complaints of current players that there is still some way to go before players are treated as well as they deserve to be but notes that there has been a vast improvement since his time.

He cites examples freely, without malice, merely by way of demonstrating the change of approach. Such as having to hide his wife in the wardrobe in the team hotel, lest it be discovered that she had not paid for her accommodation. Such as having a committee-man attempt to physically block his path as he attempted to get into a taxi rather than wait for the team bus to take him across Edinburgh when he had urgent business to attend to; the bus eventually arriving two hours late. Such as watching his second row colleague Peter Stagg put black boot polish on his leg to disguise a hole in his sock; such as lining up in the tunnel beside student Mike Biggar whose so-called white shorts were almost brown with ingrained mud; such as organising someone to stitch the sleeve of his international shirt, split at the seam all the way up the inside of his arm. All because the SRU insisted on one jersey per season "unless irreparably damaged in the course of a game" and that players supply their own socks and shorts.

Brown would be the last person to put this forward as an excuse. But a reasonable comparison is that Tony Jacklin always believed the the European Ryder Cup team became properly competitive following his insistence as captain that they be treated in first class fashion throughout the competition.

By contrast Brown thrived in the environment which saw him alongside some of the legends of British rugby, Barry John, Gareth Edwards, Mervyn Davies, Willie John McBride and Mike Gibson, to name but a handful, on three British Lions tours.

To put Brown's Scotland career in context though, the national side won only two of the 17 matches played immediately after his last appearance in navy blue, a period in which he should still have been playing but for a conspiracy of circumstances. As TV viewers who watched his performances in full kilted regalia during the 1991 World Cup know, there is no prouder Scot. But it is as a British Lion that Gordon Brown, the player, will always be best remembered.

His first tour in 1971 saw him as something of a surprise selection as a relative newcomer on the international scene at a time when every front-line member of the Lions side was a household name. His performances against England in the double-header, as the annual Calcutta Cup clash was followed by the Centenary game against England, almost certainly got him in. In the first he gave the bruising Nigel Horton such a hard time that when they went to shake hands Horton knocked his hand away warning that revenge would be gained a week later. It is part of Brown's after-dinner patter that the English selectors probably saved his life. Suffice to say Horton was left out of the England side for the return. After the win over South Africa Scotland had lost seven of their next eight matches with Brown playing in every one, but in those two meetings with the Auld Enemy he announced his presence.

Once again he was helped by the absence of his older brother from the '71 tour. Peter had declared himself unavailable due to work commitments. The pair had a slightly different philosophy. "Peter was married and had just become a partner in a chartered accountancy firm in Gala so his circumstances were different from mine then. But I had to face up to the same situation for the 1974 Lions tour. There was no paid leave of absence at the Leicester Building Society which I had just joined and I was initially told in the November that I couldn't go.

"Come the Scotland games the selectors came back to me and asked me to reconsider. I approached the chairman of the Leicester and basically told him that I really liked my job, but if the decision was upheld I was going to chuck my job." Although he had taken the precaution of lining something up with another building society, it was a gamble. "But the following day he came back to me and said 'You're going on tour'."

By 1974 Brown was, of course, an established star, but in 1971 it was fair to say that he was one of the less well-known figures in the Lions squad. If he was surprised to be going it was nothing to the reaction of some of his team-mates at the first training session. "Ray McLoughlin took it and told us to do three sets of 30 press-ups. I did three press-ups then stopped. Ray asked why. I said I couldn't do any more than that. Ray couldn't believe it. 'We're going to New Zealand with a second row forward who can only do three press-ups,' he said. By the end of the week I could do three sets of 30 all right. It's all in the mind."

It was a watershed period for rugby as Brown acknowledges. "That back division was the beginning of rugby superstars. My timing couldn't have been better. In fact it tended to work like that right down the line." The backs were not the only stars, however.

Naturally enough the 23-year-old lock took time to establish himself. But when he did it proved critical in one of the great Test series in history. He was, as the saying goes, over the moon when the name G. L. Brown was listed alongside that of W. J. McBride for the third Test. His second-row partner, however, brought him down to earth with a comment which focussed his mind on the job in hand.

"I was sharing a room with Willie John. He'd been a selector and I was saying how pleased I was to be in the side. I had replaced Delme Thomas and Willie John and Delme were like brothers. He said to me - 'Well I know the team I wanted'. I don't think he was subtle enough to use that as a ploy and I maybe took it the wrong way at the time. At least that's what I like to think now although I've never had the nerve to ask him. But did he press a button? The third Test just couldn't have gone better for me," he says of the victory which meant the Lions couldn't lose the series.

The newcomer had made such an impact that he was singled out for special attention come the final Test. "At the second line-out Peter Whiting who was their supremo in that department, belted me. I know from Andy Haden, who has confirmed it to my face, that he worked with Whiting jumping against him in a barn, hitting him and shouting abuse at him in a Scottish accent. Haden admitted that he was surprised because he expected it to be the FIRST lineout that he hit me.

"Peter Whiting is a personal friend now and he came over to apologise at the dinner and say he had to do it." Brown went off during that game, at which stage the Lions were leading, but although the All Blacks did draw level, the Lions never relinquished control in taking the series. His departure was down to a brutal premeditated assault by notorious All Black prop Jazz Muller. Brown knew it was premeditated...Muller had told him he was going to do it at the previous breakdown, before kicking a huge chunk out of his right leg.

"Linda has always said I came home from that tour a different person. Went away a boy, came home a man. I was also much more of a team man, appreciating the value of my team-mates."

Yet on that score he believes that his next Lions tour, under the captaincy of Willie John McBride and coaching of fellow Irishman Sid Millar, even surpassed the Welsh combination of John Dawes and the late, great Carwyn James in 1971. "It was even better than '71. We actually used less players in the Test series, yet there was this tremendous team feeling in '74. I can honestly say that there wasn't a single player who was an outcast."

That spirit manifested itself notoriously with the "99" call. That was the shout which went up when an individual Lion found himself isolated and under physical assault. The response to it was that the entire Lions team would lay into the nearest opponent.

It has been said that the call brought rugby into disrepute and Brown agrees. But he does not regret its usein the circumstances. "It was one of the biggest disgraces of rugby football...because we had to do it!

"The referees were so weak and we wanted to go home with our eyes in our sockets and our teeth in our heads. Not like punchbags, the way Sandy Carmichael came home after the disgraceful assault on him in New Zealand in '71. It was very much calcu-lated. We knew the referees were too weak to send the whole pack off. I absolutely would recommend it to someone else faced with the same situation."

The lack of television coverage of that tour has meant that the use of the call has been exaggerated, as Brown notes. He also believed it was a device which served a signifi-cant purpose. "It was only used around two or three times. But I believe it was because of that tour and New Zealand's tour of South Africa in 1976 that international rugby put its house in order. The mass punch-ups helped stamp out the bully boys."

More recently they have also provided a therapeutic purpose for the next generation of Browns. "When I see some of the films of the punch-ups I'm mortified. But my son Rory, when he's angry with me, goes and plays a video of me being hit by this big Springbok. I go flying backwards and the friend who edited the video has doctored it so that the guy hits me twice and I go flying backwards twice." Brown remembers the tour with great affection, nonetheless. "I was at my zenith," he says with unashamed relish.

Due to anti-apartheid protests the Lions had only one secret get-together before heading off, but spent 10 vital days of preparation at altitude in South Africa - an expe-rience described vividly by Brown. "I can only describe breathing while training at alti-tude as like swallowing a golf ball that gets stuck in your chest and then swells to the size of a tennis ball...then a football."

But when it was over he was in magnificent condition. "I played in nine of the first 11 tour games. I was not a good trainer, but you couldn't train like that at home. And I loved the atmosphere. Just loved being with those guys. I would look round at people like Gareth Edwards and not believe my luck at being there."

Among Willie John's "Invincibles" as they became known, Brown was one of the great stars. From the second-row he scored the first try of the tour and would finish third top of the try-scoring charts. "The '74 Lions were ahead of their time and I suppose on that tour, I was ahead of my time because the other locks weren't playing like that."

Two of his tries came in the second and third Tests as the Lions killed off the series. "I missed the last Test because I broke my hand on 'Moaner' Van Heerden's jaw in the third Test." Van Heerden was a hard man from Orange Free State who had been brought in for the specific purpose of intimidating the Lions pack. "But he got such a pummelling he walked off. He claimed he had a broken arm, but was playing again the next week. You should have seen the looks on the faces of the South Africans when they saw their hit man throwing in the towel." Though for the second successive Lions tour he wasn't on the pitch at the end of the series, Brown had again played a hugely significant role in a Test series win.

Despite those successes and the fact that when the Lions set off for New Zealand again in 1977 he was just 29, Brown almost missed out on a third tour. It was all down to the incident which led to a sending off and a lengthy suspension from rugby. The bitterness he still feels towards the individual still involved is almost tangible. "If Allan Hardie walked into the room now I would walk out," he says.

The effect the very name has on Brown, 17 years after the event, is remarkable. "I was speaking at a dinner in Aberdeen last year and went into a room for a drink beforehand where I was speaking to a sponsor. He said he saw that one of my old friends was out there and when I asked who he said 'Allan Hardie'. I said that either he left or I wouldn't go into the room. He started laughing then realised I was serious. He said 'But I've booked you to speak at this dinner, I'd have to sue you.' I told him he'd have to sue me, then. He then told me he was only joking and I thought 'Thanks a lot, pal.'

"Around six years ago I was in Aberdeen and was walking down Union Street when I saw Allan Hardie walking towards me. He was much closer before I realised it was somebody in a painter's outfit who just looked like him. I went into a restaurant for lunch four hours later, put the spoon to my mouth and I was still shaking." The cause of such revulsion - a former North & Midlands hooker. The details of their encounter in a District Championship match in 1976 are outlined in Brown's autobiography:

> "I was lying face down on top of one or two players when I felt someone grab my head with two hands. The hands momentarily held my head then wham! A knee crashed into my face, bursting it open from my nose to my hairline. I howled out in agony. The pain racked my whole system and the blood spurted from the wound. My assailant still had hold of my head and I instantly thought, God he's going to do it again. I struggled and twisted off the bodies and landed on the ground facing upwards with other bodies on top of me. I caught sight of my assailant's face for the first time - Allan Hardie.
>
> " 'Hardie, you bastard!' " I yelled as the blood pumped over my face. 'F—- off Brown!' he growled and then deliberately stamped on my face. The force actually lifted his other foot off the ground so that his whole weight was now being ground into my face. He then lost his balance and fell off my head."

When the book was published in the early eighties it was serialised in advance in the "Sunday Mail" and after the chapter containing that section was published Hardie attempted to take Brown to court. Brown went to his solicitor explaining confidently that it could all be seen clearly on video. Then he went to the BBC in Glasgow to discover that they couldn't find the video. An APB was issued by a panic-stricken Brown and three days before the court hearing was scheduled a friend from BBC Wales contacted him to say the sequence had turned up in a video on violence in sport. When duly delivered Brown and his solicitor breathed a combined sigh of relief. It was passed on and the case was immediately dropped.

At the time of the incident retaliation had been inevitable, but Brown accepts that even so he went too far. "The English rugby union let themselves down very badly over the recent Tim Rodber case," he reckons. Fair enough if he had hit the guy back once or twice, but to do it 10, 11, 12 times - there's a warning bell goes off in your head and you know when you've gone too far. As I chased Allan Hardie I knew I was going too far but I was just sick that I never really got him. My father gave me hell saying 'They will do you...and for what!'"

The SRU dealt rather differently with Brown's response to being assaulted. Hardie's ban was six times as long, but three months put Brown out of all bar Scotland's last Five Nations international.

"I was told before Christmas that all was not lost for the Lions tour as long as I presented myself in decent shape." He had Glasgow Rangers FC in general and Jock Wallace in particular for ensuring that he did so. Brown trained ferociously with the pros. "I owe a great deal to Jock Wallace," he says. "Not just for the physical training either. I'd had such a blow mentally that I owe a great deal to him and Linda for getting me sorted out. The guy just has such an aura. You just have to be around him. He's the greatest man's man I have ever met, although Willie John's a close second." An international rugby career was continued and a Rangers fan was born.

Though Scotland had lost two of their three Five Nations matches Brown, even when recalled to the squad, was not expecting a recall. Particularly not when he was involved in a three car smash a few days before the final squad session. He survived that fit enough to turn in a fine performance for West against Edinburgh Wanderers, conveniently at Murrayfield the day before the team was announced. "All the papers were full of my return, but I never believed a word of it."

Hope flickered though when chairman of selectors Tom Pearson came to ask after his welfare, immediately before the announcement. "So because of this the boys were all nudging me excitedly. They then announced the team and I wasn't in it. I was shattered. It was only the second time I was ever fodder for the Scotland pack and at least the previous time I'd been on the bench. Jim Telfer came over and said he needed my help. He knew I just wanted to get into the first car. But you never walk away from Jim Telfer."

Brown would never represent Scotland again.

"But after only two games for West I was selected for the Lions tour." It was a diffi-cult trip from start to finish. Early on Brown contracted shingles yet dismissed it as a heat rash and didn't have a correct diagnosis until the worst effects were over. He was also a marked man on arrival.

"I was labelled a thug in the New Zealand press before the game with Hawkes Bay. They were full of the fact that it was my first big game back. I was playing against a very experienced guy called Robbie Stuart. At the first three line-outs he belted me. He clambered all over me that day. I let it go until about 15 minutes to go. I was having a mental nightmare as well. Team-mates were screaming at me to get the ball. Eventually I belted him back.

"After the game he was at pains to come up to me and say he had to do it. It was myfirst game and he'd been told. He was beginning to think he'd get away with it for the entire 80 minutes, but if he had that would have been it for me. In Scotland nobody really noticed me as being hard before the Hardie incident, but I was a hard man on tour. And in the 70s, at international level, you could commit murder on the pitch and get away with it."

His fitness was going really well again until he suffered a serious shoulder injury which ruled him out of the first Test. The Lions duly lost. "Dawes said I was available, but I wasn't. I think he said it to make the guy who was in feel better."

Coach John Dawes of 1977 was unrecognisable from captain John Dawes of 1971 to Brown. In simple terms he told Brown he was no use to him injured and he was sent, along with Derek Quinnell who had a knee injury, to see a specialist. It was a trip which revealed a great deal about the spirit of the squad.

"It had rained every day. We were training non-stop in the mud. Quinnell was a great trouper, but when he came out of seeing the specialist, having been in for an hour, he was hanging his head and shaking it. I asked him if he was out and he said - 'No...the bastard says I've got to stay.' That was like Ally McCoist saying he didn't want to take a penalty in case he scored."

Brown was told a course of cortisone could keep him in New Zealand, but that by con-tinuing to play and train the injury would only get worse. He opted for injections, padding and an extended stay. Dawes' attitude was by no means grateful. "He just said 'Don't complain about the shoulder'."

Brown regained top form in time for the second Test and put in one of his finest ever performances. "I cleaned Andy Haden out to such an extent that he asked me if we could swap blazers. H was absolutely determined to, but I couldn't. I needed mine for the rest of the tour

"That game was one of the great character-building experiences. I shook hands with the All Blacks around me at the end and the tunnel was about 100 yards away. I just stood and looked at it and couldn't see how I was going to make it. It had been such an important game because it meant the tour was alive to the last Test.

"As I stood there someone came up and hit me right in the back. I saw him and I couldn't go after him, but if I'd had a machine gun. . . . The pain was excruciating. I couldn't go to the post-match function. Couldn't even get dressed. I couldn't handle the thought of being jostled. To avoid the crowds outside the stadiumI went out onto the pitch, right round to the far end, then through a turnstile and round to the bus where I satfor an hour in the most unbelievable agony. I thought I wouldn't play again, but after a few beers that night the pain seemed to ease off.

"Every time I see Terry Cobner who was pack leader he goes on about having to give his talks around the treatment table before games on that tour while I was getting pain-killing injections."

Haden got his revenge with a try in New Zealand's third Test win and Brown's last Test appearance came in the decisive fourth Test. Defeat by a single point meant Brown was part of a beaten team for the only time in three Lions tours, but he is vigorous in defence of their performance.

"That pack is still revered in New Zealand and during the series the All Blacks were forced, for the only time in history, to go into a scrummage with just three men, the rest standing off to defend. That is still regarded as a national disgrace and it has been reported that Colin Meads left the ground in disgust. I found it immensely disappointing to come so close after all the problems we'd had with injury and illness.

"In the final Test we had the chance to win the match right at the end with a scrum on their line. I had the ball at my feet, but the scrum started to slew so I pushed it over to Willie Duggan. The line was under the noses of our front row and our no. 8 or scrum half were bound to score, but Willie picked it up and didn't make it. The referee gave another scrum five, but they immediately collapsed it and we had to spin the ball. The chance was lost when Andy Irvine, of all people, dropped the ball. That just about summed the whole tour up."

He missed the 1977/78 season through injury. In 1978 the Brown family expanded with the birth of daughter Mardi's little brother Rory and with Linda taking ill after the birth, Gordon drifted away from the game.

In the Nineties, however, as large as life, if not larger, he re-emerged as a star of world rugby through his work as a TV pundit - "I love the TV, especially the live stuff and the spontaneity of that" - notably during the 1991 World Cup. Not bad for a man who, in his book, declared: "There has been much publicity and discussion regarding a World Cup competition in rugby. I am totally opposed to it!"

While now embracing the event he explains that comment quite logically. "I honestly didn't see how they could get a World Cup without professionalism and without filthy play. Refereeing standards are now much better than when I was playing, especially at international level. There's no financial reward for winning the World Cup although a lot are getting a killing off the park."

All in all he is quite delighted that his son has opted for rugby as his no.1 sport and will encourage him all the way. "I just pray he never comes across the tiny percentage of idiots I encountered in my career!"

And for the most part it must be stressed that there is great warmth in his tone throughout whenever he looks back on his time in the sport. "I was born and brought up with two brothers. Thanks to rugby I've got another 300...even including Englishmen like Fran Cotton, Roger Uttley, Bill Beaumont and Andy Ripley!"

Career Statistics: Gordon Brown

1969 Scotland 6 South Africa 3.

1970 Scotland 9 France 11; Wales 18 Scotland 9 [1]; Ireland 16 Scotland 11; Scotland 14 England 5; Australia 23 Scotland 3.

1971 France 13 Scotland 8; Scotland 18 Wales 19; Scotland 5 Ireland 17; England 15 Scotland 16; Scotland 26 England 6 [2];

New Zealand 13 British Lions 3; New Zealand 14 British Lions 14 [3].

1972 Scotland 20 France 9; Wales 35 Scotland 12; Scotland 23 England 9; Scotland 9 New Zealand 14.

1973 England 20 Scotland 13 [4]; Scotland 27 Overseas XV 16.

1974 Wales 6 Scotland 0; Scotland 16 England 14; Ireland 9 Scotland 6; Scotland 19 France 6;

South Africa 3 British Lions 12; South Africa 9 British Lions 28 (1Try); South Africa 9 British Lions 26 (1Try).

1975 Scotland 20 Ireland 13; France 10 Scotland 9; Scotland 12 Wales 10; England 7 Scotland 6; Scotland 10 Australia 3.

1976 Scotland 6 France 13; Wales 28 Scotland 6; Scotland 22 England 12; Ireland 6 Scotland 15.

1977 New Zealand 9 British Lions 13; New Zealand 19 British Lions 7; New Zealand 10 British Lions 9.

All appearances at lock. [1]Replacement for Peter Brown; [2]Replaced by Gordon Strachan; [3]Replaced by Delme Thomas; [4]Replacement for Jock Millican.

The White Shark

6 - J. Jeffrey

White Shark he may be called, but there's nothing he enjoys better than attacking the All Whites. Any regular viewer of television's "Rugby Special" can tell you that. John Jeffrey was among the Scots who wrapped a Wallabies scarf around his neck for the 1991 World Cup final, when Scotland, having been consigned to battling out the minor places after losing to the Auld Enemy in the semi-final, were invited guests at the Twickenham final.

All the more remarkable, then, that the first international jersey John Jeffrey pulled on was not the navy blue, but the all white. Not Scotland's change strip either - it was the genuine rose petalled England shirt. He and his good friend Hugh Parker were both part of a successful side at Newcastle University in the seventies and as a consequence, when the University Home Internationals rolled around the pair added their bulk to the English Universities cause.

"I must admit it caused a fair bit of interest when we played against Scottish Universities at Durham," Jeffrey admits. It was a remarkable beginning to a career which would become synonymous with mighty Scotland-England clashes.

"I suppose when I look back at the highlights and the lowlights they're reserved for England. The record win in 1986, the Grand Slam, losing the Triple Crown and the World Cup semi-final."

Yet, for this man born so close to the Border with all that entails, playing for England doesn't come across as having been just as traumatic an experience as might be expected. "It's just the system. You can only play for the country in which you're at University."

Make no mistake about it Jeffrey thoroughly relished his time among the enemy as a student. "I actually failed my exams, so came back here for a year," says the Kelso farmer. "But I enjoyed my time there so I went back to the department of agriculture to complete my course."

Nonetheless, while he may live little more than a Gavin Hastings clearance from the Border, there's never been much English about John Jeffrey.

There was no great rugby tradition in the family and though a Borders boy he didn't play until the age of eight because "there was no mini rugby in those days". But Jeffrey's indoctrination began at the hands of George "Chump" Murray, a teacher at St Mary's Prep School in Melrose, a man who would later become a South district official.

The promising, though by no means conspicuously large, youngster was successful through prep school and continued his education at another great Scottish seat of rugby learning Merchiston Castle. Always a back-row forward he was "mad keen" on his rugby throughout school, but suffered major setbacks just as he should have been ready to make his mark.

"If I was really going to do anything in rugby I should have been in the first XV in Lower Sixth, but I wasn't," he says. "I would have played for the first XV in Upper Sixth, but I only played for them twice.

"Early on, after one match for them. I suffered a knee problem and had an operation to have a cartilage removed. I then got back for a game but was concussed and that was me for the rest of the season. It was a great grounding, though. Both schools played a running game."

The knee injury would be a consideration throughout his rugby career and, indeed, was a factor when, armed with the ceremonial walking stick just presented to him by his Scotland colleagues, he limped out of Cardiff Arms Park after the 1991 World Cup third place play-off and Test match rugby.

Not that it ever noticeably restricted the young Jeffrey who, for all that he made little impact on the national scene at age group level, was becoming used to rubbing shoulders with class performers. First of these was the man who would become famous as one of the most elegant players ever to grace the navy blue and yet play 27 games on the wing for his country without scoring a try.

"Roger Baird followed me to St Mary's a year behind me and then followed me everywhere for a while. Then I started following him." As Jeffrey points out both players would make their internationals debuts against touring Wallabies, but a few years separated those occasions.

Meantime, at University, as well as lining up regularly alongside Hugh Parker, for whom he would later act as best man, he faced an Irish side including the likes of Phil Matthews, Keith Crossan, Trevor Ringland and Dave Irwin. In his year out of University, his first spell with Kelso introduced him to the man he regards as having been the biggest influence on his career.

"Gary Callander was a deep thinker on the game. As captain he went on to do most of the coaching at Kelso. He's forgotten more about rugby than I know. He was a bit of a tyrant as captain, but he was the real driving force behind the Kelso side which went on to win the title in the late seventies."

After school, then, it was a fairly unorthodox, unstructured rugby education. But it was one which also taught Jeffrey a great deal about the importance of the right environment for youngsters learning the game.

"When Hugh Parker and I played together we were rated as having similar prospects. I went home, to a farm five minutes from Kelso rugby club, while Hugh went back to his family's farm in Wigtownshire, a four hour round trip from Kilmarnock, the nearest top club. Almost every first division match for me was within an hour from home. It was all a very different proposition for Hugh," he notes.

On his return Jeffrey made steady progress in making up for the previous failure to win Scottish representative honours, admitting that his natural colouring helped him get noticed. "The hair colouring doesn't do any harm...as long as you're playing well. It also helps you get noticed when you do things like missing tackles as well, though."

Certainly he stood out on the trip which earned him the nickname by which he will always be remembered. "I was with the Saltires in the West Indies and we'd been out there for a while. Everyone was black...except me, of course. We were swimming in the seas and as I emerged someone, I think it might have been Kenny Macaulay, said: 'Here comes the White Shark'."

It was a moment to which headline writers would become indebted over the next few years as Jeffrey progressed through the ranks, making the South district side in 1982, earning B international honours in 1983 then, at the end of an epic year for Scottish rugby, winning his first cap.

By no means an immature performer himself by the time senior honours started to arrive, he was also helped by being surrounded by hugely experienced players. "I played my first game for the South against Wellington who ended up with two players sent off. But I think I was about the only uncapped player in the South side."

Though things happened rapidly from that stage on there were still one or two stutters before he was finally called into the Scotland side.

"I was actually in the Blues side for the international trial and wasn't selected. Then we went to Romania after the Grand Slam. I played in the Saturday game the week before the Test, against Bucharest and wasn't that bad. But Shaun McGauchey played on the Wednesday against Costanza and was outstanding. Jim Calder wasn't on the trip so Finlay Calder, Shaun and myself all felt we had a chance of getting a cap, but Shaun just had a blinder."

It would be McGauchey's only cap. Meanwhile the back-row combination which would, over the next seven years, terrorise midfielders across the globe, were together at a Test for the first time...on the sidelines! While Finlay was beginning to get a bit fatalistic about it all Jeffrey, slightly younger and who hadn't been around just as long, remained bright in his outlook.

"I still felt my chance would come. I'd only just had my first trial and I knew I was in the frame. We didn't know how much longer Jim Calder would go on. Obviously he could have gone on as long as Finlay did, but David Leslie was getting on a bit. We did appreciate that having just won a Grand Slam these guys had their places for as long as they wanted."

The call, then, came rather sooner than expected. The same year, in fact. "I had played three times for the B team and the B team were due to play against Ireland in Galway, but the South were playing the Wallabies the same day and South got precedence for selection.

"We were the only side to beat them on a Saturday on that tour. Shaun played for the district as well that day, though, so I think it was a toss-up between us for the Test."

It was Jeffrey who got the call, not in his customary position at no.8 - "the only time I ever played at flanker was for Scotland" - nor in the no.6 jersey which he would latterly make his own, but with the no.7 on his back. Despite the win with the South Jeffrey was strangely pessimistic approaching his first cap, though he describes his feelings as no more than pragmatic when faced with Andrew Slack's Grand Slam Wallabies.

"I really never expected to win that match. Really I thought we had no chance. I've always believed that once you've lost you do that much more to win your next game, so South's win didn't actually help Scotland.

"I just knew those Wallabies were such a great side and we had a changed team from that which won the Grand Slam, particularly in the back-row with David Leslie and Iain Paxton not playing. I wasn't overawed at all. That was just a realistic view."

His own first task was a particularly tricky one. The first to say that he was never an open-side flier of a flanker, he had to try to get to grips with one of the most elusive fly-halves the game has ever seen. "I did realise that playing open-side with Mark Ella at stand-off in your first international was a tough start."

If those mental machinations wouldn't have delighted the likes of a Jim Telfer the accuracy of his pre-match assessment showed why Jeffrey's analytical talent was pursued by press and television for punditry purposes immediately he departed the Test arena. At that stage, though, there was a long way to go before he reached the sort of status that made him sought after in those areas.

It wasn't just because of the margin of Scotland's defeat that day that Jeffrey was relieved to be given the chance to develop his international reputation thereafter and one of his closest confidants suggested that an extraordinarily early blunder could bring the end of his Test career after just one match.

South Sea islanders preparing for a shark
attack — Scotland v Western Samoa,
1991 World Cup

"The thing I remember most about the day was that we were singing the nation al anthem and I think in those days the boys sang the Flower of Scotland ourselves. We thought the singing was finished and I turned away and broke ranks. When I did Gary Callander said - 'That's JJ's last game.'"

It wouldn't be the last time Jeffrey would have trouble with the formalities.

His second match was the Five Nations opener against the Irish, a renewal of acquaintance with Irish debutant Phil Matthews, among others and another defeat. Jeffrey was dropped. "They told me I hadn't been dropped for playing badly, they just wanted Leslie back to captain the side. To be honest I remember even less about that game than I had about the Wallabies match."

Recalled, on the blind-side this time, for the last championship match he was part of a Scotland side which should have won at Twickenham. Among the crucial moments was one in which his Kelso colleague Baird and Iwan Tukalo both had the chance to hack the ball over the line and both missed. That was typical of Baird's luck in a Scotland shirt.

"Towards the end of his career I remember someone, it might have been Finlay, saying he was better off not scoring. He said no-one would remember the guy who went 20 odd games before scoring, but not scoring at all was quite different. I don't think Roger saw it like that."

By contrast Jeffrey would go on to become the most prolific try-scoring Scottish forward in history, his tally matched by Derek White. Those scoring exploits began in 1986, a season which saw the man who had made his first two appearances in tandem with Jim Calder, begin the more famous partnership with the other twin.

"Finlay and I had played in one B game together. We sparked off each other well, but then there was a lot of humour between Fin and everyone. We fitted well because neither of us was a genuine open-side, so we tended to play right and left. neither of us had genuine speed so we helped cover for each other. I did all the tackling though," he laughs.

"Actually if anything Fin tended to be there to spark off a move. If you watch all those videos of that period he set up a lot of the tries."

If Calder sparked them off, Jeffrey was perfectly placed to finish them off on no fewer than 11 occasions. The first of these came in the 1986 clash with Wales, ironically Scotland's only defeat of the season, despite scoring three tries to one at Cardiff Arms Park. Gavin Hastings had an off day with his kicking, in stark contrast to his perfect six on debut a fortnight earlier.

"It was an amazing game. We scored three tries in the first half and still lost. Soley scored twice in the second half and neither was given. Derrick Grant gave Gavin an awful bollocking afterwards for missing his kicks and Gav just shrugged his shoulders. He just never let that sort of thing get to him."

As his team-mates would discover such disparity in terms of place-kicking accuracy would be utterly typical of the older Hastings and the arrival of Gavin and Scott into the squad was no muted affair.

"The confidence the Hastings sisters gave you when they came into the side was remarkable. They seemed to think there was nothing to international rugby," says Jeffrey, a note of wonder still in his voice at the thought. "They genuinely believed that and it was certainly an influence on the side."

Looking back at that season, Scotland having gone on to run up a record tally against England and then beat Ireland by the narrowest of margins at Lansdowne Road, history judges it to have been a near miss. John Jeffrey doesn't really see it that way.

"We never felt we missed out on anything that year because nothing was ever really on. We lost to Wales in our second game and I think we knew we were a bit lucky to have beaten France.

"Even against England we were a bit lucky. We scored off their mistakes, particularly two by Maurice Colclough, when they could have taken control, although we did run them ragged by the finish."

Instead he regards 1987, when Scotland again lost their second match, this time in Paris, as a source of real disappointment. "We really should have won a Triple Crown that year." He notes that had the matches been played in the right order Scotland wouldn't even have had the French as their second opponents. If we'd played England at Twickenham in January as we were supposed to we'd have won. But it snowed and the game was cancelled. When the match came around at the end of the season we got wrong. In January we'd have won because England were still picking a crap team. But by April they'd got themselves sorted out a bit. Our build-up was all wrong and we made the wrong selection. The rain was piddling down, but we tried to play a running game."

Other factors were illness and injury. Iain Milne played despite a bout of 'flu ahead of the game. John Beattie suffered the knee injury which would end his career in something of a kamikaze assault on the massed English ranks early in the second half.

"What summed it up was that Tomba (Alan Tomes), who was on the bench and would normally take anyone on, was told he was going on to replace John and said - 'Do I have to'," Jeffrey recalls. "We really felt we had missed out."

In the dressing room afterwards a ceremony held by the backs to present Ian McGeechan, then the backs coach, with a dinner suit to replace his seventies glam-rock flared affair, by way of a thank you for the work he had done, fell horribly flat.

The year got no better with another infamous knee injury, that suffered by the influential John Rutherford in the Caribbean shortly before the World Cup. "Everybody knew the lads were going, though," says Jeffrey. "And no-one blamed them for going to Bermuda with the few injuries you got in those days. Not one player held it against John, he was so highly respected."

Though he already boasted a pretty respectable try-scoring record for a forward with three in 12 games, it was on that trip that a valuable lesson was learned.

"I scored a few tries over the years, but it should have been more. You remember the ones you miss more than the ones you score. The most spectacular miss was against Wales at Murrayfield in 1987 on the day of the five no. 8s. We were playing well, but Gav had missed four or five kicks. Then just before half-time John Rutherford made a break, gave it to Finlay and he gave it to me. I was already preparing my swallow dive when I dropped the ball. The whistle went for the interval, I picked myself up off the ground and when I went back I couldn't get into the huddle. Then, against Zimbabwe in the first World Cup I went to dive over in the corner when the line was clear and dropped it again. It was after that Geech made Scotland players score rugby league style. Still diving, but with the ball tucked in under the arm. None of the swallow dive stuff.

"I got concussed in the next game, against Romania, but I scored three tries and, even though I can't remember much about it, when you see the video every try I scored the ball is tucked right in."

To round off a disappointing year that concussion denied him a shot at the All Blacks in the quarter-final, but if 1987 was bad 1988 was most definitely worse for Jeffrey. Several factors contributed. Firstly, although his mentor Gary Callander at last established himself in the side following Colin Deans' retirement, not only as hooker but as captain, it was an ill-fated run. Scotland won only once, strangely enough a comfortable Murrayfield success over the French who had claimed a Grand Slam a year earlier.

Then there was Jeffrey's own failure to secure a regular place in the side, which meant that he himself accepted after the Five Nations Championship that Derek Turnbull had taken over as the first choice no.6.

But easily the nadir, of his career, never mind 1988, came with one of the most notorious post-match incidents in rugby history. The features of this most easy-going, open of men, whose frequent response to journalists is an off-hand, well-natured "write what you like", still cloud over when the matter of the Calcutta Cup Incident is raised.

To this day only a handful of people know what actually happened when the sport's most famous trophy was taken out into the streets of Edinburgh. Jeffrey and England's Dean Richards were the men held most accountable after, it was reckoned, an impromptu game of rugby with the cup used instead of a ball, resulted in it being substantially damaged.

"I will never go into detail on the Calcutta Cup Incident. I'll not go any further than I said at the time." For the record his comment then was: "I accept the suspension without complaint, but I deny damaging the cup."

Many Scots were enraged when, Jeffrey having been effectively banned from rugby for six months, the RFU opted only to suspend Richards from their next match against Ireland a fortnight later. If there was some sort of attempt to imply that the greater blame lay North of the Border then it sadly backfired. There are few in that part of the world who would not unequivocally accept the word of John Jeffrey.

For his part he believes that the situation was not helped by the severity of the punishment he received. "It didn't cost me any caps, but it cost me tours to the Hong Kong Sevens and a World Sevens tournament in Australia. It also possibly cost Kelso the Border League since I wasn't able to play in the play-off. It was an over-reaction." On his return: "I was determined to remind people about my rugby."

Ever the man with the soothing word Finlay Calder it was who would attempt to place the matter into perspective. "He said about a year later that it was a pity that I would be remembered till my dying day for dropping the Calcutta Cup and not for my rugby," says Jeffrey, good humour rapidly returning to his tone.

It is a mark of both his subsequent achievements as a player and the dignified manner in which he has conducted himself in the public eye, that Calder was proved quite wrong, something for which Jeffrey is grateful. "To be honest I don't think it's done me any harm in the long run in the way people regard me."

A repeat of his first Test proved no more successful as the 1988 Wallabies thrashed Scotland as soundly as they had four years earlier, yet this time the defeat marked the dawning of great things rather than the occasion marking the waning of an era as it had on Jeffrey's debut. This was Ian McGeechan's first match as Scotland coach. Scotland would not lose at Murrayfield again in their next 14 appearances, if the pre-World Cup meeting with the Barbarians is included. Indeed they beat every visiting side until England arrived in 1992.

The 1989 Championship saw Scotland in contention to the very end, losing the title in what proved to be a play-off in Paris as England stumbled to defeat at Cardiff. Scotland's chance of lifting the honours was presented by yet another Jeffrey try, the one which earned the 12-12 draw at Twickenham. Yet the flanker prefers the memory of his performance against the Welsh when he looks back on that season.

"I enjoyed that game more because Jonathan Griffiths came blind about 10 times from close range scrums and I stopped him every time. We'd watched him score twice for Llanelli the previous week and I was told my job was to stop, whatever he did. That was a very solid, very good performance by Scotland with a lot of new players.

"Gary Armstrong had played against the Wallabies and Craig Chalmers made his debut against Wales. Craig has never played as well as his first season," Jeffrey reckons.

The trip to London was next up and, in a return to tradition, Scotland were expected to have no answers to England's pace, yet the outstanding memory of the match is of Jeffrey out-pacing Rory Underwood to score that try.

"Actually it was Chris Oti and Rory Underwood," he says. "To be fair I got half a yard on both of them as the ball came off the full-back and I had my shoulder in front of Rory. It kept bouncing my way and he was going to have to get round me to get to the ball."

After the most entertaining match of that season's championship in which Scotland had five of the eight tries scored in the Murrayfield meeting with Ireland, answering the foolish belittling of their Twickenham performance by England manager Geoff Cooke when he described the Scots as "scavengers", it was off to the Parc Des Princes.

"We went to France believing in ourselves too much. Scotland really are always better with our backs to the wall and not expected to do too well." Yet that comment, in the context of the fact that Scotland went to France not having won their in 20 years and never at the modern Parc, says much for the mood of that squad of players. Little wonder that Jeffrey was one of nine to go on to the British Lions tour of Australia. Big wonder that so few took that same squad seriously as title challengers the next year.

"After the way we played in 1989, then having been on the Lions tour, we knew how much better we were than some of the others," says Jeffrey. Yet the game's fluctuating fortunes are summed up by Jeffrey's views on his own Lions selection. Understandably, in light of the way 1988 had ended, he held out no great hope of selection for the tour of Australia entering the new season.

"Even although I felt like that at the beginning of the season I was a bit disappointed by not winning a Test place in Australia. I was actually surprised that Mike Teague even went. I felt Phil Matthews would be the other no.6 and when they picked Teague then I knew I was first choice. Yet I never forced my way into the Saturday side at any stage and had no complaints. Teaguey was voted man of the series.

"That aspect of Test rugby has never really bothered me. On the Lions Tour there were quite a few dropped after the first Test who had never been dropped in their lives before, by anyone. I couldn't be too disappointed, though, the way Teaguey was playing."

So, having missed the boat Down Under as the Lions made history by coming from behind to win a Test series for the first time, it was on to another arena to ensure that the man who had now become his Scotland and Lions captain would not be proved right in his assessment of how Jeffrey would be remembered. The role both men played in the heroics of 1990 ensured an appropriate place in legend.

"The Grand Slam never really gathered momentum until we beat France," Jeffrey says in summarising the fairly low-key win in Dublin and the strange victory over the French. All squad members speak of the subdued way they reacted to the win over Ireland, in spite of it being a first away win in four years. As for the French game, Jeffrey plays down the significance of the dismissal of his hot-headed opposite number Alain Carminati early in the second half, France having turned only 3-0 down with the wind at their backs. He emphasises the importance of the clearance kick put in by Gavin Hastings moments after the re-start, a monster blow which actually convinced the Scots the wind hand changed.

"England hammered Wales the day we beat France and people were already talking about a Grand Slam decider. We went to Wales under a strange kind of pressure."

The difficulty Scotland had in reaching the Calcutta Cup clash with a 100% record merely served to underline Jeffrey's initial philosophy in Test rugby that no side is harder to beat than when it has just suffered a setback.

"We were always playing teams that had 30 or 40 points put past them by England," he notes. "We had to get the Grand Slam out of our minds in Wales. The very worst thing imaginable was that we would have lost down there. Geech is great at relieving that sort of pressure and was helped by the senior pros.

"We never got clear against the Welsh. I can remember looking at the scoreboard and thinking 'If they get a breakaway here that's it.'

"After the Welsh game we had a session back at the hotel with the coaches discussing the game in two weeks time. We decided to keep the press away from the younger players in the squad. We felt we knew how to deal with the attention. To be fair to the Scottish press they knew what was going on and went along with it."

As to the occasion itself, every detail of a long day which was over in the blinking of an eye for most, is etched on Jeffrey's mind. "I remember it all from start to finish," he says with relish. Just as he knew in 1984 that Scotland could not win so, now, he was certain of victory. "I couldn't actually see how we wouldn't win. Deep down I just couldn't see how we'd lose it, emotionally and analytically.

You meet all the best people in this game . . .

"To be honest I really thought they'd blow it. I thought England would believe the hype. We got there and England were getting their pictures taken with their wives and girlfriends on the pitch. Once we were into the game you could see they hadn't done their planning. They weren't sure what to do in certain situations. We always knew what we were doing.

"We talked about the march in advance. Soley told me and I said it was a great idea. The noise when we stepped out was unbelievable. Then there was that first penalty and that first drive, taking them back about five or ten yards. It wasn't that much in itself, but it was important psychologically. We said we had to be totally focussed and we were."

No triumph could have been sweeter, yet Scotland, the Northern Hemisphere champions, very nearly did go one better that summer when they travelled to New Zealand in what was an unofficial World Championship Test series. Thoughts of retirement were very much in the air for their great flankers. Indeed Calder had decided it was time to depart and wanted his colleague to join him.

"Finlay was after me to go after New Zealand. He felt we should step aside for a new team. The first Test had been like a game of ping-pong and a loose game would normally have suited us, but not that day. We were so disappointed by that. Pride was the key for the second Test. We knew we had the beating of them. Then, in that second Test, when we were in front with about a quarter of an hour to go he was saying - 'You'll have to go now. This would be the time to do it after being the first Scots to beat New Zealand. How could you beat that.' "

Even when New Zealand snatched their undeserved victory Calder persisted. Yet, a year later, JJ would have the last laugh as Calder emerged from retirement to ensure that they did take their final bow together against the All Blacks, not in the spotlight of a major Test, however, but in the strangely subdued atmosphere of a World Cup third place play-off.

"It actually wouldn't have counted for me if we'd been the first Scottish side to beat the All Blacks that day," says Jeffrey. "It was a joke game. We tried not to treat it like that, but I've heard the football boys regard it the same way."

Over the piece, for all that there were huge highs in the World Cup - "the two tries I scored against Western Samoa were the most important of my career" - 1991 was a year of disappointment.

"In the championship we really should have won in Paris. I thought we were past the Paris jinx thing, but Geech thought we got too involved with them that day. It was the reverse of the Grand Slam that way."

On to the World Cup and, as Jeffrey says: "If we didn't get to the semi-final we had done badly. It was all set up. As for the semi-final, I didn't think so at the time, but the back-row didn't play well at all. They were waiting for us and we took too much on ourselves. The backs should have been given more ball."

He also has a strange suspicion that England may have launched a successful spying mission of some sort. "At the first scrum we always, always went right. But this time I said we should go left. If you look at the videos we always went right from the first scrum, but we changed it and they were onto us. The more I think about it the more I feel they knew what we were going to do."

Though nothing had been said publicly it was known in the camp that Jeffrey was joining Calder in retirement after the tournament. The ancient knee injury could take no more of the intensity of international preparation.

"I'd been advised to stop playing rugby by a surgeon in 1989. I went in after the Lions tour and he opened it up and basically told me the knee was buggered. He said that with having the cartilage out at 17 it had been bone on bone every day for the last 10 years or more."

He was honoured to lead the team out for the semi-final, the occasion of his 39th cap. All that was left thereafter was a chance to take one last swipe at the English as the Scotland squad donned Australian scarves for the final. Only one man would not and, as ever, Jeffrey is prepared for the last word with the man he partnered through so many heady triumphs.

"Fin was the only boy who wouldn't wear a Wallabies scarf. He said it was out of order and reflected badly on the country. "He's right!" But Jeffrey did wear that scarf.

.... but unfortunately you also meet some pretty rough types.

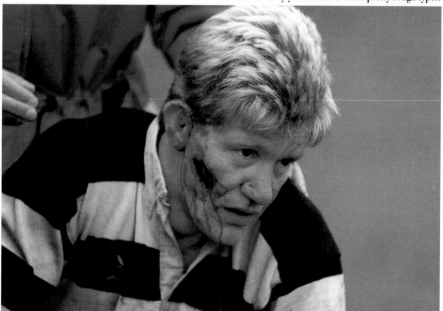

Career Statistics: John Jeffrey

1984 Scotland 12 Australia 37.

1985 Scotland 15 Ireland 18; England 10 Scotland 7.

1986 Scotland 18 France 17; Wales 22 Scotland 15 (1Try); Scotland 33 England 6; Ireland 9 Scotland 10; Scotland 33 Romania 18 (1Try).

1987 Scotland 16 Ireland 12; France 28 Scotland 22; Scotland 21 Wales 15 (1Try); England 21 Scotland 12;

World Cup - France 20 Scotland 20; Scotland 60 Zimbabwe 21 (1Try); Scotland 55 Romania 28 (3Tries).

1988 Ireland 22 Scotland 18; Wales 25 Scotland 20; Scotland 13 Australia 13.

1989 Scotland 23 Wales 9; England 12 Scotland 12 (1Try); Scotland 37 Ireland 21 (1Try); France 19 Scotland 3; Scotland 38 Fiji 17; Scotland 32 Romania 0.

1990 Ireland 10 Scotland 13; Scotland 21 France 0; Wales 9 Scotland 13; Scotland 13 England 7; New Zealand 31 Scotland 16; New Zealand 21 Scotland 18; Scotland 49 Argentina 3.

1991 France 15 Scotland 9; Scotland 32 Wales 12; England 21 Scotland 12; Scotland 28 Ireland 25; World Cup - Scotland 47 Japan 9; Scotland 24 Ireland 15; Scotland 28 Western Samoa 6 (2Tries); Scotland 6 England 9; Scotland 6 New Zealand 13.

All appearances at flanker.

CAPTAIN'S COMMENT:
On the SRU: "I don't suppose Jim Telfer did name his price to take over as director of rugby, but he should have been able to. There are few people in this game who have no skeletons, but he's one of those men. He's beyond reproach. What the Union is doing now is picking off the people who have been involved in the last decade, which is good."

The Captain

7 - F. Calder

Sibling rivalry is a wonderful thing and that was particularly true for Scottish rugby in the eighties and nineties, an era which saw three Milne brothers and two Hastings brothers capped for their country. But it was never more directly beneficial than in the case of the Calders.

It is one of the more remarkable statistics that twin brothers Jim and Finlay Calder earned a total of 61 caps between them, one scored the try which won a Grand Slam, the other was a British Lions captain, each was in a winning Grand Slam side, yet they never played together in the same Scotland side.

Although he was by no means thrown in ridiculously early, Jim, aged 23, was first to make it, gaining selection throughout the Five Nations Championship and for both Tests on the New Zealand tour of 1981. He was to provide the inspiration for his brother, in every sense, the key moment arriving in a training session in the summer of 1985.

"Jim had been injured, was trying to fight his way back into the Scottish team and I was helping him, working with him at Heriot Watt University," Finlay explains. "We had done a tremendous weight session already, working hard at it and we went for this run...about four miles.

"Jim was never a sprinter, but he would grind you down, just wear you right down. As we went on we just got faster and faster and faster," he says, reliving the sense of competition which has clearly always existed between the pair.

"We were going at a fair old lick and eventually I thought, 'no, I just can't go on.' We were getting towards the finish and I just had to stop. Jim ran on and when I got to the showers he was there. He came up to me and said, you know if I could just give you one bit of advice, if you'd just carried on another 50 yards you had me beaten. But I knew you would quit. From the day you were born you've been a quitter."

The words echoed in the head of a proud man and the mental response was unprintable. Jim Calder had just flicked the switch. "That was the last time," Finlay says now. "It was probably the worst piece of advice he ever gave anybody in his life. It was certainly the best piece of advice I ever got.

"He said to me 'You've had twice the talent of me, but I've wanted it and you haven't.' He's never beaten me at anything since...ANYTHING."

Finlay laughs heartily at the memory now, but it was clearly a galvanising moment in his rugby career. Jim, the man immortalised in Ronnie Browne's superb painting "The Turning Point" as he rises from the Murrayfield turf having scored that vital try in the 1984 Grand Slam decider against France. But through two World Cup campaigns and a second Grand Slam in 1990, the name Calder would hardly ever be missing from the Scottish back-row. "Jim was absolutely right," his twin admits.

The pair remain close, as would be expected since they had always operated in tandem from an early age and, unlike the Hastings brothers whose rugby careers were drawn together by the national selectors, the very highest level is really the only one at which their playing careers have been separated.

They were the youngest of four brothers, brought up in Haddington. Gavin, the oldest and John would both line-up alongside them in future years for Stewart's Melville FP, but neither quite had the same amount of passion for the game as the twins.

"We are very much a rugby family. I think I started playing at the age of five or six in the field next to the house. Dad played but I think it's fair to say he was a bit too much of a gentleman. He's a decent man, rather like Clifford Hastings, Scott and Gavin's father, a very decent man.

"We used to play games, the four of us. John and Jim against Gavin and myself, Gavin and Jim against John and myself, but the most enjoyable ones were when Jim and myself would play Gavin and John, who were much older and we would sometimes beat them."

A competitive edge was honed and what better preparation could there be for a brace of future Scottish internationalists than taking on the odds in that way. "We were always on the back foot a bit," Finlay says, in a tone which suggests he is talking about times way beyond those boyhood games in an East Lothian field. "I think that helps you appreciate it when you do win."

The quartet and the twins in particular, formed a close bond, while their father worked intensely to ensure that all would be properly provided for. "It wasn't a sort of father and son set-up. There was no great communication, none of the sort of bonding you try to encourage now. He took us on our holidays, but most of the time he was working. He had four young men to put through public school. He certainly had his work cut out.

"It was only when my mother went into hospital that Jim and I saw a very different side of him. We realised he was quite a good lad. But a very traditional man. I'm sure he's very proud of us, but he would never, ever...ever, say it!" Finlay emphasises. He never tried what a lot of parents do, though, try to live what he didn't have through us.

Watching some of the parents who are like that at mini rugby now, shouting and swearing on the touchlines, can be dreadful."

Robin Calder did take a pretty keen interest in the rugby careers of his two sons, though, and was by no means averse to stirring things up by pitting them against one another. "The old man would say to me, 'Did you see the way Jim played today?'. He's now at the same thing with his grandchildren. 'What about this one? What about that one?' "It was very much the old psychology."

Internationally Jim led the way, but Finlay and John were, initially at least, hot on his heels. The twins were both selected in Scotland's 1982 tour party for the trip to Australia, but they got a bit of a shock when John arrived mid-tour as an emergency replacement.

"John had an awful lot of talent, but rugby was very much a part-time interest for him, behind his personal life and his work. He never trained seriously at all. But he arrived in Australia and scored three tries in his first match. Here was a man who had the most appalling pair of hands you ever saw in you life. He picked one ball off his toes after running 50 yards, to score underneath the posts. Jim and I looked at each other and thought - 'Is this our brother?'

"The next game he scored a further three tries and then Iain Paxton went down injured on the Thursday before the first Test and John's asked to put on the no.8 jersey. You can picture the scene. Jim and I are now looking at each other and saying - 'I don't believe this'.

"He was known as John Spawn, because he spawned everything. If there was a speedboat trip going he'd get it...you'd be sitting in a rowing boat with a hole in it. It was the story of his life."

In the event, though, Paxton recovered, while Jim took his now regular place in the no.6 jersey. Meanwhile Finlay was getting a touch fatalistic about it all. "That was my first involvement at that level, but at that stage I was beginning to think, the Gods were agin me."

The international side was pretty much settled, particularly the back-row where brother Jim and David Leslie were flankers on either side of either John Beattie or Iain Paxton. A vacancy did emerge, however, in Jim's absence for the post-Grand Slam trip to Bucharest to meet Romania. "It came down to Sean and myself at that stage and Sean got it. I thought that was definitely it. He was the younger man."

However Romania, always tough on their home patch, humiliated Scotland with a 28-22 win, to have a tenuous claim at least to being European champions. That was May, 1984 and the Calder tete-a-tete was over a year away.

It is fair to say that Jim's well-received advice did not instantly have his brother believing he would be wearing a navy blue jersey the next time a Scotland side was to be selected, but that's just how it turned out.

A telephone call from Jim Telfer asking him to sit on the bench for a B international was not exactly a breath-takingly attractive opportunity, but the great coach could be persuasive. "When he asked me, I thought that was just what I needed," Finlay recalls, his voice dripping with sarcasm. "But he said if I did I would definitely get in for the trial so I reckoned that was pretty fair."

That trial was, of course, to be a major occasion in recent history. An almost symbolic blood-letting as the Reds poured through the ranks of the Blues. "We had the best team," says Calder. The selectors may not have been persuaded of that sufficiently to put them in en masse but he found himself among six new caps in the line-up to meet France.

The match was famous on two counts, for the crafty French try in the first minute from a quickly taken line-out on half-way after Gavin Hastings' kick-off flew direct into touch and for the Hastings response - eight penalty strikes in an 18-17 win. Calder's memory of the occasion is minimal. "It was over before it started," he says.

Typical of rugby though was that such a moment inspired a friendship which resulted in Calder bringing Berbizier to Orkney for a charity game some years later, after both illustrious careers were over, in a team boasting four international scrum-halves, the others being Borderers Roy Laidlaw, Gary Armstrong and Greig Oliver.

Calder always takes a pragmatic view of Scottish performances. They shared the championship with France that first season and the 33-6 thrashing of England at Murrayfield was hailed as one of the great triumphs. "It had a lot to do with the fact that they had written us off, I mean completely written us off. We ran them off the park, but that was the lowest point for English rugby in at least the last 10 years."

Scotland's performance did, though, confirm for him the veracity of the belief held by the man who would immediately precede him as Scotland captain. "Gary Callander's got a theory that Scots react best in two situations. One, when they've had a hiding or two, when they expect a hiding. That's when the Scots are at their best. Whether it be in the Parc Des Princes or Christchurch, wherever it may be. However, if they think they are going in as favourites they just can't handle it. They can't handle being liked. They like to be abused.

"That's why Jim Telfer was so good. He focussed brilliantly on players, focussed on what they were good at, cut out what they weren't good at. That was his strength. As far as vision was concerned he had none as a coach. But he could work eight forwards into a lather and get the best out of limited resources. And once you had the ball you could do something with it.

"He had a perfect foil in Ian McGeechan. When Ian was totally in charge you could go across to him and say quietly 'That is enough, get him stopped' and he would come across and would say 'All right, Jim, I think we should wind up the session now.' There was that sort of mutual trust and respect between the senior players and the coaches, when we could say if we thought they were going to leave us with nothing in our legs. In the early eighties Jim would have kept on flogging us.

"We've come a long way, although we must never forget the fundamentals which are that without hard work you deserve nothing."

Scotland's development had still not reached a particularly advanced stage by 1987, despite the presence of great coaches such as Telfer and McGeechan as well as Derrick Grant, then the national coach. Yet Calder remembers that season's championship as providing one of the highlights of his career in terms of an overall team performance.

"The game with the five no. 8s against Wales was a particularly good memory. It was a great game. The way rugby should be played. On a bone dry pitch, lovely conditions, fast forwards. That's why we should be playing summer rugby." Calder is a powerful advocate for summer rugby.

"That was as good a pack as Scotland's ever put out in good conditions and we played to the conditions," he says. Two of the no. 8s, John Beattie and John Jeffrey, got two tries. The second-row was formed by Derek White and Iain Paxton.

But as if to underline Scotland's tactical naivete as late as 1987, the year of the first World Cup, the selection of the same eight forwards, with only the bulwark Iain Milne providing large-scale ballast alongside the ultra-mobile David Sole and Colin Deans in the front-row, a Triple Crown was denied them at Twickenham by an English side which had lost all three previous matches.

"However, we went to Twickenham and got washed away," Calder says of the way the wet conditions allowed the big English pack to dominate. We had seven thoroughbreds and one Clydesdale. In those conditions we needed eight Clydesdales

The best game he thinks he ever played in was another meeting with the French - Scotland's first-ever World Cup tie later that year, which ended 20-20 in Christchurch. "It was the best because of the drama and the quality of rugby and everything. It was also the first time we'd met on neutral territory, and so emphasised how evenly matched we were "I have no complaints about the try," he says of their score which was registered as Scottish captain Colin Deans sought treatment for an injured team-mate. "If we'd done that we would have been talking about Scottish guile.

"We had a great night out that night. The French loved it and we knew we were on our way out after that. In fairness they were far better suited to go to the final. France were very tired when they played New Zealand in the final. The semi-final with Australia was one of the all-time classics. Playing New Zealand six days later they had no chance. The week before the semi they'd had a very hard game against Fiji. They had it hard the whole way through, but they were the best side to take on the New Zealanders at that time."

After a transitional year in 1988, Calder suddenly found himself with a different role in the Scottish side.

"I took over as captain more through default than anything else. Gary had it very difficult in 1988. He inherited a side that was sickening for change. He was really unfortunate, having sat on the bench all the time when he was ready for it, then struggling when he was brought in and given the added burden of captaincy.

"I was very surprised when the late Bob Munro, chairman of selectors, phoned and my wife answered it and told me who it was. My first reaction was that I'd been dropped but then I thought - 'No they never phone anyone to tell them they've been dropped.' I was the last one left in the changing room," he believes.

Admittedly there was little in terms of captaincy experience to persuade him that he was the man for the job. "I had captained the Corn Trade against the English and that was it," is his summation. "We won that game, mind you, so I was a winning captain!"

He continued to be just that, for the most part, though he takes little of the credit, suggesting that he was the last person who could have been expected to be offered the post.

He speaks of Jim Telfer with massive respect, but his relationship with him underlines why he never expected to be brought into the management camp. "I go back to the early seventies with him when I was at Melrose for five years while working in the Borders. You hear people talking about love-hate relationships, we I most probably had a hate-hate relationship," Calder jokes. "I was one of the few people who would ever nip him back. He never knew quite how to handle me which was quite nice...because I never knew quite how to handle him.

"I was a bit of a poacher turned gamekeeper. You know the expression you can't kid all of the people all of the time, well I think I'm the exception. I think I managed to bluff my way through pretty well and I've been lucky. After all I could have played that game in Romania in 1984 and never been seen or heard of again.

"I was the caretaker captain for David Sole." Yet so impressive was his handling of the side, losing just once, in Paris, that he was the obvious man to lead the British Lions to Australia, although, strangely enough, Calder doesn't quite see it that way. "I inherited the captaincy when Scotland were beginning to come together again.

"Phil Matthews was captain of Ireland and they were struggling, Wales had Paul Thorburn who had just given the 'V' sign to the press after they beat England and then poor old Will Carling got shin splints. I was the last man left in the changing room again."

He is refreshingly candid about his term of office as both Scotland skipper, which was much shorter than tends to be remembered, and captain of the Lions. "As long as you've got good players around you'll be a successful captain. On the Lions tour, for example, I let Rob Andrew and Brian Moore call the shots. They were going to do that anyway so you might as well let them.You can be the best captain in the world, but if you've got a bunch of bozos round about you you've got no chance. The reverse is also true if you're the worst captain. With 14 good ones around you, you'll get away with it

"The French game in 89, we were 9-3 down at half-time, how it wasn't 99 I'll never know. At half-time someone said 'What do we do, Fin?' and I said 'I haven't got a clue. Don't look at me. It's every man for himself.' People afterwards were questioning our tactics and I'm thinking - 'Tactics?'."

On the Lions tour he discovered what it was like to be under real pressure, especially after the first Test was lost. "Captaining the Lions, more than captaining Scotland, you're on a hiding to nothing. The Scottish press is incredibly loyal to its players. They don't go for gimmicky news but south of the Border you're fair game and you just have to accept that.

"Not only were the Press anxious for my departure from the Test side, I was getting hate mail requiring that I stood down because I was in the side ahead of Andy Robinson. Ah! The joys of amateur rugby!"

Taking on France, including le coq, at the way to the 1990 Grand Slam

Privately, at the time, Calder was actually relieved that Robinson had been selected for the tour ahead of Peter Winterbottom, who he regarded as an outstanding player and one who would have put him under tremendous pressure for the Test no.7 jersey, a distraction which did no good for Ciaran Fitzgerald on the previous Lions tour.It is worth noting that thereafter the England selectors always went for Winterbottom.

As to the success in the Test series itself and the way it was turned around after losing the opener in a three Test series, he is happy to share the credit. "It was down to good selection and better attitude." The introduction of two players, Scott Hastings, who had been struggling with injury and Rob Andrew, called upon mid-tour to replace the injured Paul Dean, made a significant difference.

"I remember watching Scott," says Calder. "Because he was within an ace of being sent home from the Lions tour because he was struggling with his hamstring. We put him in the team against Australian Capital Territories for the Wednesday before the Test and he said 'I'm just not ready'. But I took him aside and said 'Scott, if you don't play you're going home. He played, got through it and then got put in the team for the second Test." So much for being a lucky captain.

"The two men I respect most in English rugby are Rob Andrew and Brian Moore," is an opinion which was clearly cemented on that trip. "Why them...because they're winners. First and foremost they're winners. They are there to win...period. Rob Andrew beat France himself in the 1994 Five Nations match. They hardly needed the other 14. He could control a game. 1991 was murderous. He could strangle a game with that tremendous control.

"I know most people up here don't like him because his hand touched the ball in that controversial finish at Murrayfield, but I've got no complaints. I'd have been quite happy if it had been my hand that touched the ball and we'd won."

Nor does Finlay even take exception to Andrew's apparently hypocritical comments about Scotland's willingness to bend or break the rules to get results, following that match. "I haven't got an ounce of problem with what he said, because of course we cheat. We've only managed to cling on in there by being streetwise. getting your body on the wrong side of the ball and hopefully they're too decent to kick you. When you put your boots on you're there to win. After that, it's back to the old spoils of war. Motto — Winner takes all."

Further glory of that sort was yet to come for Calder, however, under another captain. "Our attitude to the Grand Slam decider was 'If you want it come and get it...come and get it!" Years after the event his tone still carries real menace. They thought they could just come and collect it, but we genuinely believed we could beat them. The whole day we used to our advantage. We soaked up the crowd. Man for man they were by far the better team, but the die was cast early on in the match."

Utterly typical was that Calder, like a man possessed, led the first charge which took the wind from English sails.

"The occasion was something we had never experienced and it would have been even more of a shock for England on the day. It certainly put Will Carling under even more pressure as captain. It would have stretched any captain."

In assessing Carling Calder notes: "He's had Rob Andrew there all the time to make the decisions and it comes back to Andrew and Brian Moore again calling the shots. But Carling had never been under real pressure up until then.

"On television during tours you hear him up in the commentary box saying things like 'England are doing OK', but in my opinion he shouldn't even be there, he should be on the touchline near his players. And if he is there then these are his boys. He should be talking about 'us'. Make no mistake he is a superb player, but under stronger captaincy England had the potential to win five Grand Slams instead of only two."

That summer's tour of New Zealand may have ended with two Test defeats, but Scotland performed magnificently and, for Calder, it was time to bow out, or so it seemed. "I knew in my heart of hearts that I wasn't going to play another championship and then go to the World Cup. I was going to be 34 by the World Cup so I made the decision to pull out altogether.

"I could have gone on to the Five Nations Championship, but I knew that if I was going to go through that grind, then the summer, then the World Cup my body wouldn't take it. I felt it would have been unfair to play in the championship then leave them with no time to break in a replacement."

Naturally he felt it wasn't his place to opt out of the Five Nations while making himself available for a second World Cup, but the coaches took that decision for him when McGeechan contacted him to ask him to play. Now he was faced with another dilemma.

"I owed Ian McGeechan and Jim Telfer," he says of his famous comment that it was 'payback time'. "And the players were tremendous. I said to myself that if they all wanted me back I had to make the effort." It was during one sprint session finding the resolve to "slog my way through" that the former captain and several of his colleagues realised that he would make the necessary fitness level. It was a huge mental effort because the standard of fitness that was needed was colossal. I got there, though, I got there."

So with Scotland reaching the semi-final as rugby reached a profile never previously known in Britain, surely it was worth it. "No...I should never have done it!"

Unusually this shock statement is delivered without a trace of a smile, or humour and he explains by outlining two of the more controversial moments of the tournament which Calder believes, rightly or wrongly, damaged his reputation.

"The Jim Staples incident looked bad, although I actually hit him with my shoulder," he says of that notorious clash with the Irish full-back during the qualifying group decider at Murrayfield. It was, though, a collision which was much worse than it looked.

"My arm swung round and it looked dramatic, but it didn't hit him. Tony Stanger had him by the ankles and it was actually the impact with the ground that knocked him out."

He also recognises that the fact the collision seemed to change the game in which Scotland had been struggling - with the shaken up Staples failing to collect the next high ball and Scotland scoring a try from it - also influenced much of the reaction. But there was hate mail again...and worse. I actually got death threats, to the house."

Retirement from international rugby for a second and final time followed and he could get back to playing just for enjoyment alongside his twin brother, by now , though, very much as equals, in terms of achievement at least.

"Up until that run I had always been in Jim's shadow, but now I reckon we are pretty even. Jim has maybe moved ahead of me a bit career-wise, but he always asks me what I'm getting paid and I always tell him about ten grand more than I'm actually getting."

He is magnanimous in comparing their respective careers, however, learning from the old Burns philosophy of seeing 'oorsels as ithers see us.' It was never more vividly brought home than on a return trip from the Borders."You wonder how people perceive you and I always say you should ask the people around you. We were coming home from Melrose on the team bus one time, when I was in the international team and they had a competition to see who was the best Calder. Suffice to say the vote went 12-1 and my only vote was because I was going to give the guy a lift home.

Victorious Lions captain welcomed home by his family in 1989.

"I wouldn't have disputed that. Jim had far more vision as a player. On the Australian tour of 1982 he was playing against Mark Ella, I was watching and Ella came towards him and Jim turned him over. I don't know quite how he did it but the ball went loose in the middle of the pitch and Jim took a step forward towards it and swung at it with his left foot. It flew into the left corner, bounced on its point and Roger Baird scooped it up and went in for a try underneath the posts. Pure magic.

"I asked him afterwards what went through his mind when he kicked, whether he was aiming for touch or what and he said that as the ball came back to him he reckoned that if Roger was in position then the chip was on and with a bit of luck he would score.

"And you look at the Grand Slam try. He had the whole thing read before the French lock had touched the ball back. He had to do that because he was painfully slow as a player. How many times did the ball not come back when Jim went into contact situations?"

Yet just the slightest nudge, like suggesting that one of Finlay's problems was the concession of too many penalties, brings out the competitiveness.

"My own game was on the brink all the time. You are bound to be giving penalties away. But Jim was a cheat as well," he says, before recounting an ancient grievance.

"He was always a cheat. We played for the JA1s at school against Leith Academy and were heading home on the bus and Jim had to write down all who had scored. Unbeknown to me I'd scored four and he'd scored two, but he couldn't handle that fact so he came up to me and said 'That was a good three tries you got today Finlay'.' The following Monday the statistics which were logged read: J.Calder 3 tries, F.Calder 3 tries. "It must have really gnawed away at him because on my wedding day he came up and said to me there's something that's been bothering me and I've got to tell you. You actually scored four tries that day for the JA1s against Leith. But that's the kind of guy he is. If he couldn't win fairly he would just cheat. He's a born cheat — but no-one has more admiration for him than me."

All of which is said through a broad grin and the Calders are men eager to get every ounce of fun out of their sport, rugby life continuing after the international days were over in Stewart's Melville FP's second XV, aka "The Dream Team".

"We played Heriot's in a game recently. There's always been a big rivalry, although that's always been more for us than them. First game of the season we beat them in the last minute. We then had the return match with them at the end of the season and normally the procedure is that you arrive no more than five minutes before kick-off, in time to pull on your boots.

"But this time I got there at 2.15 and the dressing room was full. Brother Jim wasn't able to play that day. He was golfing at Gleneagles and afterwards said his whole day was spent wondering how the boys were getting on. He said 'I'm 37 years old and can't let this wretched game out of my system'.

"But at least we can now take it for what it is. The competitiveness is still there, but we can take it for what it is."

Career Statistics: Finlay Calder

1986 Scotland 18 France 17; Wales 22 Scotland 15; Scotland 33 England 6; Ireland 10 Scotland 9; Scotland 33 Romania 18.

1987 Scotland 16 Ireland 12; France 28 Scotland 22; Scotland 21 Wales 15; England 21 Scotland 12; World Cup - France 20 Scotland 20; Scotland 60 Zimbabwe 21; Scotland 55 Romania 28; New Zealand 30 Scotland 3.

1988 Ireland 22 Scotland 18; Scotland 23 France 12;Wales 25 Scotland 20 (1Try); Scotland 6 England 9.

1989 Scotland 23 Wales 9*; England 12 Scotland 12*; Scotland 37 Ireland 21*; France 19 Scotland 3*;

Australia 30 British Lions 12*; Australia 12 British Lions 19*; Australia 18 British Lions 19*; Scotland 32 Romania 0.

1990 Ireland 10 Scotland 13; Scotland 21 France 0 (1Try); Wales 9 Scotland 13; Scotland 13 England 7; New Zealand 31 Scotland 16; New Zealand 21 Scotland 18.

1991 Romania 18 Scotland 12; World Cup - Scotland 47 Japan 9; Scotland 24 Ireland 15; Scotland 28 Western Samoa 6; Scotland 6 England 9; Scotland 6 New Zealand 13.

All appearances at flanker. * as captain

CAPTAIN'S COMMENT:
On the future of Scottish rugby: "Our whole culture has got to change if we're going to compete at world level. Until we play in good conditions we're wasting our time. Scottish rugby and Scottish football will never achieve world status while we're playing in January or February. The way things are going we're going to end up well down the pecking order. Look at what happened to Wales, having to qualify for the World Cup. That will happen to us. Maybe not next time but sooner or later. We'll drop out of the mainstream and the same as football we will not qualify for the World Cup unless there is a dramatic change of attitude. Club rugby has got to remain amateur. We shouldn't compete with English clubs. If players want to go, let them go. If a player wants to go south clubs should say 'Go with our full blessing.' For them to try to match the offers from England is, for me, 100% wrong. We have to be very careful if clubs come up with what allegedly look to be good packages, because believe me there is not the money available. I'm all for the fact that at the highest level the players must not suffer in the pocket, but the club game must remain amateur. Clubs should spend their money on facilities, not people."

Kingdom

8 - I. A. M. Paxton

A midst the rousing Jacobite anthems and references to Bannockburn which proliferate on international match days, perhaps no Scottish rugby player of modern times has embodied the spirit of Bruce more than one Iain (spelt the Scottish way) Angus McLeod Paxton, father of Seona (spelt the Gaelic way). A less determined individual could easily have been discouraged, but try, try, try again the big man did.

He first emerged on the international scene in season 1979/80 when, out of Fife side Glenrothes, he was selected for the Scotland B side to meet France at Ayr. The game was snowed off and he was never again to be selected for the B team. Following that season's international trial another newcomer, one John Ross Beattie, emerged to claim the Scotland no.8 berth. Not only that, Beattie, after only four international appearances, found himself on that summer's British Lions tour of South Africa and while he didn't play in any of the Tests he returned with his international reputation established.

Paxton meanwhile, typically determinedly, had opted to stay on in the kingdom of Fife "A lot of people have told me I should have moved earlier and it cost me this and cost me that, but they don't consider all aspects," Paxton explains. "In many ways I wasn't ready to move. I couldn't even drive and I was finishing my apprenticeship in electronics at that time."

When he did go, under the advice of Famous XV and then international selector Ian MacGregor who had been pushing him for the B international squad, he chose to join the then champion club but rejection awaited. "The initial club I went to was Heriot's. I'd worked with The Bear in Scotland squads, it was just about the time they were beginning to invite players from outwith the 21 to help out at sessions, and he also came over to the first-ever Glenrothes sevens with a Heriot's second seven."

The approach having been made a snag quickly developed. "Heriot's had a 10% policy at that time. It wasn't a completely open club. John Beattie had just come back from the Lions tour and he decided he was leaving Glasgow Accies to join Heriot's. So I was told if I wanted to go there I had to apply as a second row, not as a no.8. I told them I would only apply as a no.8. They weren't prepared to accept that.

"In fairness to Andy Irvine it was him who suggested I go to Selkirk." That was by no means the obvious move. Selkirk, despite the presence of Scotland's new play-maker John Rutherford, were by no means among the top Border sides. "But the fact they had John there and Gordon Hunter at scrum-half made it attractive to me in my position, to be working with players of that quality."

Approaches from Boroughmuir and Melrose did ensue, but Paxton had made up his mind. "District rugby was a consideration. I think Boroughmuir might have been good for me too," says a man who now lives and works, with Scottish Mutual, in the capital. "But because John Beattie was in Edinburgh I felt I had a better chance of selection in the South.

"I felt comfortable at Selkirk right away. I thought Borders rugby would be good for me as well. Toughen me up a bit. The first game I'd had in the Borders had been with Glenrothes At Gala A. We were beaten by 30 points, a good whipping and it was the first time I'd really experienced the studs going in a bit more in a club match."

Yet, a year on and Paxton found that, despite his move, he had worked his way well down the pecking order. By the time Scotland's tour party for New Zealand in 1981 was being selected John Beattie had eight international caps, Peter Lillington was second choice and Paxton even found himself behind a younger man who would also establish himself as one of Scotland's greatest ever no.8s.

"I was fourth choice for the New Zealand tour," he reveals. "Derek White had come through at Gala and when Peter Lillington dropped out because of exams he was brought into the squad."

Because Paxton and Beattie both played in the 1984 Grand Slam side and White was a member of the 1990 squad there is a tendency to regard the youngest of the trio as being of a different generation, but nothing could be further from the truth as Paxton points out. "I think there's about six weeks between us."

A study of what was being given to Scottish mums to be in 1957 might be illuminating because Beattie (27/11/57) is oldest by a fraction over a month with Paxton (29/12/57) again just over a month older than White (30/1/58).

"As I say a lot of people thought I'd moved too late, but it worked out all right in the end, although it might have been different if John hadn't burst his knee. I wasn't chosen until the Sunday session before they left took place. John went to tackle The Bear and The Bear didn't move. John's kneecap went under the strain.

"I got a phone call from John Rutherford that afternoon asking if I'd been keeping fit. I didn't take the hint, but when the call came it was a real bonus. I hadn't expected to be going out for the start of the tour. You're just hoping to be called out there."

With White picking up an injury on tour Paxton jumped at his chance. "I enjoyed touring. It wasn't a case of being the only time I was ever fully fit. Fitness was never a problem for me, but you did get even fitter," he says. "It was the closest you got in those days to being a professional sportsman. Out there every day, just working on different areas of your game. And of course we had a good coach, although I think Jim Telfer, who had taken them on a development tour of France the previous year, learned a lot on that tour as well. At that stage we were regularly going out for three hour training sessions."

Come the first Test against the All Blacks he was first choice for an international baptism of fire. White would have to wait until the following season and would not establish himself as a Test no.8 for a remarkable seven further years, proving his versatility by winning caps as both a flanker and a lock until both Paxton and Beattie departed the scene prematurely in the late eighties.

Oddly enough White had arguably had more experience of top level rugby at that stage, though. "I got capped before I'd played a game in the first division," Paxton notes, Selkirk having won promotion only that Spring at the end of his first league season with them. He had, though, faced the All Blacks at least. "That was for the North & Midlands against Graham Mourie's side at Aberdeen in 1978, so it did give me some idea of what to expect." Nonetheless Test matches against the All Blacks are always a very different affair, although Scotland did have their chances. Only stern defending by the home side prevented the Scots from overhauling them in the final quarter.

"That First Test in Dunedin was there to be won. It was quite a day. The biggest motivation for me was fear, as it so often was. Fear of letting people down. You do watch videos as well, even of games you've been involved in and wonder how you deal with some of what goes on. Till you're in the middle you don't know. That's the problem for coaches and selectors too. You never know how players will react until they're out there."

In terms of heart there were never to be any questions about Paxton's fitness for the fray, but he was found out in one crucial instance. "It was very wet. We were pressing for long stages and we had opportunities to win the game, but I learned a lesson that day that I never forgot. We had a scrummage close to our line. Colin Deans heeled it and Dave Loveridge was in among our feet to touch the ball down before I could react, to score a try." Loveridge was then considered the best scrum-half in the world. Consequently the debutant didn't get the treatment he might have expected in later years. "It was something of a shock to the system that game - just a year after playing in the lower divisions with Glenrothes.

"Funnily enough, though, Jim Telfer didn't give me a hard time for the try. He did take me aside after the second game of the tour in Wellington, though and told me there would be times I would probably hate him for the way he would treat me."

Given that Derek White was to become used to the same sort of treatment Paxton acknowledges that the British Lion of the sixties perhaps reserved special attention for those who played in the same position, but he also believes that any talented player could expect the same from the coach. "I think he was hard on guys he thought there was something worth getting out of. He also had the ability to identify the guys who could take that sort of treatment, although maybe he wasn't sure with me which is why

I got the warning. Certainly it could have worked the opposite way and I can't be sure how I would have dealt with it without that warning."

After a stuttering start Paxton's international career took off spectacularly, despite the fact that "the All Blacks really went into overdrive" in his second Test appearance. "It was quite a start," he recalls. "I started against the best side in the world at the time and after all those years with Glenrothes followed by just a year in the second division with Selkirk it was fascinating to see how the game was received there. And just over a year later I had reached double figures for caps".

At the beginning of season 1981/82 Scotland played Romania and Australia, winning both, then, following the Five Nations Championship, a two Test tour of Australia followed, Scotland winning five of those eight matches and losing only two. During that period Paxton established himself in some style, most notably in what was his shortest ever appearance for his country at the end of the Championship.

Oddly enough he was the only member of the back-row not to score a try in the glorious 34-18 win at Cardiff Arms Park, yet the match is remembered by most for "Paxton's try". You'd be surprised how many people think I scored that try," he says. "Mind you I had a pretty good record against the Welsh because I scored three of my four international tries against them as well as being involved in that move."

The move in question was the one which transformed a game in which Scotland had been under the cosh in the early stages and looking like continuing their dismal record of not having won at Cardiff for 20 years.

Then, with Wales poised to score, their skipper Gareth Davies opted to chip the ball towards their right wing with the Scots under pressure deep in their 22. Roger Baird gathered it and with a combination of dancing footwork and electrifying speed, burst down the touchline before Paxton took over on the Scottish 10 metre line, carrying the ball some 40 metres to set up the score.

It may have effectively won Scotland the game, but it cost him a trip to the Hong Kong Sevens and, very nearly, his place on the tour of Australia, where Scotland would win their first ever Test on tour.

"That try started off the day, but I did my medial ligament as I released the ball. I can still see the situation now, but I still can't see Clive Rees coming. It wasn't a hard tackle he got me with, it was just my momentum and the fact I wasn't expecting the tackle which caused the problem.

"Maybe it was just as well though. If I hadn't been tackled like that I probably would have gone myself. I had no intentions of passing initially and if I'd seen him coming I probably would have handed him off. I didn't pass until forced to and fortunately Toomba (Alan Tomes) was there in support. I was only on the field for about five

Paxton scores for the Lions against Manawatu in 1983, forcing himself into contention as first choice for the Tests.

minutes, no more than 10, but I suppose that brought me to the forefront." The record books show that rather more than 10 minutes had elapsed, but his view that the score had properly established him as a favourite among the fans was absolutely right. It was all quite a turn around, though, for a player who was the classic late developer. Prior to secondary school the Kirkcaldy-bred youngster simply hadn't had rugby as an option.

"The first time I picked up a rugby ball was in my first year at Kirkcaldy High School, aged around 12 and a half. I was there before the comprehensive days and it was a choice between rugby or cross country. I'd always played football up to that point so rugby was the obvious choice." Even then, however, there was no great commitment to the sport and when his father, a policeman, was promoted, he found himself at non-rugby playing Beath High School. "I started playing basketball," he says.

The skills which would make the no.8 such a brilliant line-out man were evident early on in that sport. So much so that he was capped for the Scottish Schools under-19 side, however history teacher Bob Hutcheson, a winger at Glenrothes, ensured that Paxton remained involved in rugby. "He was on at me the whole time about playing rugby. We started it up at Beath while I was there and got quite a good side together with a few converts from football. He got me along to Glenrothes when I was in my fifth year. That was in the November when I was 17."

Paxton made such an impression he was chosen for the first XV by the turn of the year. After one game, against Fife rivals Waid FP, he was left out for a month, but timed his return well. We were beaten 4-3 by Harris FP, but I won all the line-out ball and was spotted by Jimmy Craig who got me selected for the Midlands District Union side."

Once established there future Scottish Rugby Union President Tom Pearson pushed his case for the Midlands Schools side, quite a first for Beath HS, and rugby was playing a bigger and bigger part in Paxton's life. Then came one of the first big influences in his career, Hamish Brown - a man best described as fanatical in his approach to rugby at the evolving Glenrothes club.

"Glenrothes set me on the straight and narrow. Some people say Hamish went too far with me, but it worked out well. He was quite dictatorial, a manipulator and an organiser. He lived close to me and would pick me up for training every night. Then he'd be out with the stop-watch at Beveridge Park." Ironically Beveridge Park, close to the house in which Paxton was brought up, is the home of Glenrothes' closest rivals Kirkcaldy.

As noted, it was only with reluctance that he left after six years at Glenrothes, in which the club developed a particular reputation as a sevens side, a form of the game Paxton firmly believes in for identifying and developing young talent. "We had a lot of talented players at Glenrothes in the early days, but in retrospect it was too early in the club's history to build on it properly."

As soon as he was sure his rickety old knee could take no more of the first division in 1993 he agreed to return there as coach, setting about re-establishing the potential for a thriving rugby nursery in the new town, helping them to promotion from division V in his first season.

Having emerged so dramatically from a relative rugby backwater Paxton was, after his first spectacular year in the national squad, to find that caps would not always come as easily, the rivalry with John Beattie now firmly established.

"Looking back it was great to have got into the side in time for the 1982 championship because that was the last year of the old Murrayfield, before the East Stand was built."

He had, inadvertently, been instrumental in providing the opportunity for one of the last great moments of drama to be witnessed from the East terracing, Andy Irvine's last minute penalty which salvaged the draw with England. "English prop Colin Smart knocked me over near the half-way line. I had stopped at a ruck because the whistle had blown and he just bowled me over, right in front of the referee," Paxton explains. "He claimed afterwards he was sure I was going to kick someone, but nothing was further from my mind. I certainly wasn't daft enough to kick anyone right in front of the referee like that. Then again I wasn't daft enough to drink a bottle of after-shave either," he says of the notorious celebratory drink which, a month later, saw the same Mr Smart receive emergency treatment in a Paris hospital.

A year on, though, on the opening day of the 1983 season, with Jim Telfer's attention diverted by his responsibilities as Lions coach for the forthcoming tour and John Rutherford out with a serious shoulder injury, Scotland lost a Five Nations Championship match at Murrayfield for the first time since England clinched their 1980 Grand Slam.

"I actually thought I'd played really well even though we lost," Paxton recalls. "I felt I was certainly one of the better forwards, but I was dropped. We were at Murrayfield for a Sunday session and I came out of the treatment room, was met by Ian MacGregor and told I was out. They were 'looking for a different type of player', a 'different blend in the back-row'."

They were in fact looking to include Beattie and he was installed, but after two more defeats, in Paris as usual and at Murrayfield to Wales, the selectors knew they had to find places for both of their outstanding no.8s. This heralded the beginning of Paxton's career as an international lock forward. While he had baulked at Heriot's attempt to convert him, he was now grateful to seize the opportunity to get back into the national side. "The last time I'd played lock before that game, other than moving up during a game because of injuries, was for the Midlands District Union.

"I wasn't going to turn caps down and I don't remember being given any choice anyway. I was just selected there. I was behind Jim Aitken, which was the tougher slot simply because The Bear was on the other side. Tom Smith had been behind The Bear and they decided to leave him on that side. Every other time I played at lock after that, though, I made sure I was behind The Bear. To say I was worried about the danger of the scrums being destroyed is an understatement, but it worked out." That too is an understatement. Scotland achieved a rare triumph at Twickenham, winning, in the end, in some style as Borderers Peter Dods, with three penalties and a try and Roy Laidlaw, who scored the decisive try, provided a taste of what was to come the following year.

"Of course the other danger is that if it works out you're kept at lock," Paxton notes. He would, ultimately, win nine of 36 caps as a lock. However immediately after that win over England a first appearance for the Barbarians would, fatefully, allow him to re-establish his credentials as a no.8. "That was at Northampton and it went well. I scored a couple of tries — turned up in the right place, did the right things. The following day I was picked to go on the Lions tour with John.

"After the Irish game I thought my chance had gone. I started looking around at their other options, because I knew John would go on the Lions tour then. I really didn't think I'd leapfrog the likes of John Scott who had been around for a long time.

"I don't know how much the BaaBaas game had to do with Lions selection. Maybe the team was selected with the Lions in mind. Certainly there were a few guys there who must have been on the border-line for the Lions tour. I'm sure most of the names for the Lions tour had been inked in, but if I was on the border-line that display might have tipped it."

On arrival in New Zealand, though, it was evident who was first choice in the eyes of the management. "It was pretty clear for the first three weeks who was no.1. I didn't play till the third game. In fact I was two and a half weeks in the country without playing and John played three out of the first four matches."

Paxton acknowledges he had a lucky break in that his lone appearance coincided with the best overall performance of that first couple of weeks, the 34-16 win over Bay of Plenty, in which he scored the last try. Paxton identifies that third game of the tour as the moment which began to shift the balance and by the time he appeared against Manawatu, scoring another try, the Lions had been defeated by Auckland and had struggled in Wellington. While other Scots, notably John Rutherford, Iain Milne and Colin Deans, found themselves struggling to get past rivals from other countries to win Test places, Paxton's personal rivalry with his fellow Scot was at its peak.

"I think it's safe to say we're closer now than we were then," he smiles. "We had different styles. I'd look for space, try to run round people, John tended to run at people. He was more physical than me. I always felt I could cover the pitch better. I always wish I'd been a bit stronger, but then I knew I could get into parts of the pitch that John couldn't. Maybe the difference in running style was because I didn't like getting hurt," he adds with a laugh. "But I do find there are more benefits in trying to run past people. Percentage wise it leaves you with more options. I think Jim Telfer's ideal no. 8 was a combination of the two of us, though."

Just as Beattie nowadays magnanimously acknowledges that Paxton was the more complete player, so Paxton speaks warmly of his old rival. "There was always a mutual respect there. We were in the same teams a lot and there was never any bad feeling when it came down to it. We used to head down to breakfast at around the same time and there was always plenty banter. I do remember him putting me away in a district game, though. I went up for a kick-off and he just came straight through me. That was perfectly legitimate at the time, but I sprung a rib cartilage. It happened about five minutes after kick-off. I stayed on for about 40 minutes trying to get him back but I couldn't get near him. He did to me no more than I would have done to him. It was within the rules to hit someone in the air at that time.

"There was always a fierce rivalry, but there was never any nastiness in it and as it turned out, the way the club scene worked out, we didn't get that many opportunities to play against each other."

In the eyes of historians what will separate Paxton from Beattie is that, although Paxton went on only one Lions tour to Beattie's two, Paxton appeared in all four Tests in New Zealand, while Beattie's only Test appearance was as a replacement for Paxton in the second Test in New Zealand. In another era Beattie could easily have ended up with eight Lions caps.

Following on from the way he established himself in New Zealand for Scotland two years earlier, Paxton was clearly a top class tourist, but he acknowledges that this was by no means the happiest of Lions gatherings. "Scots are always good tourists. They always make the best of things. They never have a bad tour, even if results go badly. Maybe other countries are different, but when Scotland tour you're all in it together. The top players get no special treatment. That's the way it should be. The way Jim Telfer

Paxton's last match for Scotland, against future world champions Australia at Murrayfield, 1988

was lambasted out there by the critics," he says of the '83 tour, shaking his head. "He just didn't deserve it. His hands were tied behind his back. Some of the players out there," (more head shaking). "There were England players too busy trying to sell their blazers and other kit before the last Test to be concentrating properly.

"And Ciaran Fitzgerald was a strange captain. Maybe the way he worked with Ireland was different, but with us he didn't have a leadership quality. I went on a fishing trip with him. There were about six or seven of us on the trip, but he just took a case of beer and went and sat in the corner. There was pressure on him to keep his place so I suppose that contributed," says Paxton, unequivocal in his view that the captain should have stood down. "When you compare Colin Deans and Ciaran Fitzgerald as players . . . . .For example, the day before a game you'd have a lineout drill and with Colin it was four to the middle, four to the front, four to the back and then on to something else. With Fitzgerald you could be there for an hour as he tried to get it consistently right. I don't think that helped blend the tour."

In the event a 4-0 defeat in the Test series should have been no great surprise, although prior to that final Test when Paxton "couldn't believe the attitude" of some colleagues, he felt they were always in contention and on a personal level came away as happy as he could be in the circumstances. "When you look back over the years Scottish players don't feature that strongly in Lions Test selections so getting the four Tests was something. I tweaked a knee ligament in the second Test and possibly should have come off sooner. The final Test was no fun, but I was quite happy with my form in the first and third."

Returning home the Scots, having "looked around and compared ourselves" knew they could do something in the championship. "I think we felt we were better than the other Home Unions," says Paxton. Though he played at no. 8, with Beattie at openside flanker for another epic meeting with the All Blacks later that year, the drawn match at Murrayfield, the Scottish selectors continued to swither. "I got dropped into the Whites for the trial. You don't remember trials normally, but that one sticks in my mind. Whether they felt I needed a gee up or what, I don't know. Anyway the Whites beat the Blues."

David Leslie returned to the side and once again, as history was made, Beattie had to make do with a cameo appearance, coming on only as a replacement for Bill Cuthbertson in the Calcutta Cup match during the Grand Slam campaign. Paxton set things rolling, enjoying another memorable moment against the Welsh, diving in extravagantly for the first try in the Cardiff win and setting the tone for a magnificent series of exhibitions of back-row play, alongside Leslie and Jim Calder.

"Going down to Wales was always tough, we certainly weren't supposed to beat England, but the Dublin game was amazing. We were all looking round at one another and asking each other if it was really happening. They were never going to catch up the way we started and although they had their spell, as all international teams do at some·

stage, we finished with two good tries." Paxton believes that day meant most to the supporters, if not the players.

"The Triple Crown was bigger than the Grand Slam for a lot of my friends who were over there. I have a friend who is a director of Johnston & Johnston and he had to go on one of these management courses where they were asked to describe the most emotional experience they ever had. The rest were going on about their weddings and things like that. He picked the Triple Crown game and had them all in the palm of his hand telling them about the day.

"We enjoyed the moment, all right, but I would have thought there would have been a lot more whooping and hollering in the changing room. It wasn't a quiet changing room exactly, but I think minds were already on the task ahead. David Leslie's always the boy for the quotes and I think that day it was 'Another day, another dollar.'

"At the end of the season if we'd just won the Triple Crown it still would have been a very special season, but we were aware of the opportunity." The true meaning of what was achieved, a first Triple Crown for 46 years, first Grand Slam for 59, has only come home in the intervening period.

"I only really appreciate what we did now, much more than then," says

At the tail or as main lineout target, Paxton delivered what Scotland required

Paxton. "Maybe it's the Scottish presbyterian mentality, but you always seem to have this wariness of over-celebrating in case somebody pulls the rug from under your feet. That said I was at college and didn't get back till the Wednesday after the France game."

A decade on he feels safe to reveal that there may just have been a glimmer of doubt over the deciding try. "The ball definitely touched my hand on its way to Jim," he says. "Joinel definitely got the big touch, but my finger-tips were on the ball. I suppose it was a knock-on."

Another outstanding memory, an inspirational moment in many ways, epitomised the courage of Iain Milne. "I remember running away from a scrum and hearing The Bear give a shout of pain. The second-row were putting the fists through. He never hit back, but he never budged an inch."

When the rug was pulled from under Scotland's feet, in Romania a couple of months later, Paxton, unable to go because of exams, watched it with friends in Mull. "It was a good one to miss."

Immortal status having been conferred Paxton still found that cut little ice with the selectors and after he missed the defeat by Australia through injury at the start of the next season, he only got back in when Beattie was injured during the Murrayfield defeat by Ireland. Despite Paxton's brace of tries against the Welsh, Scotland were on course

Paxton draws the back row cover.

for a whitewash and come the 1986 Championship and the dawning of a new era, he was dropped yet again.

Following the narrow defeat of France, Jeremy Campbell-Lamerton was the only one of the six newcomers not to establish himself. Paxton, then, found himself in the second-row once more, this time for a protracted run of eight matches, returning to no. 8 only for the World Cup, serious injury meaning Scottish rugby would, following the 1987 championship, be deprived of the services of his great adversary Beattie.

Scotland's perennial shortage of lock forwards produced one very exciting experiment, the pack remembered for the "five no.8s" - Beattie, Finlay Calder, John Jeffrey, Paxton and Derek White - who faced Wales and England. "I would agree that might have been the best side of the lot, although there was always a question-mark over the line-out. I was all right jumping in the middle in Scottish rugby, but against real specialists like Robert Norster I was always going to struggle. The Wales game in 1987 saw the ideal conditions for that pack, ideal for open play. But we were found out in bad weather at Twickenham."

Alongside the England game of 1986 - "We were written off again, there. The critics don't know just how much fuel that gives us!" - he selects the World Cup opener against France, when reinstalled at no. 8, among the most enjoyable of matches. "It was just something special. The very fact it was the first game and Derrick Grant and Ian McGeechan had things set up well. The build-up was excellent. It was a new challenge. They caught us with a sucker punch, scoring a try from a penalty when one of their players was lying injured, but it was a good day being involved in something so special, so far away from home.

"We were played out by the time we reached the quarter-final with the All Blacks. I played all four games, as did a number of the guys. Four Tests in quick succession like that is hard. Even against weaker sides you can't drop the pace. It was a hard trip but as ever the Scots had no problems, just made the most of the trip."

Playing with an injury "when I shouldn't have" against Ireland in 1988 spelt the beginning of the end and when he returned after two matches out Paxton languished in one of the most turgid internationals ever. "England won at Twickenham with guys just lying down on the ball all day. Dean Richards was just killing it all the time."

The final appearance came in a heavy defeat by the Wallabies, Paxton missing the championship before, at the age of 31, going on a "development tour" to Japan where things went well until an embarrassing defeat in the unofficial Test. "I was written off after that by a certain member of the press. That was of no consequence in itself, but it isn't nice to read when you feel you've contributed something over the years.'

However Paxton refused to become bitter about that, finding that once he had finally given up hope of re-selection, the game was still there to be enjoyed. "I started playing some of my best rugby at club and district level after that. After playing in the 1989 trial I could sense things were going against me. Nobody's ever told me why I was left out, but I had a couple of really good seasons with Selkirk. I had nothing to lose, the rules had changed which was beneficial to my style and I think I started enjoying my rugby more once I was out of the squad system."

He also enjoyed his first year of coaching with Glenrothes and, in emergencies, donned the boots once or twice. Six years after his last cap he still couldn't quite give up and Scottish rugby was continuing to benefit from that indomitable spirit.

Career Statistics: Iain Paxton

1981 New Zealand 11 Scotland 4; New Zealand 40 Scotland 15; Scotland 12 Romania 6; Scotland 24 Australia 15.

1982 Scotland 9 England 9; Ireland 21 Scotland 12; Scotland 16 France 7; Wales 18 Scotland 34 [1]; Australia 12 Scotland 7; Australia 33 Scotland 9 [2].

1983 Scotland 13 Ireland 15; England 12 Scotland 22+; Scotland 25 New Zealand 25

New Zealand 16 British Lions 12; New Zealand 9 British Lions 0; New Zealand 15 British Lions 8 [3]; New Zealand 38 British Lions 6.

1984 Wales 9 Scotland 15 (1 Try); Scotland 18 England 6; Ireland 9 Scotland 32; Scotland 12 France 21.

1985 Scotland 15 Ireland 18 [4]; France 11 Scotland 3; Scotland 21 Wales 25 (2 Tries); England 10 Scotland 7.

1986 Wales 22 Scotland 15+; Scotland 33 England 6 +; Ireland 9 Scotland 10+; Scotland 33 Romania 18+.

1987 Scotland 16 Ireland 12 +; France 28 Scotland 22 +; Scotland 21 Wales 15+; England 12 Scotland 21+;

World Cup - France 20 Scotland 20; Scotland 60 Zimbabwe 21; Scotland 55 Romania 28; New Zealand 30 Scotland 3.

1988 Ireland 22 Scotland 18+; Scotland 6 England 9+; Scotland 13 Australia 32 [5].

All appearances at No. 8 except + at lock. [1]Replaced by Gordon Dickson; [2]Replaced by Eric Paxton; [3]Replaced by John Beattie; [4]Replacement for John Beattie; [5]Replaced by Graham Marshall.

CAPTAIN'S COMMENT:
On rugby: "I enjoyed my rugby. I still enjoy my rugby, but it's only a game. I mean when the chips are down I am prepared to get stuck in like anybody else. But I take it for what it is."